WHEN WE WON
THE WAR

WHEN WE WON THE WAR

The Story of Victory in Europe, 1945

NORMAN LONGMATE

HUTCHINSON OF LONDON

Hutchinson & Co (Publishers) Ltd
3 Fitzroy Square, London W1

London Melbourne Sydney Auckland
Wellington Johannesburg and agencies
throughout the world

First published in Great Britain 1977
© 1977 by Norman Longmate

Set in Monotype Fournier

Printed in Great Britain by
The Anchor Press Ltd and bound by
Wm Brendon & Son Ltd
both of Tiptree, Essex

ISBN 0 09 128510 0

To all those who helped to win it
especially
Corporal A.G.L., RAF and Wren P.R.L., WRNS

CONTENTS

	Introduction	13
1	Hitler Kaput	15
2	Chaos or signature	25
3	Waiting for Victory	43
4	The German war is therefore at an end	60
5	We want the King	71
6	Bonfires over England	82
7	*Bless 'em all*	94
8	Flowers over Europe	103
9	The wonderful 9th of May	116
10	Postman's knock in Red Square	127
11	New light for Miss Liberty	136
12	Burma Looms Ahead	144
13	Outlook: 'Dry'	158
	A Note on Sources	177
	General Index	186
	Index of Place Names	190

ACKNOWLEDGEMENTS
FOR TEXT

Grateful acknowledgement is made for the use of the copyright material as follows: to the British Broadcasting Corporation for the extracts from news bulletins and other broadcast material; to Weidenfeld and Nicolson Ltd for Giles Romilly and Michael Alexander, *The Privileged Nightmare*, Susan Mary Alsop, *Letters to Marietta*, Robert Rhodes James (editor), '*Chips*'. *The Diaries of Sir Henry Channon* and Albert Speer, *Inside the Third Reich*; to Hamish Hamilton Ltd for David Niven, *The Moon's A Balloon*; to Laurence Pollinger Ltd and Hamish Hamilton Ltd for Alan Moorehead, *Eclipse*; to Faber & Faber Ltd for William Sansom, *Westminster at War*; Wm Collins Sons and Co. Ltd for *The Memoirs of Field-Marshal Montgomery* and *Harold Nicolson: Diaries and Letters 1939–1945*; to The Bodley Head for Kay Summersby, *Eisenhower was my Boss*; to Granada Publishing Ltd for Humphrey Lyttleton, *I Play as I Please*; to A. D. Peters and Co. for J. L. Hodson, *The Sea and the Land*; to William Heinemann Ltd for Harry C. Butcher, *Three Years with Eisenhower*, and Jane Gordon, *Married to Charles*; to André Deutsch Ltd for Derek Lambert, *The Sheltered Days*; to Hodder and Stoughton Ltd for Elizabeth Nel, *Mr Churchill's Secretary*; to W. H. Allen and Co. Ltd for R. C. F. Maugham, *Jersey under the Jackboot*; to Mr Leslie Sinel for *The German Occupation of Jersey*; to Laurence Pollinger Ltd for Alan Moorehead, *Eclipse*, and to Laurence Pollinger Ltd and the estate of the late Dr Hewlett Johnson for *Searching for Light*; to David Higham Associates Ltd for Edward Ward, *Give Me Air*; to New English Library for Carel Toms, *Hitler's Fortress Islands*; to the editor of the *RAOC Gazette*; to the editor of *The Oak Tree*; to

9

the Shropshire and Herefordshire Regiment; to the Trustees of the Buffs Museum; to Macdonald and Jane's Ltd for Patrick Forbes, *The 6th Guards Tank Brigade*; to Mr Nigel Nicolson for *The Grenadier Guards*; to Thomas Nelson and Sons Ltd for Desmond Flower, *The History of the Argyll and Sutherland Highlanders, 5th Battalion, 91st Tank Regiment, 1939–45*.

Apologies are offered for any inadvertent breach of copyright where, owing to the lapse of time, it has proved impossible to trace copyright-holders, and appropriate amends will gladly be made in any future edition.

ACKNOWLEDGEMENTS
FOR ILLUSTRATIONS

Imperial War Museum: 1, 2, 4, 5, 6, 7, 8, 9, 10, 26, 29
Fox Photos Ltd: 15, 25, 35
Associated Press: Line drawing p. 31; 3
Leeds Public Library: 11, 18
Manchester Public Library: 12, 13, 17, 33
Syndication International: 14
Popperphotos: 16, 30
Roger Viollet, Paris: 19
Novosti: 22, 24
Keystone Press Agency: Dustjacket, 20, 21, 23
Frank Falla: 27
Jersey *Evening Post*: 28
Radio Times Hulton Picture Library: 31, 32, 34

ILLUSTRATIONS

Between pages 48 and 49
1   The liberators: Holland
2   The liberators: Prisoner of war camp in Germany
3   The vanquished: The German delegation at Lüneburg
4   The victor: Field Marshal Montgomery meets the Germans
5   Surrender: Von Friedeburg at Lüneburg
6   Accepting surrender: General Eisenhower and Air Marshal
    Tedder at Rheims
7   Where it ended in the West: Schoolhouse at Rheims
8   Where it ended in the East: College in Berlin
9   The German delegation at Berlin
10 Montgomery in Copenhagen

Between pages 80 and 81
11 Waiting for the fun to start: Leeds
12 Celebrations in full swing: Manchester
13 VE Day in London: in Fleet Street
14 VE Day in London: Piccadilly
15 On the balcony: Prime Minister and Royal Family
16 Outside Buckingham Palace
17 Victory tea party: Camberwell
18 Victory bonfire: Leeds

Between pages 112 and 113
19 VE Day in Paris
20 New York celebrates: Ticker-tape on Wall Street
21 New York celebrates: Dancing in Times Square

22 Moscow celebrates: Crowds in Red Square
23 Moscow celebrates: A British sergeant is tossed in a blanket
24 Prague celebrates: Czechs welcome Russian troops
25 The Forces celebrate: ATS girls near Cairo
26 Surrender on shipboard: The Channel Islands
27 Into captivity: Admiral Hüffmeier leaves his Guernsey headquarters
28 Into captivity: German soldiers leave Jersey

Between pages 144 and 145
29 The price of defeat: The Dönitz government is arrested
30 The price of defeat: Captured U-boat in the Thames
31 'Send him back to finish the job': Election meeting in Abingdon
32 'Let us face the future': The new Prime Minister addresses his supporters
33 The trials of peace: Bread queue in Manchester
34 'Demob': Officers collect their civilian suits
35 'Demob': A soldier's homecoming

INTRODUCTION

More than thirty years have elapsed since the Second World War, the life of a generation. The majority of people now alive in Great Britain can have no memory of the war; almost half were not even born when the events described in this book took place. The war marks, by general consent, a major watershed in both national and personal experience, separating those who lived through it from those who did not. Of no part of it is this more true than of the 'victory season' of 1945. It seemed that summer that Britain's power and prestige in the world were unchallengeable, that no internal difficulties existed that could not be overcome with sufficient resolution. One could – strange as it must now seem to those who do not remember that era – sing with total sincerity and conviction 'God, who made thee mighty, make thee mightier yet'.

VE Day and VJ Day marked the victorious culmination of a national enterprise unselfishly undertaken and carried out with courage and dedication. This book is the story of how we won and how we celebrated.

For help in tracing many of the lesser-known sources used in this book, and in locating unfamiliar illustrations, my thanks are due to the following: Mr T. C. Charman and Mr E. Hinds of the Imperial War Museum; Mr A. B. Craven, Director of Library Services, Manchester, and Mr D. Taylor, Local History Librarian; Mr J. Alan Howe, City Librarian, Edinburgh; Miss Naomi Evetts, Liverpool Record Office; and Mr Robert F. Atkins, Director of Libraries, Sheffield. I am also grateful to Mr Harold Harris for his reminiscences of Hamburg at the end of the war; to Mr Bill McCoy for his account of his experiences in Changi Jail: to Miss Christine

Vincent, for help in collecting photographs and other visual material; to Mr David Risner, who kindly read through the manuscript for me and, above all, to Miss Idina Le Geyt, for her patient and enthusiastic research into the printed sources. I believe that all those who worked on the book found it, as I did, refreshing to be immersed in a period when Britain was unmistakably a major power and the British people were optimistic and self-confident, a time of both achievement and hope.

N.R.L

I

HITLER KAPUT

'War speeds with giant strides towards its end.'
– News Chronicle *headline, Tuesday, 1 May 1945*

AT 10.30 pm on Tuesday, 1 May 1945, it began to seem to listeners to the BBC's Allied Expeditionary Forces programme that the end was in sight at last. At that moment, 'Your Hit Parade', consisting of 'The ten most popular American tunes of the week', was faded out for a sensational news flash:

THE NORTH GERMAN NEWS SERVICE HAS JUST TOLD THE GERMAN PEOPLE THAT HITLER IS DEAD.
THEY SAY HE'S BEEN KILLED IN THE BATTLE OF BERLIN.
ADMIRAL DÖNITZ, THE COMMANDER-IN-CHIEF OF THE GERMAN NAVY, HAS BEEN NAMED AS HITLER'S SUCCESSOR.

The programme was then resumed. So, too, was the General Forces Programme, intended for listeners at home, which now continued with 'Music While You Work'. There was no reverent pause or solemn music, such as usually followed an obituary announcement. The Führer departed this life, so far as most of the British public and the men in arms against him were concerned, to the sound of dance music. Those tuned to the BBC Home Service had, however, to wait a little longer, to the next break between programmes at 10.40 pm, to hear the glad tidings. Even the death of the most hated man in the world could not, in the BBC's eyes, justify interrupting 'Evening Prayers'.

On German radio Hitler had a more impressive send-off, the breaking of the news being preceded by a selection from Hitler's favourite composer, Wagner, and the solemn strains of Bruckner's Seventh Symphony. Admiral Dönitz also paid the expected tributes to his predecessor: 'In proud reverence and sorrow we lower our flags before him. With his passing one of the greatest heroes of German history has passed away.' But the call to arms which followed was surely the least stirring in German history. The military struggle, announced Dönitz, continued only 'to save the German people from annihilation by the advancing Bolshevist enemy. Inasmuch and as long as the attainment of this aim is being hindered by the British and the Americans, we shall have to continue to defend ourselves against them as well.' One group of listeners at least were singularly unimpressed, the 6th Battalion, the Royal Welch Fusiliers, who were advancing on Hamburg, from where Dönitz was broadcasting. They heard the announcement after 'an officer in battalion headquarters', a captured farm, had been 'twiddling the knobs' of the command radio set and were first off the mark next morning in commemorating the Führer's demise. 'On the village monument', commemorating a visit by Hitler in 1935, one soldier, a stonemason in civil life, added an unsympathetic postscript: 'Kaput, 1945'.

The news of Hitler's death dominated the front pages of the morning newspapers in Britain that Wednesday, 2 May, and he was given what might be called enthusiastic obituaries. There was also speculation as to why Dönitz, hitherto known only as Commander-in-Chief of the German Navy and thus the directing force behind the U Boat offensive, had been chosen as Hitler's successor. The full story was not to be known for years. The weird sequence of events which had culminated in the Grand Admiral's totally unexpected, and equally unwelcome, elevation had really begun on 20 April, Hitler's birthday, a major date in the Nazi calendar when all the leading figures in Germany traditionally brought the Führer presents. It had not been a very happy occasion, since everyone realized it was likely to be the last birthday Hitler ever celebrated, but it had brought together the three obvious claimants to the succession, Göring, Himmler and Goebbels. Göring rapidly disqualified himself, although officially Hitler's heir. He was already out of favour due to the calamitous collapse of the Luftwaffe he commanded and left the birthday party early on the plea of 'urgent tasks' in the south – these being in fact to organize the evacuation of his private collection of works of art and to ensure that he was captured by the Americans, not the Russians. On 23 April, assuming Hitler to be powerless in Berlin, he sent him a signal proposing, unless he heard that Hitler still enjoyed 'freedom of action', to 'take over at once the total leadership of the Reich'. Hitler, suspecting treason, retorted by denouncing Göring as a traitor and stripping him of all his offices. Himmler went next, north-west to Schleswig-Holstein, where on 23 April he opened secret negotiations with the allies for the surrender of the German forces in the west. When Hitler learned what had happened, from a BBC news bulletin on 28 April, 'he raged like a madman', wrote one eye-witness and Himmler, too, was, like Göring, declared to be a traitor and formally expelled from the Nazi Party. That left Goebbels, but Goebbels, the only one of Hitler's intimates to remain truly loyal to him, planned to remain in Berlin, so though promised the formal post of Reich Chancellor in succession to Hitler he could not become executive head of a new government. Both the Luftwaffe and the Wehrmacht having failed him, Hitler decided that this honour should go to the Navy, which still displayed the true 'National Socialist spirit', while its head was known to be utterly devoted to Hitler. The succession settled, Hitler shot himself at about 3.30 pm on Monday, 30 April 1945. Shortly afterwards, making no mention of Hitler's death, Hitler's close associate, Martin Bormann, who shortly afterwards left the Bunker and was never seen again, signalled Dönitz informing him that the Führer had chosen him as the next ruler of Germany. At 11 am on 1 May, Bormann followed this up with a somewhat vague telegram: 'The testament is in force', meaning Hitler's will, which became operative on his death, but it was not till 3.15 pm that day that Dönitz received real authority to take over as head of the German state in a telegram from Goebbels – who five hours later killed himself – informing him unequivocally that Hitler was dead.

With this message authority finally passed from Berlin to the little town of Plön, in Schleswig-Holstein. At 9.30 Hamburg radio warned the German people to stand by for 'a grave and important announcement'; at 10.20 Dönitz announced to the German people and the world that their beloved Führer had fallen that afternoon fighting at the head of his troops. Both statements were untrue. Hitler had in fact shot himself in private the day before. His reign had, most appropriately, ended in a blaze of lies.

Dönitz had already taken his first important decision. As the Commander-in-Chief of the armed forces he had overruled a Field-

Marshal, Ernst Busch, who wished to counter-attack the British divisions now advancing on Hamburg. German troops, he declared, should only go into action to help keep open the escape routes for refugees fleeing from the east before the Russians. A plea to display the 'Hitler spirit' left Dönitz unmoved and next day it became clear that by no means all the Führer's followers shared his death-wish. The Gauleiter, or Nazi ruler, of Hamburg threatened to call on the civilian population to attack the German troops defending the city if they did not agree to hand it over without a struggle, a decision Dönitz formally endorsed.

The surrender of Hamburg reduced still further the narrow isthmus of territory not yet wholly washed away by the British advance. Albert Speer, arriving in Plön on the evening of Wednesday, 2 May, eager to secure Dönitz's signature to an edict banning any further destruction of bridges and other key facilities, found that the seat of government had already moved from Plön to Flensburg, only three miles from the Danish frontier. Dönitz had taken up residence in a liner, the *Patria*, in the nearby fjord, while the new administration established its headquarters in the naval school at nearby Mürwik.

At Flensburg there now arrived a long procession of important, or at least self-important, refugees, including several prominent Nazis begging for a submarine to take them to safety in South America. Speer himself dreamed briefly of being flown to Greenland, but finally dismissed the plan as a 'combination of panic and rank romanticism'. Fear also prompted some surprising transformations: a former SS commander suddenly blossomed out in the innocuous uniform of a general in the Red Cross. Another arrival was Alfred Rosenberg, the oldest surviving senior official of the party and its former philosopher, who was discovered soon after his arrival on the floor of his office and assumed to have taken poison, though later the 'suicide' awoke; he had merely been dead drunk. More sober reinforcement was provided by Hitler's two top generals, Keitel, Chief of Staff to the OKW, or High Command of the Armed Forces, and Jodl, Chief of the Operations Staff.

The most unwelcome visitor was Heinrich Himmler, for no one wanted the head of the Gestapo around when the allies arrived, and, after he had persistently ignored all hints that he was unwanted, Dönitz on 6 May wrote him a blunt letter of dismissal:

Dear Herr Reich Minister,

In view of the present situation, I have decided to dispense with your further assistance as Reich Minister of the Interior and member of the Reich Government, as Commander-in-Chief of the Reserve Army, and as chief of the Police. I now regard all your offices as abolished.

To be on the safe side, Dönitz also dismissed Goebbels, who, unknown to him, was already dead, and other absent Nazi ministers. But Himmler still lingered around Flensburg, setting up a headquarters of his own and pestering the senior local commanders to help him.

Although it was no longer any real business of his the former Reichsführer SS was deeply conscious of the humiliation of governing Germany from this small provincial town which had been annexed from Denmark only eighty years before. He proposed that the whole government should fly to Prague, an ancient imperial city, but rejected a counter-offer to fly him there alone, suspecting, rightly, that his colleagues planned to land him on an airfield already in allied hands. Other ministers favoured a move into Denmark. But Dönitz firmly rejected any suggestion of leading a government in exile. Their job, he believed, was to wind up the war and hand over to allied authority as speedily as they could, and it was one that needed to be done on German soil.

The political upheaval which had produced the Dönitz government had taken place against a backcloth of military defeat. By the time of Hitler's death, on 30 April, the war was clearly and irretrievably lost. One of those who realized this was William Joyce, better known as Lord Haw Haw, whose aristocratic tones – though his origins were in fact humble – had attracted a large audience to his broadcasts on German radio earlier in the war. On the day his hero died Haw Haw made his last appearance at the microphone, in Hamburg, roaring drunk. 'You may not hear from me again for a few months', he admitted, his voice slurred, then, with an access of his old arrogance he shouted in a mixture of English and German: 'Long live Germany! Heil Hitler, and farewell!' Another servant of the Reich in Hamburg also remained faithful to his trust to the very end. Two days later, at 5.50 in the afternoon of 2 May, only a few hours before the city fell, British intelligence, who had long since captured and 'turned round' all the

German spies in the United Kingdom, were astonished to receive a message addressed to one of them encouraging him to send further information about mine-laying, and assuring him that a suitcase he had left in Hamburg in 1939 'had been safely delivered to his sister'.

The sequel to Operation *Overlord*, the invasion begun on D Day, had been code-named *Eclipse* and now, as its final stages unfolded, not even the respective headquarters knew precisely where the front line was, indeed there *was* no continuous line, only a swirling pattern of separate actions. But the general strategic pattern was clear. The British 21st Army Group, under Field-Marshal Montgomery, was driving northwards towards the Danish frontier, with only a small area between the North Sea and the Baltic, including Kiel and Hamburg, left in German hands, but far behind the front, much of German-occupied Holland, including Rotterdam and Amsterdam, was still holding out. On the right flank of the allied front were the 12th US Army Group, under General Bradley, and the 6th US Army Group under General Devers. After crushing the last large pocket of resistance behind them, in the Ruhr, the American armies had reached the Elbe, the great river barrier across the middle of Germany, which provided, as Bradley said, a 'visible line of demarcation', thus removing any risk of the Russians and Americans firing upon each other in a calamitous misunderstanding. There was, however, a serious difficulty. At the Yalta conference in February the zones of occupation had already been laid down and the Elbe lay ninety miles inside 'Russian' territory. Eventually, after twelve frustrating days on its banks, Bradley's leading units crossed the river and at 4.10 pm on the afternoon of 25 April a patrol of the 1st US Army found itself in contact with the advance troops of Marshal Konev's 1st Ukrainian Army Group in the city of Torgau on the Elbe, a historic moment modestly celebrated by General Bradley with 'a coke from the cabinet under the bench in my van'. Later celebrations were less restrained. Soon after the first link-up at Torgau there had been a joint victory banquet of the divisional staff, and then, Bradley noted, 'as the ritual spread, each echelon of command strained to surpass the one beneath it in the variety of its food and drink'. Conscious, when his turn, near the very top of the command pyramid, came, of 'the vodka victory toasts that had already felled several previous US staffs', Bradley prepared for his first meeting with his allies, on 5 May, 'with a heavy breakfast of buttered wheat cakes and a tumbler of canned milk'. Before leaving the members of the party, as a final precaution that their heads would do the United States credit, were issued with 'a small bottle of mineral oil', to ensure, they were told, that they could 'drink anything' put before them. A stern test of sobriety for their hosts came after dinner when a chorus of Red Army soldiers sang *The Star-Spangled Banner*, despite a total ignorance of English; they had learned it, not understanding a word, by heart.

What the Americans considered, probably with reason, a deliberate 'dragging of feet' by the Russians also presented problems in Austria, since the eastern part, like Czechoslovakia, 'belonged' to the Russians under the terms of the Yalta agreement. On 22 April, part of the US 1st Army, under the flamboyant General Patton, had swung southwards and two days later crossed the Austrian frontier and advanced down the Danube towards Linz, halfway to Vienna. Patton's aim was to cut off the retreat of the German forces into the Bavarian mountains where, it was believed at SHAEF (Supreme Headquarters, Allied Expeditionary Force), the most fanatical SS divisions, led by a few top Nazis, might hold out for months in a bloody last-ditch stand. This 'Southern Redoubt', to quote Bradley, 'existed only in the imaginations of a few fanatic Nazis' and in those of the allied intelligence chiefs and later Bradley confessed himself 'astonished that we could have believed in it as innocently as we did'. Hitler had at one time contemplated awaiting events, and the resurgence of German might which his horoscope promised for August, in his mountain retreat at Berchtesgaden, on the Austro-Bavarian border, and Göring had actually fled there, but the area was almost empty of German troops. When 'the voice of the Wehrmacht', a general famous as a radio commentator on military matters, floated himself across the Elbe in a small boat to surrender to the 9th Army he revealed that the first he had ever heard of this imaginary fortress, which dominated allied strategy in the closing days of the war, had been in a Swiss newspaper.

By now, for many commanders, coping with the floods of willing prisoners desperate to fall into American hands before the Russians arrived was proving a greater problem than fighting. Some refused to accept any more and the 11th Panzer Division, in Czechoslovakia, on offering to lay down its arms, was told that it would only be welcomed if it brought its own field kitchens with it and could feed and support itself.

Permission to cross into Czechoslovakia itself was not given until the evening of 4 May, by Eisenhower in a personal telephone call. According to US Army legend the ordinary doughboy had forced his hand. Knowing nothing of the Yalta agreement, but sick of the non-fraternization rules which made it a military offence to speak 'unofficially' to a German of either sex, the GIs on the Czechoslovak borders had spent their enforced idleness in wandering across them in search of 'dames'. The Germans, it was said, had assumed them to be the advance guard of a far larger force and had abandoned their strong defensive position in the mountains. Patton's response was typical. 'On to Czechoslovakia and fraternization! How in hell can you stop an army with a battle cry like that?' Patton's troops, his immediate superior General Bradley believed, could have been in Prague within twenty-four hours, but he was instead ordered to stop at Pilsen, a few miles inside the border, the Russians refusing to allow him to go any further.

Prague, it had briefly seemed, might become another Warsaw, for there, in 1944, the local resistance had risen against the Germans and appealed for allied help, but the Russians, at the gates of the city, had waited and let them be crushed. On 5 May the Czechs rose against their oppressors and broadcast a similar plea, which the Americans were not allowed to answer, but this time, happily, history did not wholly repeat itself. The Russians, whether by choice or unwillingly, failed to break through but before the Czechs could be massacred the Germans in Prague had capitulated.

It was growing allied anxiety about Russian intentions which precipitated the formal ending of the war. Although Scandinavia, excluding neutral Sweden, quite as clearly 'belonged' to the British as Czechoslovakia did to the Russians, the allies had watched with growing uneasiness the progress of the Russian armies along the shores of the Baltic, which seemed all too likely to culminate in the Red Army occupying Denmark. At this time, because the Western allies were determined not to make a separate peace, they were reluctant to accept the surrender of only part of the German forces, although, from 1 May onwards, there was no longer any real central command and the Germans facing Montgomery's forces in the north and those still holding out in Austria and the south were really fighting two separate battles. Eisenhower firmly rejected, however, suggestions that he should proclaim that the war was over, in the hope that the few enemy troops still fighting would then give in. 'VE Day', he told a party of American editors who visited him after touring Buchenwald and meeting liberated prisoners of war, on 27 April, 'is going to be a day of relief for a lot of soldiers and their families. I don't believe we should have that relief until we are sure that our men are not losing their lives trying to defeat large numbers of enemy forces which may be dug in somewhere.'

By now most German prisoner-of-war camps had long since been overrun but one group still in captivity were the 'Prominente', well-connected individuals whom the Germans hoped to use as hostages. In mid-April they had been removed from the legendary Colditz Castle and were thereafter shunted about southern Germany from one refuge to the next. One of those in the party was Michael Alexander, nephew of the future Field-Marshal, who has described how the general in charge of Prisoner of War Affairs personally informed them, at a halt near Berchtesgaden, that 'he had received a direct order from the Führer that we were to be shot'. To the relief of his audience he went on to add that he had decided to defy the order and eventually the party were loaded into two lorries and set off eastwards into Austria:

We drove across the bridge and towards the widening Inn valley. In a meadow to the left was an old wooden barn. Creeping towards the barn were two figures carrying rifles. They were Americans. We cheered. Round the next corner was a troop of three American tanks. A dusty steel-helmeted figure was peering out of the turret of the leading one. A raised hand and a slowly swivelling gun signalled us to stop. . . . The American soldiers gave us chocolate and bottles of wine taken out of their tanks. They were the spearhead of the 53rd Division, whose headquarters were in Innsbruck [captured on 3 May] about thirty miles down the valley. . . . They said, laconically, that they were way ahead of their main body because the officer in charge was anxious to get a name for himself. . . . Innsbruck was all gold in the morning sun. At the cross-roads in the Maria Therese Strasse American military police in the snowdrop helmets and spacemen boots casually flipped the traffic by. Groups of GIs, heavily armed with Leicas, sauntered along the sidewalks in the style of Gary Cooper. The citizens, looking at the shops or sitting in the cafés,

seemed already to have adapted themselves to the new climate of life. . . .
Next morning . . . the Prominente travelled in an open truck to Augsburg
. . . where, as they arrived, a British major said curtly: 'You're very dirty.'
An American colonel, more intelligent and more practical, indicated the
washroom.

2

CHAOS OR SIGNATURE

'I see no alternative – chaos or signature'
– General Jodl to Admiral Dönitz, Sunday, 6 May 1945

AT the beginning of May, Supreme Headquarters, Allied Expeditionary Force, lay at Versailles, just outside Paris. Eisenhower had established it there, just as fifteen months earlier he had moved his staff out of Grosvenor Square into a hutted camp at Bushy Park, ten miles away, so that they might work and live together as a team, away from the distractions of a great city. SHAEF Rear, as it was somewhat ingloriously known, was still there, with a few offshoots even further from the battlefront, in South Kensington and the West End. SHAEF Forward, from which the main battle was directed, was at Rheims, eighty miles from Paris, in the heart of the champagne country, occupying an undistinguished redbrick building, the co-educational Ecole Industrielle, or Industrial College. The northern front was being commanded from Lüneburg Heath, nearly 400 miles to the north-east, where Field-Marshal Montgomery had assembled the cluster of caravans and office lorries that made up the advanced headquarters of 21st Army Group.

It would have been appropriate for the war to have ended in the Hall of Mirrors where the Treaty of Versailles had been signed in 1919, an idea that was all the more tempting because Hitler had, in 1940, forced the French to capitulate in the very railway carriage, and on the very spot, where the German emissaries had surrendered twenty-two years before; but dramatic gestures were not in Eisenhower's line and the closing stages of *Eclipse* were to be played out in more mundane surroundings.

The collapse of the Third Reich began to seem an accomplished fact at 11.30 am on Thursday, 3 May, when a four-man delegation, sent by Admiral Dönitz, arrived at Lüneburg to discuss surrender terms for the armies in the north. It was led by Admiral von Friedeburg, who had succeeded Dönitz as Commander-in-Chief of the German Navy, but the negotiations, it was made clear, were to cover all three services. The Luftwaffe was considered part of the Army, which sent General Kinzel, Chief of Staff to the German commander opposing Montgomery. For the Navy there was Rear-Admiral Wagner, while the fourth delegate (a fifth, a colonel, arrived later) might be said to represent the Führer's ghost; he was a mere major, but, having been one of Hitler's personal aides, was felt, as one correspondent put it, to provide 'the last expression' of his past power. Major Friedel's prime preoccupation was not, however, to honour his dead master's memory but to get himself promoted before the war finished, and he finally 'made' colonel on the very day of the armistice.

'The German delegation was, I must say, an impressive sight coming down the road,' felt the same correspondent. There was a British armoured car, provided by the subordinate commander whom they had first approached, at both the head and tail of the convoy, and in between, 'sitting waxed-faced, tense and bolt upright in their cars, the German envoys presented a perfect caricature of the Junker officer on parade. Monocles, thin, tight contemptuous lips, jack boots, long grey belted coats, a general atmosphere of pent-up defiance.' Montgomery himself described the scene which followed:

They were brought to my caravan site and were drawn up under the Union Jack, which was flying proudly in the breeze. I kept them waiting for a few minutes and then came out of my caravan and walked towards them. They all saluted under the Union Jack. It was a great moment; I knew the Germans had come to surrender and that the war was over. Few of those in the signals and operations caravans at my Tac headquarters will forget the thrill experienced when they heard the faint 'tapping' of the Germans trying to pick us up on the wireless command link – to receive the surrender instructions from their delegation.

I then said to my interpreter: 'Who are these men?' He told me.

I then said, 'What do they want?'

Admiral Friedeburg then read me a letter from Field-Marshal Keitel offering to surrender to me the three German armies withdrawing in front of the Russians between Berlin and Rostock. I refused to consider this, saying that these armies should surrender to the Russians. . . . Von Friedeburg said it was unthinkable to surrender to the Russians, and they were savages, and the German soldiers would be sent straight off to work in Russia.

I said the Germans should have thought of all these things before they began the war, and particularly before they attacked the Russians in June 1941.

Von Friedeburg next said that they were anxious about the civilian population in Mecklenburg who were being overrun by the Russians. . . . I replied that Mecklenburg was not in my area and that any problems connected with it must be discussed with the Russians. I said they must understand I refused to discuss any matter connected with the situation on my eastern flank between Wismar and Domitz. . . . I then asked if they wanted to discuss the surrender of their forces on my western flank. They said they did not. They said they were anxious about the civilian population in those areas, and would like to arrange with me some scheme by which their troops could withdraw slowly as my forces advanced. I refused.

I then decided to spring something on them quickly. I said to von Friedeburg:

'Will you surrender to me all German forces on my western and northern flanks, including all forces in Holland, Friesland with the Frisian Islands and Heligoland, Schleswig-Holstein and Denmark? If you will do this, I will accept it as a tactical battlefield surrender of the enemy forces immediately opposing me, and those in support in Denmark.'

He said he could not agree to this. . . . I then said that if the Germans refused to surrender unconditionally the forces in the areas I had named, I would order the fighting to continue; many more German soldiers would then be killed, and possibly some civilians also from artillery fire and air attack. I next showed them on a map the actual battle situation on the whole western front; they had no idea what this situation was and were very upset. . . . I thought that an interval for lunch might be desirable so that they could reflect on what I had said. I sent them away to have lunch in a tent by themselves, with nobody else present except one of my officers. Von Friedeburg wept during lunch and the others did not say much.

Afterwards, Montgomery met the delegation again, this time in his conference tent, 'with the map of the battle situation on the table', and repeated his demand for unconditional surrender as a prelude to any other discussion. 'They saw at once that I meant what I said,' he recorded, 'but said they had no power to agree to my demands. . . . Two of them would go back to O K W [High Command of the Armed Forces], see Keitel, and bring back his agreement.' Armed with an agreed record of the meeting von Friedeburg and Major Friedel then left for Flensburg, under orders to be back at Luneburg by 6 o'clock the following day, while Montgomery telephoned Eisenhower to report the day's events.

The Supreme Commander had spent that Thursday working on a newsreel speech, planned for VE Day, which he had already re-drafted three times, with occasional interruptions from his Scots terrier Telek, named after his former retreat, Telegraph Cottage on Kingston Hill outside London. His private staff had given him the dog as a birthday present two years before and since then Telek had, most appropriately, acquired an American mate, Caacie, pronounced 'khaki', but said to stand for 'Canine Auxiliary Air Corps', since she had arrived from Washington by plane. The pair had now produced four pups who had for an hour that evening, in Eisenhower's office, 'chased and bedevilled' their mother, but no doubt helped 'Ike' to relax.

His speech written, the Supreme Commander discussed with his immediate aides, after receiving, without emotion, news of the surrender of the Germans in Italy that day and the fall of Berlin, his post-war future, 'his No 1 plan' being 'to sit on the bank of a quiet stream and fish'. His companions thought that fate might have other plans for him, though no one guessed that they might include the Presidency of the United States. The little group spent an enjoyable evening, 'Ike being interrupted a couple of times by phone calls from Monty and Bradley, who had good news to report and questions to ask'. The questions concerned what had happened that day at Lüneburg and were answered as the British Field-Marshal had already anticipated. If the Germans returned from Flensburg with a favourable answer 'Monty . . . should accept it as a battlefield surrender in the name of the Supreme Commander'. This decision given the Supreme Commander went to bed, reluctantly carrying with him for final correction the manuscript of his victory speech, instead of the 'western' which he usually read in bed.

Montgomery had never been averse to publicity and at lunchtime on Friday, 4 May, a telephone call reached S H A E F in Paris from 21st Army Group reporting that the surrender was duly 'on'. 'We've got everything in hand. The correspondents are all set.'

Among them was Alan Moorehead, who had already covered several of Montgomery's campaigns and now witnessed his final triumph:

Shortly after five o'clock on 4th May, while the firing died along the front and a tacit truce was being preserved, the war correspondents gathered in a tent at Montgomery's headquarters. It was a wild hill-top on Lüneburg Heath, especially wild in those alternate gusts of cold rain and watery sunshine, and the lovely colours of the countryside spread away for miles, pools of dark green in the clumps of pine, purple in the heather.

Calmly, almost breezily, Montgomery began to tell us of the events leading up to the armistice. Half-way through his talk Colonel Ewart came in to say that the German delegates had arrived back with their answer.

'Tell them to wait,' Montgomery said, and he went on addressing us for the next half-hour. Montgomery was finishing his war exactly as he had begun it – absolutely convinced that he was right and that things were going his way.

'And now,' he said at last, 'we will attend the last act. These German officers have arrived back. We will go and see what their answer is.' He led the way to his caravans on the hill-top.

In the night Montgomery's officers had managed to get hold of a copy of the document of surrender which Alexander's head-quarters had drawn up in Italy. Based upon this a similar instrument had been written to meet the present situation. Friedeburg, cigarette in hand, slowly led his delegation across the heath to Montgomery's caravan, where he saluted, mounted the steps and went inside. There followed some discussion as to whether Dunkirk and the Channel Islands might have been included in the surrender, but the subject was dropped as this would have caused delay. The four other envoys, tight-waisted, rigid and silent, stood nervously in a semicircle at the steps of the caravan. Inside, Friedeburg had asked for a German copy of the terms, but he scarcely glanced at them.

Presently he came out, nodded to the others and muttered something as if to say, 'It's just as we thought', and the five men walked slowly past us to the conference tent. Its sides had been rolled up, and six chairs had been placed at a trestle table covered with a plain army blanket. The Germans took their place at the table. Never had I seen Montgomery more sure of himself than at this moment. As he came past us he murmured pleasantly, 'This is a great moment', and he proceeded calmly to the tent, the terms of the surrender in his hand. He conducted the proceedings rather like a schoolmaster taking an oral examination. As he went into the tent the Germans rose and saluted. Then sitting at the head of the table, spectacles on nose, Montgomery read the terms slowly, precisely and deliberately in English. The Germans, who spoke hardly a syllable of English, sat there without a word, for the most part staring vacantly at the grey army blanket. Camera lights flicked on and off. The reading took a full three minutes.

At the end Montgomery picked up an unpainted post-office pen, dipped it in the ink-pot and said: 'You will now sign the document. First General-Admiral Friedeburg', and he handed the pen across.

'Next General Kinzel.' Each man leaned over Montgomery's chair to fix his signature. 'Next Rear-Admiral Wagner. Next Colonel Poleck' (who represented Keitel, the new commander in chief of the Wehrmacht). 'And last Major Friedel' (Montgomery mispronounced it 'Freidel').

Finally: 'I will now sign for General Eisenhower, the Commander-in-Chief of the Allied Forces,' and the Field-Marshal added his signature with the same pen.

The instrument of surrender was signed with what Montgomery called 'an ordinary Army pen that you could buy in a shop for twopence' and it later disappeared: 'I suppose someone pinched it.' The document itself was typed on ordinary Army foolscap and Montgomery defied orders to send it to Supreme Headquarters, adding it to his private archives; Eisenhower had to be content with a photostat. This clearly revealed that Montgomery had at first got the date wrong; being forced to cross out the 'fifth', the date the surrender took effect, and substitute that of the actual signing, the fourth. Montgomery later recalled, too, one other small incident at that historic ceremony. One of the Germans 'wanted to smoke to calm his nerves' and 'took out a cigarette. I looked at him and he put the cigarette away.'

After the signing the delegates left Lüneburg, though only one of them, Wagner, who later obtained a senior post in the West German Ministry of Defence, long survived that day. Von Friedeburg and Kinzel, true to their exacting soldiers' code, killed themselves, while the ambitious Colonel Friedel did not live long to enjoy his new rank, dying soon afterwards in a motor accident.

When the Germans had gone Montgomery spent the evening composing a signal of thanks to his senior commanders and then 'My Last Message to the Armies', which ended on a characteristic 'Monty' note: 'It has been a privilege and an honour to command

this great British Empire team in Western Europe. . . . Good luck to you all, wherever you may be.'

It had seemed possible that the surrender to Montgomery might be followed immediately by another, of the German armies still in contact with the Americans to the Russians, but as the hours passed it became apparent that the war was likely to drag on into another week. In London it was a restless time. Even the Prime Minister was affected by the uncertainty. That Friday afternoon he cancelled his proposed week-end visit to Chequers and 'very much later than usual', as his bodyguard, Inspector Thompson, noted, 'went down to the [Downing Street] Annexe for his dinner. As I joined him, I searched his face for some hopeful sign and thought that he might drop a word with an indication of the position.' But the Inspector was disappointed; the Prime Minister finally 're-mained in town all week-end', though 'constantly on the telephone'.

Most people in London found it hard to settle, among them the wealthy Tory MP, 'Chips' Channon. He wrote in his *Diary*,

After dinner I went along the corridor of the Ritz, being, like everyone else, in a restless mood – all London has been on edge these last few days, waiting for the final announcement – and went to read the latest news on the tape machine. There I read that at 9.13 a communiqué had been issued at SHAEF that the Germans had capitulated in Holland, Western Germany and Denmark . . . We were all immensely moved and celebrated in Kümmel.

Ordinary families learned rather earlier that the British Army's war was over, in a brief BBC news-flash at 8.40 pm, a fuller report following in the 9 o'clock bulletin. Alert listeners noted that the BBC at least now considered the 'emergency' over. The news-reader, John Snagge, failed to give his name and at the end of the news confirmed that henceforward he and his colleagues would again be anonymous.

Nowhere had uncertainty prevailed more that Friday afternoon and evening than at Rheims, as Eisenhower's secretary and personal assistant, Kay Summersby, an Englishwoman originally assigned to him as a driver but later, at his insistence, commissioned into the American Women's Army Corps, described:

All afternoon we waited tensely for Monty's call. Air-Chief-Marshal Tedder (the Deputy Supreme Commander) joined the General in his tiny office; Butch (Eisenhower's naval aide, Captain Harry Butcher) joined me in my office. We waited and waited. Finally, General Ike declared he was going home and could be reached there. Afraid of missing the big surrender, I succeeded in urging him to wait just another five minutes. The phone rang exactly five minutes later, about 7 pm. I answered it. It was Monty. Butch and I eavesdropped shamelessly through the open door. The ceremony had gone through. . . . Although dead tired, the General sat down and dictated a special message to the Prime Minister praising the courage and determination of the British people. . . . Then he and Butch went off for dinner.

But after dinner came the development they were all eagerly awaiting: 'Another message from Monty . . . saying the Germans were flying to Rheims the following day, due in about noon, to discuss the general surrender of all German forces.'

For Denmark, as a result of the German surrender to Montgomery, the war was already over. The news that it was free at last reached Copenhagen around 7.30 that evening when everyone, as usual, was, illegally, listening to the BBC. With the need for concealment gone the announcement was followed by the Danish 'freedom song', composed during the war in honour of this long-dreamed-of day, then – the need for concealment of their listening habits gone – the population poured into the streets, swarming across the Town Hall Square, close to which stood the German headquarters.

Alan Moorehead, having enjoyed a ringside seat at Lüneburg the afternoon before, now, on 5 May, witnessed the liberation of Denmark, by a token force from Montgomery's army and the advance guard of the SHAEF Military Mission, intended to smooth the country's path back to peacetime conditions.*

While still the cease-fire order was only a few hours old the machines took off – a dozen Dakotas, the fighter escort ranging high and wide on either side. Past Lübeck and Kiel and out over the Baltic. German ships seeing us coming ran up the white flag and turned apprehensively away. Then, one after another, the green Danish islands. Every house on that liberation morning flew the national flag on a pole, the white cross on the

---

*The main body of the Mission, of which I was a member, was to follow by road and was still in South Kensington, loading packing cases with office equipment.

red background, and from the air the effect was as if one were looking down on endless fields strewn with poppies.

Over the suburbs of Copenhagen there was at first not much movement in the streets; fearing just possibly this was the final air raid of the war the people ran indoors. But then as we came lower they gathered confidence and poured out into the open. A thickening procession of cars and bicycles and pedestrians came careering down the road to the airfield. One after another the Dakotas slid into a landing between the stationary German aircraft and drew up on line before the airport buildings. The airborne troops jumped down, and with their guns ready advanced upon the hangars. The scene did for a moment look slightly ominous, especially as none of us quite knew what to expect. Armed German guards were spaced along the runways. Two German officers stood stiffly in front of the central office and began to advance towards the landing aircraft. General Dewing, the leader of our mission, met them half-way and in two minutes it was clear: we would have no trouble in Denmark. . . .

At that moment the Danish crowd burst on to the field. The Danes have a curious staccato bark for use at moments of ecstasy. It sounds like 'Wa-wa . . . Wa-wa'. They roared 'Wa-wa' at the airborne troops and then threw flowers at them. They danced among the aircraft and sang 'Tipperary'. The Germans were forgotten. A long line of young Danish soldiers in umbrella-like black steel helmets and armed to the teeth with tommy-guns and hand-grenades were drawn up for Dewing's inspection. While this was going on the two German officers walked back to their staff car only to find it stolen and the last I saw of them they were trudging unhappily back towards the city on foot.

Meanwhile our procession of some twenty or thirty cars with Dewing at the head was driving at an alarming speed into a kind of cavern of waving arms and legs and flags and flowers. 'Wa-wa.' 'Wel-kom.' 'Hello, boys.' The General disengaged himself from a wreath of chrysanthemums and we passed on rapidly over the bridge into the lovely city. It seemed to us that we had never seen such pretty girls, such gay dresses, such glistening shops and gardens.

Dewing headed for the Hotel Angleterre, which he intended to make his headquarters, and once we were there the crowd swarmed forward, making it impossible to get in or out of the building. The scene in the lobby bordered on hysteria. One has a disconnected series of recollections, of corks coming out of champagne bottles, of tables laden with smoked salmon and caviare, of grilled steaks and strawberries, of singing and a receding and advancing wall of laughing faces, of bright flowers under the electric light and the sun streaming down on the people chanting in the street outside.

In the midst of all this a German admiral roamed about the corridors of the hotel vainly trying to find someone – anyone – to whom he could surrender the cruisers *Nürnberg* and *Prinz Eugen*, their attendant destroyers and 600000 tons of mercantile shipping then lying in the bay. It did not seem of much consequence to anyone at the time, and a good half-hour must have passed before the German tracked down our admiral in his suite.

Then there were the Danish quislings who seemed to be pretty thickly quartered in the Angleterre. They were plucked out of bedrooms and out of restaurants in the middle of their meals. Flying columns of Resistance boys kept plunging through the lobby with their hand-grenades. One mounted the staircase to find a line of people with their hands up on the first landing, their faces to the wall, and a Danish soldier prowling about with a tommy-gun.

Unwisely one or two of us ventured out of the hotel, hoping to see something of the town. We were seized by the crowd and hoisted shoulder-high around the square. When we pleaded to be put down they dumped us on the roof of a car and began to parade us round the streets. At last we got down and made for the apparent security of the Palace Square, a beautiful courtyard by the canal. At once the guards abandoned their posts and came rushing at us. We bolted into King Christian's rooms and stayed there with the chamberlains until the way back to the hotel was clear again.

The liberation of Copenhagen, felt Alan Moorehead, had 'a special flavour, a more simple and lighter spirit than usual', because there were 'fewer shadows under the gaiety': Denmark, the 'Model Protectorate' of Hitler's Empire, had suffered least of all the occupied countries and, materially, the population had had a far easier war than the people of Britain. The scene in Holland was very different. The population had barely been kept alive that winter by food sent in, wherever it could be, by the allies, the resistance movement had been everywhere penetrated and crushed by the Germans, and the deportation of Jews to the gas chambers had continued until the very last: Anne Frank and her family had been dragged from their attic in Amsterdam only nine months before. Much of the country was still in the grip of a large and determined enemy garrison, backed by a particularly vicious force of local traitors, and the civil ruler, Seyss-Inquart, was a man of iron. Despising escape, he had made a night dash by motor-torpedo-boat to consult Dönitz in Flensburg days before, and then gone back to his doomed province where, as he rightly foresaw, only death awaited him; he was convicted as a war criminal and hanged.

The Germans in Holland, almost alone among those still fighting in the west, were slow to give in. After the news of the surrender to Montgomery, which clearly included Holland, 'German SS troops', the war correspondent J. L. Hodson learned, had 'shot . . . and killed or wounded' the Dutch civilians who, hearing the news the night before, had poured into the streets 'to celebrate in Utrecht, Amsterdam, Rotterdam and Dordrecht'. The Dutch SS recruited from local traitors and even more hated than the Germans had, Hodson was told, forced 'their countrymen to pull down the flags of rejoicing, and stand with their hands above their heads'. Even more worrying to the allies was the fear that the Germans would, as they had threatened to do, open all the dykes still in their possession and let in an even more ancient enemy, the sea.

Only on the afternoon of Saturday, 5 May, were all these doubts finally resolved, when the war correspondents were summoned to witness the surrender of the German commander in Holland, General Blasowitz, to the Canadian General Ffoulkes. On their way there the journalists observed two signs of the times: a long convoy of allied trucks carrying food and fuel into Holland, and Prince Bernhard, German-born husband of Princess Juliana, the heir to the Dutch throne, looking 'very pleased with himself' in 'a luxurious open car that a brief while back was used by Seyss-Inquart'.

The setting for the ceremony might have been chosen to remind all those present of the misery and ruin which the Germans had brought to this once contented countryside:

At 4 pm we assembled in the empty bar and restaurant of a partly-destroyed hotel at Wageningen where the surrender terms were to be given to General Blasowitz, commanding the German army in Holland. The windows were out, brickwork near one window was precarious. Men were busy fixing up a BBC microphone and electric lamps for photographs. The room was dusty and dirty, and a litter of basket chairs strewn about. . . . General Ffoulkes and his men were fresh complexioned, ruddy, with rather plump faces, looking like businessmen who had put on soldiers' uniforms, men brisk but essentially human. Seated opposite across these shoddy tables was General Blasowitz, a short man about sixty, with a lean, hardbitten face, hard grey eyes, slightly hooked nose, thin, protuberant lips and sharp chin. Such hair as we saw was cropped close. Rechelt, his Chief-of-Staff, was almost as hungry-looking. Both personified war, men whose trade was war. They wore leather overcoats dyed grey, had red leaves on their jacket collars and iron crosses at their throats. The proceedings were brisk, and General Ffoulkes was blunt. But there was nothing grim, no attempt to humiliate, no stamping or clanking. Indeed, at times the atmosphere was rather akin to a business board meeting. The terms held many interesting points – that the Germans must accept further orders without argument or comment, that the Dutch SS must be disarmed and the Germans be responsible for their behaviour, that the Germans would be responsible for guarding all pumps at the dykes until we went in, and that the Germans must feed and maintain themselves until the enemy are moved out of Holland. Among Ffoulkes's admirably blunt remarks were: 'I want to make it clear only one person will give orders and that's myself.'

But, despite these stern words, co-operation between victor and vanquished during the take-over was essential and as Hodson left he noted that already 'the Canadian and German staff officers had to get their heads together over the details of location of units, etc.'

The German surrenders, following the earlier capitulation in Italy, prompted a pleasantly worded signal from Winston Churchill in London to his Foreign Secretary in San Francisco: 'In three successive days 2500000 Germans have surrendered to our British commanders ... quite a satisfactory incident in our military history.' But at Rheims there was as yet little rejoicing. The day had dawned damp and dismal and Captain Butcher, after an early breakfast, was in the office by 8.45 preparing plans, if the Germans' plane had to be diverted to another airfield, for Eisenhower to join them there by train. 'It looked,' he decided, 'a bit as if the actual signing could take place today, but it might be on a train', a far from satisfactory location, especially for the newsreel cameramen.

Preparations meanwhile went ahead at Rheims, in the hope that the weather would clear, observed by Captain Kay Summersby:

There wasn't much work being done in our red schoolhouse when I arrived the next morning. Most of us sat around talking about the surrender ceremony ... Butch was outranked out of his office, which had been taken over by the Russian representatives, General Susloparov, and his bald-headed interpreter, a Soviet colonel also bearing the first name of 'Ivan'. . . .

Just before noon, we learned the German party's plane had run into foul weather and landed at Brussels. They would ... come on to Rheims by car, due to arrive about five o'clock.

The Headquarters staff found themselves, after all, eating alone. 'Lunch was quiet,' Captain Butcher observed, 'Ike being contemplative as to the dilemma he would be in if the Russians refused to accept the surrender', but after the meal everyone was soon 'running round like crazy', especially in the place chosen for the surrender, 'the War Room, where Ike generally has met with his top commanders and staff each morning at 9'. Here the photographers had brushed its usual occupants aside and 'pushed a huge table, normally in the centre of the room, to the far corner to permit more coverage for their lenses'. To Captain Butcher, and to Eisenhower's Chief-of-Staff, Lieutenant-General Bedell Smith, who was soon threatening to call off the whole affair if the intrusive newsreel men were not put in their place, this military holy-of-holies now 'looked exactly like a movie set in Hollywood or Elstree', instead of the military nerve centre more familiar to Butcher:

The room is about thirty feet square and has pale blue walls covered with battle maps showing the disposition of the forces on all fronts. There are charts showing the current day's air operations, casualty lists, records of supplies landed, railway and communications systems and today's, tomorrow's and the next day's weather. On one wall there was a thermometer, mounted on a background of swastikas showing the mounting millions of German prisoners in allied hands.

The Germans arrived at last shortly after 5 o'clock to be met by two British officers 'who saluted smartly, the Germans responding promptly and precisely'. The visitors were then politely shown to a toilet, where 'The German Admiral', one observer reported to his interested colleagues, was 'humming softly as he washed ... and changed his collar, but Colonel Poleck [the 'fifth man' at Lüneburg, representing Keitel, the last Commander-in-Chief of the Wehrmacht] appeared nervous'.

Twenty minutes later, after an initial conference presided over by Bedell Smith, there came another anticlimax. Von Friedeburg, it was learned, was only authorized to parley, not to surrender, and they had no means of communicating direct with Dönitz back in Flensburg, while he in turn would require time to pass on the news of any surrender to his forces, now scattered and in flight. Poor von

Friedeburg, eager to surrender but lacking either the authority or the means to do so, 'indicated that at least forty-eight hours would be needed before he could sign and spoke feelingly of the hardships of the German civilian population'. But the Americans were no more sympathetic than the British had been two days before. 'Beetle [i.e. General Bedell Smith] replied toughly', recorded Butcher approvingly, 'that the Germans still are our enemies and would remain so until the surrender. . . . Beetle told Friedeburg either that he would have to receive full authority from Dönitz to make complete and unconditional surrender in all theatres or Dönitz should send to Rheims his . . . commanders-in-chief with necessary authority to make a complete surrender.' Von Friedeburg retired to 'the office assigned him and called for whisky', no doubt much needed, while the rest of the cast assembled in the war room. 'The movie cameras were in focus, the lights lit, and all was in readiness.' But instead of von Friedeburg, come to make peace, there appeared Eisenhower's Chief-of-Staff, who 'blinded by the glare' announced another postponement. 'There was nothing to do now but wait until Friedeburg heard from Dönitz.'

This was far from easy to arrange, but finally the Admiral sent off his message, in Supreme Headquarters' code, to Second Army Headquarters, who would pass it to their nearest unit to Flensburg, for delivery by courier.

It had been a disappointing day. The cameramen dismantled their equipment and went to bed; so did Eisenhower and his staff though the Supreme Commander was roused soon afterwards by a telephone call from Churchill, who had been ringing all day to discover what was happening. The Germans, who had not yet eaten, retired to No 3 Rue Godenot, a billet used by military officers. Their every move was now being scrutinized and it was duly reported they had dined at eleven on tomato juice, pork chops, mashed potato, carrots and peas, fruit, red wine and coffee, and had then listened to the radio until after midnight.

Next morning, Sunday, 6 May, began peacefully at Rheims, but that afternoon there was a violent, high-level argument about 'all that Hollywood equipment in the War Room', honour being satisfied by leaving the lights, which were clearly vital, intact, but reducing the number of microphones on the table. Another twenty war correspondents were summoned from Paris, and Captain

Butcher found himself entrusted with a new appointment, hitherto unknown to military organization, 'superintendent of the fountain pens', one gold and one gold-plated, given to Eisenhower by a friend especially for use in the ceremony. The big event of the day, around 6 pm, was the arrival of Dönitz's new emissary, General Jodl, German Chief-of-Staff, who 'strode arrogantly from the car... expressionless' and greeted von Friedeburg, one officer with an ear near the keyhole reported, with a non-committal 'Ah-ha'. After this, a little ominously for anyone who remembered recent history, 'the Admiral came out, asked for coffee and a map of Europe'.

Far away in England it had been an unsatisfactory Sunday; everyone had expected this would be the first week-end of peace-time. One Marylebone man, going out to tea in the country, noted that 'it was a dull, rather rainy day but the country looked fresh and the rhododendrons and azaleas were in full bloom'. The late afternoon news 'told us that the end of hostilities was very near', which they knew already, but the party cheered up after 'our genial host on the strength of this news produced a bottle of champagne'.

At Rheims as yet there was no champagne. The evening dragged slowly on. There was a ninety-minute conference between the Germans and Bedell Smith, then another between Bedell Smith and Eisenhower, followed by further consultations with the Russian General Susloparov. Eisenhower remained firm that he would accept nothing less than a general capitulation, but the Germans had asked for more time – likely to be at least three hours – to consult Dönitz, in their own code. Finally, around 9 pm, they pleaded for another forty-eight hours before making up their minds. This was too much for Eisenhower. 'You tell them,' he ordered General Strong, his senior British staff officer, 'that forty-eight hours from midnight tonight, I will close my lines on the Western Front so no more Germans can get through, whether they sign or not.' With this ultimatum he left the office. Despairingly Jodl signalled Dönitz: 'General Eisenhower insists that we sign today ... I see no alternative – chaos or signature. I ask you to confirm to me immediately by wireless that I have full powers to sign capitulation.'

It seemed that the war was to last at least one more night, but already the first of the victory parties was under way, given by the WAC officers to their male colleagues. 'Actually,' acknowledged Kay Summersby, one of the hosts, 'the party was not very abandoned or gay. . . . The Rheims champagne disappeared surprisingly slowly, although one of the Russian officers, attempting to drink American vodka, got so drunk that he and his colleagues had to leave', a nice reversal of what usually happened at Russian parties. Eisenhower had at first planned to go straight to his quarters but was persuaded to put in an appearance at the party, on learning that Susloparov and 'Ivan' were to be there – disastrously as has been seen – 'but stayed only a few minutes', his thoughts clearly elsewhere and the party finally broke up completely soon after midnight.

But no one had much sleep at Rheims that night. Kay Summersby was soon busy in Eisenhower's office, while Captain Butcher, as custodian of the fountain pens, was summoned at 1.30 am by a telephone message from General Bedell Smith's secretary: 'The big party is on.' As he climbed from his car he found himself in the middle of 'a hornet's nest of correspondents' who 'had driven up from Paris on the chance that they would be permitted to cover the ceremony', although a pool of seventeen, acting for the whole of the world's press, were already 'on hand for the job'. Once inside, Butcher discovered that the general responsible for public relations was, not very successfully, 'trying to work out details of the procedure for complying with the order of the Combined Chiefs-of-Staff that announcement of the end of the campaign was to be made simultaneously at a later date by the governments at Washington, Moscow and London'. Butcher had to hurry to be in time for the ceremony itself, at which Bedell Smith would preside; Eisenhower himself remained aloof from direct contact with the German emissaries, as he had done throughout.

General Strong placed the documents for signature in front of General Smith, before whom I laid the solid-gold fountain pen. Beetle spoke briefly to the Germans, which was interpreted for them by Strong. It was merely that the surrender documents awaited signature. Were they ready and prepared to sign? Jodl indicated assent with a slight nod. . . . Generals Smith, Susloparov and Sevez [for France] then signed both documents. At the conclusion of the signing, General Jodl stood at attention, addressed General Smith, and said, in English: 'I want to say a word.'

Then he lapsed into German, later interpreted as:

'General! With this signature the German people and German armed forces are for better or worse delivered into the victor's hands. In this war, which has lasted more than five years, both have achieved and suffered more than perhaps any other people in the world. In this hour I can only express the hope that the victor will treat them with generosity.'

The official ceremony over, Eisenhower addressed a final admonitory word to the German delegation.

After the necessary papers had been signed . . . Field-Marshal Jodl was brought to my office. I asked him through the interpreter if he thoroughly understood all provisions of the document he had signed.
He answered '*Ja.*'
I said: 'You will, officially and personally, be held responsible if the terms of this surrender are violated, including its provisions for German commanders to appear in Berlin at the moment set by the Russian High Command to accomplish formal surrender to that government. That is all.'
He saluted and left.

Having brought the greatest war in history to a triumphant conclusion, Eisenhower still had other duties to perform that morning. He posed for the photographers, holding up the famous pens in a 'V for Victory'. He had to record a short statement for the radio and the newsreels, which involved a retake, since, as Butcher reminded him, technically what had taken place was not an 'armistice', as he had described it, but a 'complete and unconditional surrender, and that's what we've been fighting for'. Then, after some jocular discussion about the terms of his formal signal to the Combined Chiefs-of-Staff – 'We have met the enemy and they are ours', was one not-too-serious suggestion – Eisenhower dictated the cable in the simple and direct terms that came naturally to him: 'The mission of this allied force was fulfilled at 0241 local time, May 7, 1945.'

3

WAITING FOR VICTORY

'It's a fact, but not official'
– CBS announcer, on American radio, 12 noon, Monday,
7 May 1945

MONDAY, 7 May 1945, was for Eisenhower's staff, and everyone else important enough to be in the know, the day that it was all over. For the rest of the world it was the day that it ought to have been over, but wasn't. The Germans were allowed to know that they were beaten; the peoples of Britain and the United States were forbidden to learn that they had won. Officially the day was labelled VE – 1. Unofficially it deserves a title all of its own, as the day of the greatest, most disastrous and most unnecessary muddle in the history of mass communication.

The trouble began at Rheims as soon as the capitulation had been signed, shortly before 3 am British and local time. The public relations officers were eager to release the news, the correspondents desperate to send it. But the politicians, in the shape of Churchill and Truman, had promised the Russians that the news would be held up until 'a time to be fixed later', when the surrender had been formally ratified by the Russians in Berlin. This intention was obviously doomed from the start. All Eisenhower's staff, especially those with press experience, understood very well that a story of such magnitude was almost certain to 'leak'. The public had a right to know that the war was over, the press and broadcasting organizations had a duty to tell them. But the Supreme Commander could not be persuaded to ignore the unwelcome, and unworkable, embargo. 'To a soldier,' realized Captain Butcher, a strictly hostilities-only officer, 'an order is an order' – the self-same argument that was soon to be heard on other lips in the dock at Nuremberg.

Even so the truth would have got out, had the cease-fire orders been dispatched, as intended, 'in clear', for they would have speedily been picked up by the civilian listening organizations which monitored all plain-language broadcasting. Butcher, loyally if misguidedly, pointed this out to his master, whereupon Eisenhower ordered them to be sent in cipher. Butcher's further suggestion that cease-fire orders and correspondents' stories might both go out together at 7 am, a convenient time for the broadcasting organizations and for many newspapers, was turned down. As though nursing some vast military secret or the report of some major disaster, the correspondents were refused access to telephones or teleprinters and, like 'Ike's' staff, went to bed irritated and frustrated, conscious that they were 'sitting' unwillingly on the greatest story of their lives.

Most of those involved were up early, after only a few hours' sleep. At 9 o'clock Captain Butcher, already dressed and breakfasted, found General Eisenhower, still in bed, busy on the telephone, though he had woken earlier and been relaxing with a western, *Cartridge Carnival*. This was to be his, or anyone else's, last peaceful moment that Monday: the day which should have been the happiest of the whole war at SHAEF was, by universal consent, to prove much the most stormy.

Kay Summersby realized early on that she was in for a difficult time:

I found VE Day [it was in fact VE – 1] to be the worst day I ever put in at the Supreme Commander's office. One glance at the messages awaiting the General indicated that there would be no parties that day. Everything was in a muddle. One message stated the Germans in Czechoslovakia refused to surrender to the Russians opposite their lines. . . . A second message noted that . . . the German radio announced the Nazis had made a separate peace with the Western allies, not with the Russians. The latter not only complained bitterly at this report, but advised SHAEF they no longer felt General Susloparov had been an acceptable Soviet representative at the Rheims ceremony.

Around 3 pm the final blow fell. Beetle roared into the office like a madman: Ed Kennedy of Associated Press had smuggled into America a story of the Rheims surrender. The 'scoop' already hummed over AP wires into the United States, leaving a pack of angry correspondents in France, a group of very upset gentlemen in the Kremlin, 10 Downing Street and the White House – and a very irate Supreme Commander at Rheims . . .

The rest of 7 May was all like that. Even the Prime Minister added to the general chaos in our office, by telephoning a total of eight times from London. I didn't get to opening a single 'fan letter', although they covered my desk. We all went home late that night, agreeing it was the most harrowing day SHAEF ever experienced.

General Eisenhower's reaction to the results of the monumental blunder he had permitted, though was hardly responsible for, was one of sorrow rather than anger. He had always trusted the press, he complained to Captain Butcher, and now they had let him down. Many of his senior officers, however, ever ready to raise the cry of 'duty' when it suited them, seemed slow to understand that journalists had duties to perform too, and, like so many people in trouble, blamed the newspapers for their own misdeeds. 'Ed Kennedy's premature release of the surrender story,' wrote Butcher that night, 'has caused the damndest snafu* I've ever experienced. I've learned the hard way it's much easier to start a war than to stop one.'

That day at Rheims, and at SHAEF Main in Paris, the demand was for a scapegoat and, since the real culprits, Churchill and Truman, could hardly be indicted, one was rapidly found. An immediate investigation revealed that the culprit was a highly regarded and enterprising foreign correspondent from New York, Edward ('Ed') Kennedy, who, after throwing up an intended career as an architect, had joined the Associated Press agency and, since his arrival in Paris in 1935, had covered the fight against Fascism all over Europe, in Spain, in Greece, and during the long slog back through Sicily, Italy and France. He had left Rheims and had written, after the ceremony, his 1500-word story in Paris, where it was duly 'filed' with SHAEF for dispatch, but left unsent. But now, with rumours of the surrender spreading all over Paris, the Germans had taken a hand. Anxious that their forces, cut off from their normal communications, should cease fighting, the Dönitz government had, at 2.30 pm British time, announced the surrender by radio from Flensburg. Kennedy pointed out that there was now no possible military justification for holding up his dispatch and

---

*'Snafu' was an American Army expression, also widely used by civilians. It stood for 'situation normal, all fouled up'.

warned the censors that if they would not release his story he would
try to get it out himself, and did so by the simple means of phoning
it to his agency's office in London. 'This is Ed Kennedy,' he told
them. 'Germany has surrendered unconditionally. That's official.
Make the dateline Rheims, France and get it out.' For the London
office, Kennedy's voice was authorization enough and since his
message had originated abroad it was automatically passed by the
London censor. While a telephonist in London was taking down
Kennedy's full story, the advance flash reached New York, which
held it up for ten minutes, fearing a mistake, then released it. At
9.36 am New York time, 3.36 pm in London and Rheims, the
message clattered off teleprinters all over the United States:
GERMANY SURRENDERED UNCONDITIONALLY
TO THE WESTERN ALLIES AND RUSSIA 2.41 AM
FRENCH TIME TODAY.

Curiously enough, due to a previous false alarm, on 28 April,
when a casual remark by a senator in San Francisco had led the same
agency to report prematurely that the war was over, Kennedy's
epic scoop was received with scepticism, over which the desire to
believe that it was true gradually triumphed. Alistair Cooke was in
San Francisco, where it was still only 6.30 in the morning, covering
the United Nations conference for the *Manchester Guardian*:

The sudden flash from Associated Press shortly after daybreak set the
telephones ringing in delegation bedrooms, radio commentators piling
into driverless cabs and the presses of local papers triumphantly stamping
out the enormous headlines they had set up weeks ago. . . . Sleepy
workers leaving their homes saw extras on sale at the street corners and
nodded with much relief that peace was making its final appearance.

Before long, however, doubts began to spread, especially after, at
11.15 am New York time (8.15 am in San Francisco), SHAEF
transmitted a carefully worded message to American news agencies
and radio networks:

Supreme Headquarters authorize correspondents at 16.45 Paris time
(10.45 am Eastern Daylight Time) today to state that SHAEF has made
nowhere any official statement for publication to that hour concerning
the complete surrender of all German armed forces in Europe and that
no story to this effect is authorized.

This deliberately misleading statement did not, of course, actually contradict Kennedy's message but, with memories of that earlier fiasco, it was enough. Alistair Cooke watched the spread of doubt in San Francisco:

Within the hour the radio networks were spreading to all homes and restaurants and factories of this land a harrowing turmoil of rumour. The city police, put on the alert at dawn, relaxed again. Before noon it was established that the Associated Press had once again repeated its unlucky haste in announcing VE Day too early.

The American itch to 'jump the gun' has never been rewarded with such public humiliation. . . . The delegation heads who had announced press conferences today promptly postponed them and it was not until the radio networks returned to their reassuring daily routine of morning serials and cooking recipes that San Franciscans knew that they were back in the world of reality and that the conference delegations could take up the business of peace where they left it last night.

In New York it took far longer to damp down the rejoicing. 'Officially,' wrote the *New York Herald Tribune* next day, 'it was V Day minus one, but to these New Yorkers, it was The Day.' The *New York Times* described what happened as the news spread:

It swept the city with gale velocity. Men and women, utter strangers, shouted it to one another . . . housewives screamed it from the windows. Clerks and typists shrilled it from the skyscrapers. River craft east and west took it up and fed the din with siren and whistle blasts. Cabbies pounded it out on their horns. Women ran down 23rd Street and Eighth Avenue excitedly shouting, 'It's over! The war's over!'

People stared at one another. . . . Then the great paper and cloth throwing orgy began. Paper in every possible form and description cascaded from a hundred thousand windows – scrap paper, ledgers, playing cards, torn telephone book fragments, stationery, streamers, tickertape.

By 10 am paper was piled high in the street, but more solid symbols of celebration followed from the windows of dress manufacturers and wholesalers, whose workers 'threw bale upon bale of textiles into the street: rayon, silk, woollens, prints, foulards – every conceivable remnant in every possible shade and hue – turned and squirmed in the thin morning sunlight'.

Within the hour, Sixth, Seventh and Eighth Avenue and Broadway were eight to ten inches deep in multicoloured fabrics. Thrifty passers-by forgot their delirium long enough to salvage some of the larger remnants. ... Passing trucks, pleasure cars and cabs were draped with the material. It clung to ledges, sills and cornices and the wind played with it and tore at it. Men and women in the streets tore it from their hats and ... shoulders.

This was not the only largesse available in New York, not usually the place to give much away, that day. Opposite Macy's women hung from windows waving bottles of liquor, screaming 'Hey, soldiers! Hey, sailors! Come on up and get a drink!'

A Times Square jeweller, seized with the common fever, ran up to a passing news photographer shouting, 'I have two sons overseas. They'll come home to me now' ... dashed into his shop, came out with a handsome wrist watch and pressed it on the photographer. 'Keep it,' he cried, 'I want you to have it.' The bewildered photographer had not quite absorbed this welcome shock when a few yards down the street a stationer charged up to him with a carton of cigarettes and thrust them at him. The stationer was in much the same state of hysteria as the jeweller. 'Take that, keep that,' he insisted.

By lunchtime Times Square was thronged with joyous crowds and people trying to pass a movie theatre encountered an unfamiliar obstacle; the whole queue was on its knees uttering prayers of thanksgiving. The incomparable New York Telephone Company found its switchboards swamped as rejoicing subscribers broke the news to their friends. The rejoicing continued into the afternoon, observed by the correspondent of the *Manchester Guardian*:

In Times Square thousands of people, yelling ceaselessly, packed the streets, stopping all traffic as far as the eye could see. Milling crowds blocked all thoroughfares. Press photographers clambered on to windowledges to snap the fantastic scene of men and women going wild in the mid-morning sunshine.... Outside one Broadway hotel a group of allied servicemen, Americans, British and Canadians, formed a grinning line while an endless queue of girls marched past to give them congratulatory kisses.

The city authorities described the celebrations as 'bigger than 1918' and the *New York Times* estimated that, between 10 am and 5 pm, 'a million or more New Yorkers danced in the streets'. Then came retribution, a stern telling-off from Mayor La Guardia, as the *New York Times* recorded:

The liberators
British tanks enter the Dutch town of Ede

US troops at a British prisoner of war camp

On Lüneburg Heath

The German delegation arrives at Montgomery's headquarters to surrender. On the right is an escorting British officer

Montgomery meets the German spokesman. In the background is his camouflaged command lorry

Top left
Von Friedeburg signs the instrument
of surrender at Lüneburg

Top right
Eisenhower and Tedder formally
announce the surrender at Rheims

Left
The schoolhouse at Rheims
accommodating Supreme Headquarters

Below
The college in Berlin where the final
surrender took place

The German delegation at Berlin

Field Marshal Montgomery in Copenhagen shortly after the liberation

'I want all the people of the City of New York who have thoughtlessly left their jobs, to go home. . . . Maybe there's still some fighting going on. You don't know and I don't know. . . . Let's be patient for just a few more hours.' A hush closed on the Square and men, women, soldiers, sailors, marines, bobbysoxers and high school fresh-men in the tremendous throng looked sheepishly at one another.

In Washington, a more sober city, 'Victory Day that never was' hardly got off the ground. 'Hours after the news was known,' wrote one observer, 'there was little excitement in the vicinity of the White House.'

All over the United States, as elsewhere in the world, the public turned that day to the radio for definite news – and were disappointed. Many of the radio networks which had at first mounted special victory programmes later abandoned them, and restored their normal schedules. At noon the CBS announcer, after broadcasting another infuriatingly inconclusive report, allowed a distinctly sour note to creep into his commentary:

It's obviously a fact. But not official. Official is official is official. And there, for all the purposes of absolute definition, goes the day we thought might be called VE Day . . . If the objective of the supernatural powers had been to snafu the actual end of the war in Europe, so as to save all the waste of climactic hysteria, nothing could have worked out better.

But the people of Europe, who had endured so much more than the civilians of North America, were not to be cheated of their hour of rejoicing. 'Authorization or no authorization,' cabled home the *New York Herald Tribune*'s correspondent, 'Paris was Bedlam. Hundreds of thousands of Parisians jammed the streets, pistols were fired into the air from moving cars, planes overhead dropped multicoloured flares and fireworks boomed in all directions.' It was not until 10.30 that night, however, that what seemed to be official confirmation reached Paris, with the result one American resident observed:

In the Allied Servicemen's Club in the Grand Hotel an orchestra leader whose men had just finished playing and singing *And the tears flowed like wine* suddenly shouted to the dancers that the war was over. . . . A wild groan of joy went up from the men in uniform. They then began capering extravagantly, their girls in their arms, to the tune of *Hallelujah*. Afterwards, tumbling out into the boulevards they started spreading the news to all [GI] Joes and to anyone French who would listen. But that night it was only the Americans, the optimists from across the Atlantic, who believed the good news.

In Rome that day people were more ready to accept it but the atmosphere was anything but one of holy quiet, as 'the great bells of St Peter's and those of a hundred other churches rang out in jubilation. . . . Sirens which last were heard as a warning of the approach of allied planes, also sounded for ten minutes.' Vatican radio, adding more modestly to the din, introduced its victory report with Beethoven's Fifth Symphony, whose opening 'V for victory' bars had heralded many a British broadcast to occupied Europe. In Milan there was said to be concern over the condition of the famous painting 'The Last Supper', still invisible behind sandbags in the partly destroyed refectory of Santa Maria delle Grazie. A little further north there was, reported *The Times*, apprehension at possible revenge by the Yugoslav partisans who had taken over Trieste and the French Senegalese occupying Turin. At Udine the Germans were, very understandably, anxious to surrender to the British Army rather than to the Italian partisans. In Naples, the musical comedy star Cicely Courtneidge, on an ENSA (Entertainments National Service Association) tour to entertain the troops, was singing *Home is where your heart is*, when the news reached the San Carlos theatre. 'A British soldier got hold of a huge Union Jack from somewhere,' Miss Courtneidge remembers, 'and rushed up over the orchestra and on to the stage and hung it round me. I went on singing, and soon it seemed the whole of Naples was singing that song, with tears streaming down many a cheek, including mine.'

Even in neutral Stockholm confetti showered down on Drottninggaten, the city's Oxford Street, and the Danes and Norwegians who had found refuge there ran through the streets, displaying their national colours. One second-floor restaurant contributed to the jollity by lowering by rope six magnums of champagne, from which passers-by could help themselves. A little belatedly, perhaps, Sweden also announced that she was breaking off relations with Germany, as – evoking an even more cynical response – did Spain and Portugal. Finland, who had actually been on the 'wrong' side since Russia had entered the war, could hardly celebrate her ally's defeat but made what amends she could by proclaiming 9 May a public holiday to celebrate the liberation of her Scandinavian neighbours.

Only in one non-German city in Western Europe was rejoicing less than wholehearted. In Dublin, around 2 pm (3 pm in Britain) after news of the German radio announcement had reached Trinity College, about fifty students, almost certainly English, appeared 'on the roof of the main entrance, waving Union Jacks and singing *God Save the King*, and the *Marseillaise*' while a crowd gathered outside. Soon a number of small fights broke out among them and eventually there was a more serious disturbance, when, offended by the Irish tricolour being flown beneath the Union Jack and other allied flags, a crowd attempted to storm the gates and had to be dispersed by the police, who 'drew their batons and cleared College Green and the greater part of Dame Street. Several people were knocked down in the scramble to escape . . . and were taken to Mercer's Hospital for treatment.' Later 'a crowd of about fifty young men attacked the doors of the Wicklow Hotel', yelling threats at 'the traitors' presumed to be inside, and 'with hundreds of reinforcements from neighbouring streets, the crowd marched down Nassau Street to Jammet's Restaurant, outside which they sang the *Soldier's Song* in Irish' and broke several windows. The trouble was only ended by the police clearing the streets.

The German people, as already mentioned, learned the news at 2.30 pm when the new German Foreign Minister, Schwerin von Krosigk, broadcast from Flensburg:

German men and women, the High Command of the armed forces has today, at the order of Grand-Admiral Dönitz, declared the unconditional surrender of all fighting German troops. . . . After a heroic fight of almost six years of incomparable hardness Germany has succumbed to the overwhelming power of her enemies. To continue the war would mean only senseless bloodshed. . . . No one must be under any illusions about the severity of the terms to be imposed on the German people by our enemies. We must now face our fate squarely and unquestioningly. . . . In our nation justice shall be the supreme law and the guiding principle. We must also recognize law as the basis of all relations between the nations. . . . Respect for treaties will be as sacred as the aim of our nation to belong to the European family of nations. . . . Then we may hope that the atmosphere of hatred which today surrounds Germany all over the world will give place to a spirit of reconciliation among the nations. . . . May God . . . bless our difficult task.

Von Krosigk's broadcast, a not undignified acknowledgement of German guilt, was followed by a three-minute silence for his audience to reflect on what they had heard. To the newsrooms of the rest of the world it added only one more complication to the burning question, was the war over or not? The BBC, as on D Day when a similar situation had arisen, played for safety. It reported without comment at 3 o'clock that the Germans were saying that the war was over, and Harold Nicolson, at home at Sissinghurst in Kent, hurried with his wife and son to 'climb the turret stairs, tie the flag to the ropes and hoist it in the soft south-west breeze. It looks very proud and gay after five years of confinement.' His neighbours, not possessing homes with towers, did their best to match the Nicolsons' lead. On his way to London that afternoon he observed 'a handful of children fluttering little flags' and, on reaching the capital, 'flags everywhere'. He also learned the reason for the mysterious delay which was now infuriating the whole nation. 'At Cannon Street I saw the BBC's Chief Engineer . . . escaping exhausted from London. He says that everything is completely tied up, that we cannot get Moscow to agree to a simultaneous announcement and that everything is to be postponed until tomorrow.'

But for some citizens the BBC announcement of von Krosigk's speech was enough. Showing better sense than all the 'top brass' at SHAEF, the news-vendors at Liverpool Street that afternoon, remembers one woman travelling back from her wartime home in Bishop's Stortford to her peacetime house at Barkingside, were already shouting that the war was over. A young woman journalist, shopping in Woolworth's in the Strand, recalls a man bursting in, crying excitedly, '"The war's over!" By the time I walked up Kingsway,' she remembers, 'toilet rolls were streaming out of the windows and everyone was talking to strangers, sharing the excitement.' Another woman, near Chatham, was busy spring cleaning her mother's pantry. 'I put down my whitewash brush and we opened the bottle of sherry we had been saving for that moment. Just two women – my father had died during the war – and a sleeping baby girl. The ones who suffer most from man's folly.' Another woman, married to a Ministry of Information official and living in St John's Wood, sternly addressed her small daughter:

'Marian,' I said, 'you must remember this all your life. It's history. . . .
Come on now we'll hang out flags.' I ran with Marian up the drive to
hang them on the trees by the road. Now she understood. 'The war's
over and it's my birthday,' she told any passing pedestrians. But nobody
seemed quite sure the war *was* really over, except Marian and myself.

For people due to return to wartime duty that afternoon the
government's refusal to give a clear lead was particularly madden-
ing. Another young mother, who had been enjoying a brief break
from her wartime job on a cargo-carrying canal barge, 'could', she
confessed, 'think of nothing worse than having to spend two days'
holiday . . . down the Newdigate arm which is scarcely more than a
ditch, narrow and malodorous, with coal and cinders on the one
hand and rats in the muddy bank on the other, but although the
evening papers were full of headlines there was still nothing definite
by the time I was due at Euston for the 4.25.' So she dutifully set
off and after a long train journey on a 'roasting hot' afternoon, and
'a walk of half a mile down the towpath carrying my bag and
wearing a very uncomfortable pair of heavy boots that my husband
had had in the Home Guard I got to Hawkesbury. . . . The others
took one look at my draggled form and said in chorus: "Whatever
have you come back for. Don't you know the war's nearly over and
it will be V Day tomorrow?"'

The British public had so far that day been starved of news. The
press that morning had, inevitably, to carry just the sort of non-
committal headline that journalists detested. 'End of war in Europe
at hand' promised *The Times*; 'Germany's surrender imminent'
predicted the *Daily Telegraph*; 'It may be today' reported the *Daily
Mail*. The *Daily Express*, after its monumental 'No war this year'
blunder in 1939, was this time taking no chances. Its headline was
vaguest of all, 'The last hours'.

Long after the surrender was common knowledge all over the
rest of the world, including ex-enemy and neutral countries, the
British people, who had taken up arms earlier than any other and
suffered longer, were still not allowed to know that their long ordeal
was over. The man they had so long trusted to tell them the truth
still felt that his ill-judged promise to Stalin came first. His detective,
never far away, noted how 'the Premier waited throughout the day,
hoping to be able to release the news at 6 pm of the end of the war',
but 'frequent telephone conversations with President Truman and

Marshal Stalin resulted in the decision that the announcement was to be made the next day'. The Western leaders were, understandably enough, reluctant to begin the peace by going back on a pledge, however misconceived, given to the Russians and – even more understandably – determined that the Germans should have no excuse for claiming that they had only surrendered in the West.

No one that afternoon had a more frustrating time, as the crowds in central London became visibly larger and more impatient, than the announcers at Broadcasting House. What should have been a happy occasion had already been marred by a major internal row: Joseph Macleod, who had introduced many editions of the nightly 'War Report', had been told by higher authority that he would not be allowed to take part in the special 'Victory Report', 'because your voice is unsuitable'. Macleod, suspecting that the real reason was his well-known left-wing views, had vigorously protested, but in vain, and eventually spent VE Day in the BBC equivalent of Siberia, at Wembley, revising the proofs of the special victory edition of *Radio Times*.

Churchill had, as Macleod noted, a well-deserved reputation at Broadcasting House for complete 'disregard of people's arrangements' and that Monday he surpassed himself, refusing 'up to the very last fifteen minutes to say whether he would broadcast at 6 o'clock. . . . G. [another announcer] and I stood by from early morning, gradually shelving alternative plans at 1, 3, 5, 6 and 7 pm.'

Puzzled and angry people went home from work, their big moment spoiled, grumbling at the government instead of rejoicing in victory. A *Manchester Guardian* reporter described the confused scene in central London:

All day people in London sensed that the end was near. In Piccadilly Circus, in Whitehall, and in the Westminster area thousands gathered and waited for hours in the expectancy of hearing the great news. Mostly the waiting people were Londoners, but servicemen and women of all nationalities mingled with them.

Buckingham Palace became the focal point. The area outside the massive railings and the royal parks around were thronged with waiting crowds, who seized on every movement inside the Palace gates. They saw the red carpet being placed on the balcony on which the King and Queen were expected to appear. The Royal Standard fluttered from the roof of the

Palace, the windows of which still carried black-out hoardings, some being bricked up.

When no announcement was made on the six o'clock news the crowds in Piccadilly Circus dispersed quietly, and at half-past six the crowds outside the Palace also began to disperse and by seven o'clock only a few people were left.

In Whitehall, where thousands of civil servants and others leaving their offices added to the throng, the crowd waited on patiently until just before seven o'clock. Then a number of police inspectors walked along informing the people that Mr Churchill would not speak that night. Disappointed but in good humour the crowd gradually drifted away.

This was the moment when, having caused the maximum inconvenience all round, the British government at last plucked up courage to risk incurring Stalin's displeasure. At 7.40 pm the Ministry of Information issued, instead of the full-blooded tidings of victory that everyone expected, a clumsy and pusillanimous piece of bureaucrats' prose, which limped on to the air in the middle of a piano recital:

It is understood that, in accordance with arrangements between the three great powers, an official announcement will be broadcast by the Prime Minister at three o'clock tomorrow, Tuesday afternoon, 8 May.

In view of this fact, tomorrow, Tuesday, will be treated as Victory-in-Europe Day, and will be regarded as a holiday. The day following, Wednesday, 9 May, will also be a holiday. His Majesty the King will broadcast to the people of the British Empire and Commonwealth, tomorrow, Tuesday, at 9 pm.

So here, at last, if not the news of final surrender, was at least a firm promise of it. For some it came too late. At St Paul's, twelve ringers who had waited all day to ring a victory peal on its great bells had already gone sadly home. Many citizens, thwarted so often that day, tuned in again at 9 o'clock to the BBC, which offered only its ordinary programmes – 'Monday Night at Eight', an anthology of Elizabethan poetry and Oscar Rabin and his Band – to hear only the same announcement, plus a deliberately vague dispatch by Frank Gillard, who, muzzled like his colleagues at SHAEF, was only allowed to report from General Bradley's headquarters that 'we await developments', and that 'the Germans are announcing that they have surrendered to the allies'. For years the British public had been taught to distrust everything the Germans said. Now it was all they were allowed to hear.

Everywhere it took a little time for the news to sink in. One Scotswoman who had been spending a few days in the small town of Kirriemuir, to be near her soldier fiancé, witnessed its impact on her fellow guests:

We were all gathered round the fire in the lounge of the hotel. We were just waiting to hear the final announcement and, when it came, the feeling that we had was that of enormous thankfulness. . . . It was some time until the party spirit took over, but when it did it seemed to occur spontaneously all over the little town. People gathered in its little main square and suddenly a rash of flags and bunting appeared. It was a lovely evening, with the mauve and pearly light which is a characteristic of good weather in this part of the country.

It was the 9 o'clock news, the traditional source of authoritative information, which really touched off the rejoicings: 'London,' reported the *Daily Mail*, 'dead from six till nine, suddenly broke into Victory life. . . . Suddenly, spontaneously, deliriously. VE Day may be tomorrow, but the war is over tonight.' 'By nine o'clock,' agreed *The Times* in its more sober prose, 'the crowds were even bigger than those which had dispersed two hours earlier.' The pavements were soon jammed with citizens wearing paper hats, and the buses crawling slowly through the pedestrians who had overflowed on to the road were filled with cheering passengers.

The only people the crowd would make way for were lines of shouting, singing girls, arm in arm with servicemen, waving flags and yelling at the tops of their voices. Cars trying to press through the crowds emerged with dozens of men and women clinging to the bonnets, the sides and the backs and others standing on top trying to wave flags and hang on at the same time. . . . When cars came to traffic lights which were red they sounded the V sign on their hooters.

Even in the West End, however, conditions varied greatly between different streets. Pall Mall, the heart of 'clubland', was a conspicuous desert in a sea of rejoicing. Most of the clubs, the *Liverpool Daily Post* reported next morning, had been gloomy and deserted, and with the little champagne still in the cellars costing £3 or £4 a bottle few could afford to buy it.

Harold Nicolson, dining at Pratts, found it 'empty and dull' though he noticed on his way home 'a few drunken soldiers' and 'a fat Jewess in a paper hat . . . strolling down St James's Street turning a rattle'.

Trafalgar Square, however, at the other end of Pall Mall, presented a distinctly more cheerful appearance, as the lady secretary of the Hungerford Club, which provided shelter for the tramps who clustered around Charing Cross, discovered:

From the windows of my flat just behind St Martin-in-the-Fields, there came a surge of sound, as of a great crowd of people singing and cheering, and the steady shuffling of hundreds of feet. . . . I rushed down to Trafalgar Square, with my torch. . . . There an astonishing sight was vaguely visible in the darkness. The whole Square was filled with people. . . . One could just see groups of men and women, their arms linked together, whirling round and round. Others leapt about on their own in their irrepressible relief and joy. . . . An enormous tide, or river, of humanity filled the Square in ever increasing numbers, as others heard the news and flocked in from neighbouring streets. . . . The great lions, occasionally visible in the flare of a torch . . . seemed the right background to the spontaneous expression of relief of those thousands who, for so long, had endured the shattering sorrows of war, the darkness and gloom contrasting with the light and joy in the hearts of the people.

Travelling towards the capital at the same moment was that dedicated Londoner, A. P. (later Sir Alan) Herbert, Member of Parliament and more recently naval Petty Officer, who had that day delivered a small ship to Grangemouth Docks, but had then announced that 'enough was enough' and refused to take it further 'through the canal to the Clyde'. The decision was prompted partly by Scotland's eccentric calendar and barbarous licensing laws, for 'whatever day it was in Scotland, the pubs, it seemed, were always shut'. (Monday, 7 May, was in fact a Scottish Bank Holiday, when it was illegal to buy a drink.) Also, he and his crew 'all seemed to smell the end of the war . . . and . . . wanted to be back in London', and, with great relief, they boarded the night train from Edinburgh due at King's Cross at dawn.

But even for native Scots it had been a disappointing day. The Bank Holiday had brought more people than usual on to the streets, but, agreed the *Scotsman* next day, 'Edinburgh yesterday evening could be said to be more negative than positive'. The public there, as everywhere, had expected 'the eagerly awaited announcement . . .

sometime in the afternoon', as it seemed 'an unavoidable deduction from . . . later messages that general surrender was already a fact. Some sanguine people proceeded to celebrate in various ways, but the public generally seemed to take the matter philosophically or phlegmatically and preferred cautious attendance on events to any emotional exuberance.'

Even when the cautious citizens of Edinburgh decided that perhaps the war might be over after all, the realization hardly ushered in scenes of riot and debauch:

A large number of private houses blossomed into appropriate bunting, generally on a modest scale . . . but in the main thoroughfares the heavier permanent flagstaffs remained free of coloured cloth. The city was in its normal condition in the evening, except possibly for a certain amount of animation and enveloping cheerfulness on the part of those walking abroad in the streets.

But at last, following the official announcement, repeated in the 9 o'clock news, things did begin to liven up a little:

At the King's Theatre the news was announced by loudspeaker and greeted with an enthusiastic burst of hand-clapping. There was no undue excitement. . . . In the Regal Cinema, Lothian Road, the showing of the main film was interrupted after nine o'clock to permit an announcement of the news by the manager. . . . The entire audience stood in tribute to those who had made the supreme sacrifice and the National Anthem was played. It was announced that a special victory film would be screened today.

In Leith a number of vessels in the harbour made . . . a display of their bunting and there was a distinctly festive aspect imparted to the grey piers and quays. In the evening there were scenes of great rejoicing in the centre of the city. At the Mound, a crowd numbering thousands assembled and there was dancing and singing for several hours on end. At the East End (of Princes Street) American sailors entertained the company by climbing the Duke of Wellington statue, and joining the Duke on his horse. . . . The youthful portion of the population, not easily deflected from any occasions of celebration, took matters into their own hands in many quarters, and bonfires were lighted in the streets, to be extinguished as soon as practicable by the NFS [National Fire Service].

The Glasgow Fire Brigade, one of the busiest and most efficient in the world, had that night no fewer than seventy calls to bonfires out of control, and, the *Glasgow Herald* reported, people could be seen singing, dancing and wearing paper hats in George Street, though they were sadly disappointed when, after only a thirty-minute test, the fairy lights festooning the buildings were switched off. The city's most distinctive contribution to celebrating victory came at midnight, when it was officially VE Day at last:

Hundreds of ships, warships, merchant ships, tugs, steamers, motorboats and anyone possessing a horn, hooter or an old ARP rattle opened up in the Firth of Clyde to create the most tremendous victory din likely to be heard in any part of the country. For miles around and far inland the noise was heard and people on the coast, excited by the din . . . suddenly defied the coast blackout ban and allowed their lights to blaze out into the streets.

4

THE GERMAN WAR IS THEREFORE AT AN END

'That will remind you of a glorious day'
— Winston Churchill, signing small boy's autograph book,
4 pm, Tuesday, 8 May 1945

THE first day of peace began with a great storm. Stuart Hibberd, who had come off duty at Broadcasting House only at midnight, was awoken an hour and a half later by the crashing thunder, while all over southern England the rain tore at the recently erected flags and noisily extinguished the lingering embers of a thousand bonfires. To many people, also disturbed by it, it brought instantly back that other great storm on that last night of peace, when the rain had dripped down the newly filled sandbags and flooded the floors of the still untested Andersons and trench shelters. While the storm raged the Prime Minister, still up, was dictating to a secretary and, she remembers, 'once or twice he said with a twinkle, "What was that? Oh, only thunder", or "Might as well be another war".' But clearly the noise did not affect his usual flow of eloquence, for 'it was 3.45 before he went to bed and 4.30 by the time I had finished typing'.

By morning the storm had blown itself out, and though in many places the sky was overcast, in London, where most people's thoughts were centred, the sun broke through. At Kew, on the outskirts, the temperature reached 78°F that day and over most of the country it hovered around 70°F, making it warm enough to sit outside. Around the Kent coast and in the Midlands there were thunderstorms and Scotland and the North had a good deal of rain, but nowhere was the weather bad enough to wash out the celebrations and in London, at least, after some early showers, it stayed dry.

The morning was everywhere a quiet, but busy time, of expectation and preparation, also recalling irresistibly that far-off September Sunday when the whole long saga had begun. Just as then, one could hear everywhere the sounds of hammering, though instead of making blackout shutters or strengthening shelters neighbours were now helping each other to nail up shields proclaiming 'God Save the King' or to stretch strings of bunting across the streets. The materials of celebration were, in the classic phrase of the time, 'in short supply' so that anything that looked festive was pressed into service. All the Oxford Street stores had been stripped bare of flags and bunting on the previous day but most houses managed some sort of display, and Red Flags flew alongside the Stars and Stripes, or home-drawn Hammers and Sickles perched, a little incongruously, alongside the royal coat of arms. Also as on that last half-peacetime Sunday the womenfolk were hard at work, not cooking the joint, but struggling, from carefully hoarded stocks of fat, sugar and dried fruit – plus the more plentiful, but less festive, dried egg, Spam and 'Household Milk' – to make cakes and custards, sandwiches and trifles for that afternoon's communal tea party.

In middle-class districts people were traditionally less sociable and the war correspondent J. L. Hodson, just back from reporting the fighting, found his neighbourhood 'as quiet as on a Sunday' and some people ignoring the whole event. 'The chimney-sweep I met in the road had done fifteen jobs since five o'clock this morning, and was going home at 1 pm £3–£4 better off.' Nor was it a day of rest for the clergy, who everywhere held special Victory Services. The one I attended, in South Kensington at eleven that morning, was packed and, in my private's uniform, due to go overseas on the following morning, I remember feeling an intruder among these comfortably-off civilians, celebrating the end of their war. But even this undemonstrative congregation overcame its customary reserve to join heartily in *All people that on earth do dwell* and *Now thank we all our God* – the same hymn with which the German general staff, led by Field-Marshal Keitel, later hanged at Nuremberg, had in 1940 greeted the news that the French had asked for an armistice.

For those at home the BBC provided its customary Daily Service, from Bedford, where the Religious Broadcasting Department was still evacuated. Its theme, too, had been joyful, with Isaiah chapter 35 – 'The wilderness and the solitary place shall be glad and the desert shall rejoice' – accompanied by *Jesus shall reign* and *Let us with a gladsome mind.* The broadcasting day had begun, as usual, with the early news at 7 am, read by Stuart Hibberd. The King, it was reported, had sent a message of congratulations to General Eisenhower, Mr Eden had broadcast from San Francisco, reminding everyone of the need 'to summon up all our strength for the final overthrow of our other enemy, Japan', and Mr Molotov, his Russian opposite number, had told a press conference in the same city that 'the United Nations should speed up their task of laying the foundations of world security'. In the Far East American troops were advancing on Okinawa and the Australians had gained ground on Tarakan, off Borneo. In Europe King Leopold of the Belgians, whose sudden surrender in 1940 had endangered the British Expeditionary Force and been bitterly resented by his allies, had been released from German captivity by the American 7th Army.

There was good news, too, from the eastern front where fighting was still continuing. The city of Breslau had surrendered to the Russians and in Prague and throughout Bohemia the Germans had also offered to capitulate. Nearer home, confessed the BBC, the mood of the previous night in London had been one of 'bewildered satisfaction' due to the lack of real news. But there were at least definite plans for that day. The main-line railways were promising 'normal services today with special late relief-trains', plus Sunday services on the following day, while London Transport would be running Sunday services on both days, though 'last trains, buses, trams and trolley-buses will leave the central area earlier than on ordinary days'. The Post Office's contribution to the celebrations was of a similarly despairing nature; cheap night telephone calls would be suspended, telegraph services would be reduced, and 'people are asked not to use them except for really urgent matters'.

The morning newspapers appeared as usual that Tuesday, though, to allow their workers the Wednesday off, they would not, it was announced, be published on the Thursday. (Evening newspapers, by contrast, were not published on the Wednesday.)

From *The Times* to the *Daily Worker* the headlines were almost identical, the *Daily Mail*'s 'It's all over' perhaps reflecting Fleet Street's relief. The most striking front page, however, was that of the American Forces newspaper, the *Stars and Stripes*, which bore in four-inch letters the simple headline: GERMANY QUITS!

The papers had little new to tell that morning, though they

described at length the premature celebrations of the previous day and the twin American and Russian advances into Czechoslovakia. Events in the Far East attracted little attention: the 'Forgotten Army' in the Far East that day seemed to merit its bitter nickname. Even in the *Manchester Guardian* its activities received only a brief mention in one corner, under the headline '14th Army held up by rain'. But other matters were not overlooked. 'Country Diary' in the *Manchester Guardian* recorded for posterity that morning that a turtle-dove had been seen at Altrincham and Knutsford on 19 April, 'an exceptionally early date', while 'sedge-warblers and a grasshopper warbler had reached Knutsford on the twenty-ninth'. That day, too, the *Daily Mirror* fulfilled a long-standing prophecy that Jane, its famous strip cartoon character, would finally reveal all on the day of victory. There, sure enough, that Tuesday morning, she stood, in naked splendour, though only at the expense of the story, which had, mysteriously, leapt several days forward.

One matter which, rather surprisingly, the press did not explain was how VE Day had got its name. The term had in fact been coined, three months after D Day, by the Director of the United States Office of War Mobilization as the target date from which American industry could begin to return to peacetime production. Its brevity, so convenient for headline-writers, ensured that it soon caught on, replacing both 'Armistice Day', already in use in both countries for a different occasion, and the more clumsy 'Unconditional Surrender Day'. One British newspaper, the *Manchester Guardian*, did, however, explain next day why the official cease fire was to come into effect at one minute past midnight. The Army sensibly timed messages at 2359 or, as in this case, 0001, to ensure that no confusion arose as to whether 'midnight' meant the start of a particular day or its end. When, later on VE Day, Mr Churchill referred to the surrender taking effect at 'one minute after midnight on Tuesday, 8 May', he was, the purists happily pointed out, making a mistake; 'one minute after midnight' was not on 8 May but the ninth.

The West End that morning was strangely quiet. To one woman, coming up from Sussex for the day, 'the crowd seemed friendly but lethargic. Their pace, physically and emotionally, was that of a Sunday stroll. There was no wild excitement, no frenzy.' 'Chips' Channon, walking through Mayfair to his customary Mecca, the

Ritz in Piccadilly, found 'the streets almost empty' though the hotel was 'beflagged and decorated' and 'everyone kissed me', including a duchess. Harold Nicolson, lunching at the Beefsteak Club near Leicester Square, was struck by the prevailing air of normality, but by the time he emerged to walk to Parliament was confronted by 'a very different scene':

The whole of Trafalgar Square and Whitehall was packed with people. Somebody had made a corner in rosettes, flags, streamers, paper whisks and above all, paper caps . . . of the comic variety . . . I observed three Guardsmen in full uniform wearing such hats. . . . And through this cheerful, but not exuberant, crowd I pushed my way to the House of Commons. The last few yards were very difficult, as the crowd was packed against the railings. I tore my trousers in trying to squeeze past a stranded car. But at length the police saw me and backed a horse into the crowd, making a gap through which, amid cheers, I was squirted into Palace Yard . . . and seeing that it was approaching the hour of 3 pm I decided to remain there and hear Winston's broadcast, which was to be relayed through loudspeakers.

All over the country the clattering of crockery and cutlery, hastily being assembled for the forthcoming street parties, died away as 3 o'clock approached and windows in the surrounding houses were flung open to await the Prime Minister's broadcast. To many it must have recalled those pre-war Armistice days when the nation also fell silent in anticipation of a great shared emotional experience.

Nowhere was the sense of expectation greater than at No 10 Downing Street, as Churchill's secretary, Elizabeth Nel, later described:

The entire staff turned up at Number 10 from the Annexe for the occasion and we all stood outside the Cabinet Room door. Just before three we heard a great trumpeting sound over the loudspeaker as he blew his nose, then some remarks, 'Pull down that blind', 'What are you doing with that? No leave it there. Move a little further away please', but, of course . . . he was not yet on the air . . . this was only coming out to us.

Matching the moment, the sun came out over central London, and carrying clearly through the summer afternoon, echoed the chimes of Big Ben, which had in the past introduced, in the 9 o'clock news, so many a tale of hardship and calamity. Then, from the Cabinet Room at 10 Downing Street, from which the doleful tones of Neville Chamberlain had apologetically announced the declaration of war, and from which Churchill himself, 'in a solemn hour for the life of our country', had, in May 1940, first summoned his countrymen to resist, the familiar voice rang out clear and confident:

Yesterday at 2.41 am the representative of the German High Command and government, General Jodl, signed the act of unconditional surrender of all German land, sea and air forces, in Europe, to the Allied Expeditionary Force and to the Soviet High Command. Today, this agreement will be ratified and confirmed at Berlin. . . . Hostilities will end officially at one minute after midnight tonight, Tuesday, 8 May, but in the interests of saving lives the 'Cease Fire' began yesterday to be sounded along the fronts. . . . The German war is therefore at an end. Our gratitude to all our splendid allies goes forth from all our hearts in this island and the British Empire.

We may allow ourselves a brief period of rejoicing but let us not forget for a moment the toils and efforts that lie ahead. Japan, with all her treachery and greed, remains unsubdued. The injustice she has inflicted upon Great Britain and the United States, and other countries, and her detestable cruelties call for justice and retribution. We must now devote all our strength and resources to the completion of our task both at home and abroad. Advance Britannia! Long live the cause of freedom! God Save the King!

It was in every way a classic Churchill speech, from his sturdy mispronunciation of the name 'Jodl' (the Germans sound the 'J' as a 'Y') to its rousing conclusion, which Harold Nicolson noted, caused a gasp of astonishment or admiration, among the listening thousands in Parliament Square. Then, as Churchill finished speaking, the haunting notes of the Cease Fire, sounded by the buglers of the Royal Horse Guards, rang out and, as they died away, 'God Save the King'. Fervently everyone, self-consciousness for once forgotten, sprang to attention and sang it, just as they had on that melancholy Sunday, 3 September 1939.

Some people felt a desire to return that day to the place where they had heard Chamberlain's very different broadcast. One volunteer nurse who had been at Paddington Green Hospital on that distant day returned there on her day off, feeling that she 'would like to be there . . . to hear Mr Churchill tell us that Germany had surrendered':

The nursing staff had decided to listen to the Prime Minister's announcement in the ward with the children, so as soon as I had put on my cap and apron I went straight up to the ward. As the hands of the ward clock neared the hour, the nursing staff automatically moved apart. For once the ward was silent – the children stopped chattering and not one of them was crying. When the Prime Minister's voice came on the air I glanced at the women in uniform. Each one stood quietly and you could tell by their eyes that their thoughts were far away from the hospital.

The announcement finished, I felt a tug at my hand, which was being held by a small girl in the cot I was standing by. A little face was gazing up at mine. 'What does it mean?' she asked anxiously.

'The war has ended,' I tried to reassure her with a smile.

'What does that mean?'

'Well it means,' I hesitated for a moment, searching for something she would understand, 'it means you will see lights at night in the streets and windows lit up.' She looked dazed and I stumbled on: 'It means you will never hear a siren again.'

'Never hear a siren again?' she repeated in a voice of utter astonishment. 'Never again?' And I could see by the look in her dark eyes that she did not believe one word I had told her.

At Downing Street, oddly paralleling that scene in the bunker in Berlin when the defeated Hitler had bidden farewell to his personal staff, the Prime Minister's helpers gathered to acclaim him:

After his statement . . . we all rushed downstairs and out into the garden, to line the path to the garden door and when he came out to go to the House to give his statement again we clapped and clapped and I think there were tears in his eyes as he beamed and said 'Thank you all, thank you very much.' Outside, through the Horse Guards Parade, along Birdcage Walk, and Great George Street . . . the whole place was jammed with people waiting to welcome him. They cheered and shouted, 'Good old Winnie' and some pressed forward to pat the car and jump on the running board, so that it was almost impossible to move, and it took quite thirty minutes to drive the quarter of a mile.

Sitting inside, with Churchill, his detective found that 'no engine power was necessary' for the vehicle was 'literally forced along by the crowd' with 'everyone determined to shake his hand. In Parliament Square the cheering thousands closed right in. Mr Churchill came forward to stand on the front seat of the open car with me while mounted police cleared a way. Eventually we reached the House after a terrible struggle, which Mr Churchill, looking very happy, thoroughly enjoyed.'

His colleagues, inside the Chamber, were less happy, for when Questions finished, at 3.15, the Prime Minister was not yet in his place and 'for a few embarrassed minutes', wrote 'Chips' Channon, 'we had nothing to do. Members, amused, asked desultory questions, keeping their eyes on the door behind the Speaker's chair.' The officials were already dressed for a great occasion, 'the Serjeant-at-Arms ... in Court Dress ... the Speaker wore his robes with gold braid etc.' The pause in the proceedings was resourcefully filled by A. P. Herbert, safely in his place after his overnight dash from Scotland, who rose to ask the Leader of the House when the government proposed to proceed with the Outlawries Bill, an imaginary measure, 'formally read at the beginning of each Session ... to preserve the right of members to discuss what they will'. Sir John Anderson, a solemn if not pompous man, rose to the occasion and, as Herbert commented, was luckily equipped with 'a slow delivery', which helped to spin out time. Other questions in a similar vein followed, including one on the forthcoming Water Bill – 'unsuitable business this week' commented one MP – and then, at 3.23, as Harold Nicolson, by now also in his place, noted, 'a slight stir was observed behind the Speaker's chair and Winston, looking coy and cheerful, came in. The House rose as a man and yelled and waved their Order Papers.' Some in their excitement even leaped on the benches and pulled out and waved handkerchiefs, while a few MPs were moved to tears. Even the occupants of the Galleries, supposed to behave as though they were non-existent, joined in, uttering strictly non-parliamentary 'Hurrahs'. The Prime Minister 'responded', observed Nicolson, 'not with a bow exactly, but with an odd shy jerk of the head and a wide grin. Then he ... begged to move "That this House do now attend at the Church of St Margaret, Westminster, to give humble and reverent thanks to Almighty God for our deliverance from the threat of German domination".'

And so, with the Serjeant-at-Arms with the mace on his shoulder preceding, 'Mr Speaker, in his resplendent, rarely-worn State robe and train of gold and black', followed by the Prime Minister and the acting leader of the Labour Party, Arthur Greenwood, then by

Privy Councillors, in groups of four, and finally by the ordinary MPs, two by two, 'we all strode out', Nicolson wrote, 'through the Central Lobby . . . through St Stephen's Chapel and out into the sunshine of Parliament Square through a lane kept open for us through the crowd'. He had expected 'some jeers or tittering', but instead they were received with cheers. Today, even politicians were popular.

Nicolson's colleague, Tom Driberg, who had entered the House after a famous by-election at Maldon, three years earlier, described the scene which followed:

The windows of the church were still drably darkened; but the violet gown of the Speaker's Chaplain – a Doctor of Divinity of St Andrew's University – caught the eye vividly as he stood before the blushing peonies and azaleas massed on the altar. The service had an almost Presbyterian flavour, a restrained dignity. . . . The singing was rich and exultant. The dramatic climax was at the end; the organ was playing, the west doors were flung open, the warm, living sunshine poured in, there was a second of suspense – and then, simultaneously, the bells pealed out clamorously, rocking the roof above us and the crowds cheered wildly as they saw the Speaker and the Prime Minister emerging.

For many MPs the most moving element of the ceremony had occurred when the Speaker had read out the House's own roll of honour: the names of twenty-one MPs who had given their lives. Then, its duty done, the House adjourned. The Prime Minister, hurrying back through the central lobby, was loudly clapped and, even more unprecedented in these sacred precincts, was intercepted by a small boy (his name was duly recorded by Tom Driberg for posterity, Peter Bland of Golders Green) 'who contrived to pursue the Prime Minister from St Margaret's into the Member's Lobby itself and, taking no notice whatever of his thrice-repeated and emphatic refusal, eventually obtained his autograph'. Churchill, knowing when he was beaten, ruffled the boy's hair and remarked as he signed, 'That will remind you of a glorious day.'

London that day was looking its best. 'The trees in the Mall and St James's Park,' noted the *Scotsman*'s London correspondent, 'were showing the freshest green of Spring. . . . The tulip beds were gorgeous masses of bloom.' In the sunshine people stood and gazed hopefully at the long, grey façade of Buckingham Palace with 'its bomb-spattered stonework' and bomb-blasted 'windows as yet unglazed', but above it floated the Royal Standard and in the centre of the main frontage the balcony was already 'draped with a crimson and gold hanging'. The more adventurous swarmed all over the Queen Victoria Memorial, which was largely taken over by newsreel cameras with projecting lenses; those already weary subsided on the grass or the kerb. They were in a mood to cheer everyone who appeared and they did: the Palace Guard marching 'along the Mall with fifes and drums' before the old one marched away, led by the band of the Irish Guards; the Prime Minister, arriving in morning dress and an open car for lunch and later leaving to make his broadcast; loudest of all, perhaps, the airmen arriving to be decorated at an investiture, one of whom shyly revealed that he had made twenty-seven trips over Germany before being wounded, and was carried shoulder-high by a group of GIs through the wildly-applauding crowd. 'Anything did for laughing and cheering', observed the *Manchester Guardian*. 'At one time it was a shabby horse-cab clumping along with a shabby cabbie in a shabby billycock and inside, superb Edwardian sight, an Army officer with a pointed, brown beard. Or it was medical students in procession with their red lion carried high, or carts with decorated ponies.'

After Churchill's broadcast there was a lull in the streets outside. The war correspondent, J. L. Hodson, walking 'through Whitehall, Trafalgar Square and Piccadilly' in the bright sunshine, found 'London was gay and densely thronged, but . . . comparatively quiet'. He saw 'only half a dozen people tipsy and these hung from a second-storey window in Piccadilly Circus, one woman beating time and wearing a large imitation policeman's helmet'. Outside Rainbow Corner, the American servicemen's club on the corner of Shaftesbury Avenue, there was rather more excitement, for GIs 'were throwing oddments down from the windows of their clubs . . . suddenly a great streamer of paper came down . . . then we saw it was a roll of toilet paper, and everybody laughed'.

Streets were crowded and looked, from a short distance, impassable. But in the main one could move about. It was a crowd light-hearted, wearing its red, white and blue rosettes as on a Cup Final Day, and wearing, too, a host of comic little hats, silver cones, tricoloured cones and, in one instance, small royal crowns. Two soldiers sported a badge, 'Pity the poor unemployed'. . . . There was little singing . . . but I heard *Marching through Georgia* in Whitehall and the *Volga Boatmen*'s song in the Haymarket. . . . Girls had climbed on to various clumps of stone and turned themselves into living statues: the lions' heads in Trafalgar Square were being sat upon and in Whitehall a girl had clambered on to a stone ledge twenty-five feet above the street. In Piccadilly we slipped into a News theatre and heard the only bitter comment, from the woman taking our tickets, who said 'All celebrating like fools and the war not over.'

This thought was at the back of many people's minds, though rarely spoken. The writer John Lehmann, walking 'right across Hyde Park . . . pouring with sweat . . . with a heavy suitcase in one hand and a briefcase in the other' after 'queuing for a bus in Paddington that never came', was struck by the 'not quite full-hearted nature of the celebrations. The crowds,' he decided, 'aware that Japan . . . had still to be conquered . . . at what cost no one could reckon', were more dazed than excited, 'like cripples taking their first steps after a miracle healing, not fully grasping yet the implication of the new life ahead of them.'

5

WE WANT THE KING

'Today we give thanks for a great deliverance'
– King George VI, 9 pm, Tuesday, 8 May 1945

THE morning had been mainly a quiet, domestic time, the afternoon
had been dominated by the Prime Minister's broadcast, but the
evening was everywhere devoted to rejoicing. In London the
atmosphere really began to liven up around teatime, though it
required all one's ingenuity and persistence to secure a cup of tea.
Most cafés were open, including the ubiquitous 'Joe' Lyons, which
offered a refreshing cup for 2d, though with sugar strictly limited
and with a chained communal spoon for stirring, but they were
packed out, and many people gave up the struggle and went thirsty.
It was Churchill and the King whom everyone wanted to see and
soon after 4 o'clock the Prime Minister emerged from the Palace
of Westminster to drive to Buckingham Palace, after a diversion
via Downing Street for a cigar. As he told his detective, he had,
most unusually, come out without his cigar case, and the crowd
would be disappointed if, on this day of all days, he appeared without this customary accessory. Having duly collected one he made
the most of it: 'A crowd waited for him to leave the building and he
paused to light the cigar in front of them.' Then on down the Mall
to Buckingham Palace, where soon afterwards he appeared 'on the
balcony with the royal family, the King, bareheaded and in naval
uniform . . . Her Majesty in soft powder blue, Princess Elizabeth
in her uniform of second subaltern of the ATS and Princess
Margaret in blue'. After this wildly-applauded occasion, the tide of
humanity flowed back towards Whitehall, where word spread that
the Prime Minister would be making a second speech and thousands
of people were soon jammed in front of the Ministry of Health
building, shouting 'We want Winnie'. When, just before six, he

walked out on to the balcony, complete with cigar at an impressive angle, a deafening roar went up, growing even more frenzied when he gave the 'V' sign. 'He was,' the BBC reported later that evening, 'unable to make himself heard until his colleagues on the balcony with him signalled for silence and in a minute the vast audience was uncannily quiet.' Then, 'in a strong firm voice', Churchill told them:

This is your victory. It is the victory of the cause of freedom in every land. In all our long history we have never seen a greater day than this. Everyone, man or woman, has done their best. Everyone has tried. Neither the long years, nor the dangers, nor the fierce attacks of the enemy, have in any way weakened the deep resolve of the British nation. God bless you all.

During the early evening residents from the suburbs, their local celebrations forgotten, poured into London and joined the hundreds of thousands of people of all ages now milling about between Buckingham Palace, Piccadilly and Whitehall. Many tried to push their way into the crowded pubs which, after opening at 6 o'clock, had in some cases already been drunk dry. There was, however, astonishingly little drunkenness and the President of the Board of Trade, Hugh Dalton, mingling with the crowds that evening, found 'everyone most orderly and happy' with 'not a single drunk to be seen or heard'. It added up, he decided, to 'a grand ending, and we have been saved from "darkness for a thousand years"'.

Due to the double summertime introduced during the war, it did not get dark until astonishingly late; lighting-up time, which many people still thought of as blackout time, was not till 10.30 pm, but as dusk fell the floodlights, doubly astonishing after nearly six years of darkness, were switched on, throwing into dazzling relief all those great public buildings which had miraculously survived all that Hitler could hurl against them. One by one, as the lights came on, they burst upon the eye, revealing that London had not merely taken it but that all the essential features of its skyline were still there: the Tower of London; the Royal Exchange; the Mansion House, the Royal Mint; the dome of St Paul's with its cross picked out high above it; and then, halfway down the Strand, Somerset House, followed by the great cluster of buildings around Whitehall – the river front of the Houses of Parliament, the Horse Guards frontage of the War Office, the Middlesex Guildhall. Most impressive of all, most people felt, was the stately quadrangle of buildings around Trafalgar Square, with the pillared front of the National Gallery 'alive with every stone outlined in the floodlighting', and Admiralty Arch, 'rising out of the ground and Horatio Nelson standing aloft in a greenish ray of light . . . as romantic as even he could have wished'. As the darkness deepened the searchlights began to sweep across the night sky as once they had searched for enemy bombers, performing 'a kind of geometric dance of rejoicing', and creating, as they crossed and criss-crossed in the sky, narrow pyramids of light, enclosing triangles of blackness.

Almost as exciting as the floodlights were the rows of coloured bulbs over the entrances of cinemas and theatres and the lights streaming from their foyers and from pub doorways, freed at last from their blackout curtains. (One woman, struck by the brightness that night, recalled hearing a soldier describe forcing one's way through them to get inside as 'like getting mixed up in the skirts of a nun'.)

Among those enjoying the unfamiliar brightness was Tom Driberg:

In the orange glow that streamed down from the Tivoli to the pavement of the Strand, a buxom woman in an apron made of Union Jacks and a man of respectable middle-class and middle-aged appearance did an exaggeratedly Latin-American dance while an accordion played *South of the Border*. The trees in Leicester Square were silvery-green in the festive light. . . . As I picked my unobtrusive way along Coventry Street, a cheerful woman bawled 'MPs – ye're off duty tonight!' I started guiltily; but she was addressing two redcaps [Military Policemen]. On the roof high above Scott's dignified oyster house an airman and a Yank did a fantastic Harold Lloyd act, elaborately sharing a bottle, tossing coins down to the people, who screamed each time they swayed over the parapet. . . . An ambulance came clanging along and waited, but was fortunately not needed.

In the luxury restaurants of the West End the shadow of austerity and rationing still lay heavy over every frayed tablecloth, for it was illegal to serve more than three courses or to charge more than 5s for a meal, or 15s including all extras except wine. The Savoy Grill offered only a modest victory dinner: soup, chicken, and peach, for 11s, including 6s house-charge. For more lavish hospitality one had to attend a private party like that given by 'Chips' Channon in his magnificent drawing-room, lovingly copied from the Amalienburg Palace in, most appropriately, Munich. Harold Nicolson, among the guests, left early in disgust after watching his host and other appeasers 'celebrating *our* victory over *their* friend Herr von Ribbentrop', not yet captured, but later to be tried and executed as a war criminal.

Churchill's speech at 3 pm had provided the first climax of the day; the second came six hours later, after a thanksgiving service and a thirty-minute 'Tribute to the King', with the King's broadcast:

Today we give thanks to God for a great deliverance.

Speaking from our Empire's oldest capital city, war-battered, but never for one moment daunted or dismayed, speaking from London, I ask you to join with me in that act of thanksgiving.... Let us remember those who will not come back . . . the men and women in all the Services who have laid down their lives. . . . Then let us salute in proud gratitude the great host of the living who have brought us to victory. . . . Armed or unarmed, men and women, you have fought, striven and endured to your utmost. No one knows that better than I do; and I as your King thank you with a full heart. . . . With these memories in our minds, let us think what it was that has upheld us through nearly six years of suffering and peril: the knowledge that everything was at stake, our freedom, our independence, our very existence as a people.... We knew that if we failed the last remaining barrier against a world-wide tyranny would have fallen. But we did not fail. Let us . . . on this day of just triumph and proud sorrow . . . take up our work again, resolved as a people to do nothing unworthy of those who died for us and to make the world such a world as they would have desired, for their children and for ours.

It was not merely one of the longest of the King's broadcast speeches, lasting thirteen minutes, but also, by general consent, his best, delivered with a moving sincerity and conviction. 'Though our royal and official tradition of attributing all to God does not endear itself to me,' confessed one journalist to his diary, 'the King . . . does his work well' and 'his stammer does win one's heart'. The ordeal of his 'live' broadcast over, the King appeared as expected on the Palace balcony, lifting his hand – rather shyly, I thought, as one of the watching thousands – in response to the roar of the crowd. Then the cheering redoubled as, in naval uniform, he led out his two daughters and his wife, her diamond tiara sparkling in the floodlights as she smiled down at the crowd. A collective sigh of regret went up as they went indoors again, but it was not long before the same chant, 'We want the King', was being raised again, often in a noticeably American accent, although the GIs, who usually took the lead in any celebration, were this evening content to take second place. One woman remembers an American wedged beside her predicting that the royal family would not be drawn out again, while she stoutly asserted that they would, and she felt, she confessed, a glow of patriotic triumph when once again the balcony doors swung back and that slight figure in naval uniform came smilingly forward. 'We went out eight times altogether,' the King recorded in his diary, and 'were given a great reception.' It was nearly eleven before the royal family went indoors for the last time and then, unknown to the crowds, the two princesses, one a fourteen-year-old schoolgirl, the other a nineteen-year-old ATS subaltern, were allowed to slip out to see the sights, escorted by two young officers. 'Poor darlings,' commented their father affectionately, 'they have never had any fun yet.'

The BBC was meanwhile providing those at home with a picture of VE Day all over the British Isles. After the King's speech an unusually cheerful 9 o'clock news followed. The Admiralty, it was announced, had issued surrender instructions to the German Navy; a British tank column was 'having a triumphal passage' across Denmark, and allied delegates had arrived in Oslo to accept the surrender in Norway; the hated Seyss-Inquart had been captured in Holland; and Zagreb in Croatia, one of those now far-off campaigns that had once seemed so important, had fallen to the Yugoslav Army. The RAF had been busy, carrying 350 tons of food to Holland and flying home the first 4500 former prisoners of war to be brought back direct from Germany. The BBC added, 'as a tailpiece to Victory Day news . . . something you haven't heard about since the war began . . . Britain's weather on the day it happened . . . most of the time it's been sunny and very warm.' But listeners must have felt that normal times had indeed returned with the weather forecast which followed, the first since 1939: 'Sporadic rain over the whole country with thunder in places: outlook for Thursday, unsettled, local thunder and somewhat cooler. There's also news today,' added the BBC, unwontedly skittish, 'of a long-lost friend –

the large depression; it has turned up again between Ireland and
the Azores where it's reported at the moment to be almost
stationary.'

Among the crowds now thronging the pavements of the West
End, the principal desire seemed to be to make a noise. Dustbin lids
and the metal covers placed over sandbags were both pressed into
service and anyone with any kind of musical instrument was soon
surrounded by an enthusiastic group of supporters. That night the
future band-leader Humphrey Lyttleton, who had come up from
the Guards depot at Caterham where he was under training as a
subaltern, armed with his trumpet, formed his first, distinctly
impromptu, orchestra:

Inspired by . . . a picnic champagne supper in the park I took the trumpet
out and started to play. . . . Soon other instrumentalists began to materialize. A man appeared out of nowhere with a big drum strapped to his
chest, a soldier turned up with a trombone and then an extraordinary
grunting noise heralded the arrival of a sailor carrying what looked like
the horn of an enormous old-fashioned gramophone. He puffed away
into the small end and produced a convincing, if monotonous, bass note.
After a while we got the wanderlust and set off in procession round the
Memorial, with a huge crowd amassing behind us, to the tune of *High
Society*. Then someone brought up a handcart and I was lifted bodily on
to it, still blowing lustily. There was only room for one on the cart so
the rest of the band had to footslog beside it. They pushed me along the
Mall, by St James's Street, to Piccadilly Circus, on to Trafalgar Square
and back to the Palace. . . . I dimly remember blasting off a chorus of
For He's a Jolly Good Fellow in the direction of His Majesty.

Also in the West End that night was another young man, only a
few years younger, whose experiences were less fulfilling. A nine-
year-old evacuee when the war began he was now, when it ended, a
public schoolboy of almost sixteen, and had come up from his
home in Banstead with a party of schoolmates, all hoping to make
the evening doubly memorable by gaining their first sexual experience. The evening had begun well enough, when they stood on
the table of a restaurant off Tottenham Court Road singing their
school song – *Deo non fortuna* – By God, not luck – after they had
drunk, and pretended to enjoy, their first champagne. Later there
was a modestly encouraging encounter in Trafalgar Square where
'some girls grabbed us to dance the hokey-cokey; sheepishly we put

our left legs in and our left legs out, we did the hokey-cokey and we turned about'. But disillusionment lay in store:

With sly grins and self-conscious swaggers we tried to get ourselves solicited. . . .

The woman had dark hair, grey near the roots. . . . She wore ankle straps and a fox fur and radiated desiccated sex, cupidity and 'Evening in Paris'. Effervescing with beer and victory, I approached her.

'Excuse me . . .'

'B—— off,' she said, without removing the cigarette from her mouth. 'B—— off or I'll tan your backside for you.'

The others were full of admiration. 'What did she say?'

'We discussed terms,' I said, 'but I told her it was too much.'

One place that night distinctly more respectable than on an ordinary evening was Piccadilly Circus. Since the arrival of the GIs Piccadilly had acquired a second reputation as a market place for illicit sex, but on VE Night this was little in evidence. The famous Circus did not, it must be admitted, look its best that night, in spite of the lighted buildings all round and the theatre crowds pouring out to join the fun, for the statue of Eros was still boarded up and bore such unseasonable exhortations as 'Save for victory'. One then teenage girl who had come up from Palmers Green remembers it as being 'packed with people. Some had climbed Eros, others had climbed lamp-posts and the railings round the entrance to the underground station. When someone began throwing fireworks I became nervous and sheltered in a shop entrance.' Happily a Sir Galahad was at hand in the shape of 'a tall handsome officer in the Royal Canadian Air Force who . . . offered to escort me to a safer place. He took my hand and fighting his way through the crowds . . . dragged me to safety and then we had a much needed celebration drink.'

There was little violence and vandalism; less than on many a pre-war Boat Race night. For once policemen's helmets, so irresistible to high-spirited undergraduates, were not a great attraction. *The* prize on VE Night was the curved white steel helmet which gave the American 'Snowdrops' (Military Policemen) their nickname. Other unusual headgear seen that night included 'a detachable iron crown' worn by a sailor, who had apparently removed it from an heraldic beast guarding a gateway, leaving his own flat cap, looking even odder, in exchange. But anything which aroused memories of the defeated Axis rulers was considered fair game. In the New Zealand Forces Club in Charing Cross Road someone discovered behind the portrait of that country's Prime Minister 'a scowling bust of Mussolini', which was soon providing a target for missiles. But the Duce, whose death had been reported on 29 April, proved a tough nut to crack and it needed a whole barrel even to chip his brow.

The prevailing mood that night was joyous, not riotous. Typical was the scene which one woman came upon in a traffic-free street in Soho, the home of the foreign community, 'traditional dances of central Europe . . . being performed with all the skill and seriousness of Highland reels. Foreigners, as grateful for victory as any of us . . . advanced and retired and turned and skipped to their own thin mournful chants. Their old people stood around in the firelight, clapping in time.' Less cheerful was her husband's landlady, whom they encountered later in Bloomsbury, for 'part of her back wall had collapsed. "Today of all days," she exclaimed at the injustice of life. "They'll never accept it as war damage now. Why couldn't it have fallen down yesterday?"'

Part of the legend of Armistice Night, 1918, was that, in their frenzied relief that the slaughter was over, complete strangers had met and made love in the streets and parks. If such incidents occurred in 1945 they were few, and unpublicized. Far more typical was the experience of one young woman, who, despite some family opposition, came up from Guildford for the evening and remembers going 'home on the train intact, despite my parents' *dreadful* warnings'. *Her* most riotous experience was to join a conga line swaying down normally sedate Whitehall.

This had remained throughout the evening the other great centre of excitement, with the Ministry of Health balcony providing for the crowds an attraction second only to Buckingham Palace. After his appearances at 3 and 6 o'clock, Churchill emerged again, surrounded by members of his government, soon after 9.30. Richard Dimbleby, perched in a window opposite, described in 'Victory Report' how the crowd, twenty-five to thirty thousand strong, formed 'one sea of waving hands and handkerchiefs . . . all the way from the Cenotaph to the House of Commons'. On a neighbouring balcony stood the Chiefs-of-Staff who had so often grumbled in private about their overlord's tyrannical demands, but now, in the most unmilitary way, were 'smiling and clapping' along with the civilian ministers who surrounded Churchill, among them Lord Woolton, Herbert Morrison and Sir John Anderson, all key members of what Churchill had called 'this famous Coalition'. Ernest Bevin, in his sturdy proletarian accent, called for three cheers for victory, given with a willing roar that poured noisily from a million loudspeakers, and then conducted the crowd in singing *For he's a jolly good fellow*.

Churchill's remarks on this occasion were not broadcast because, as Dimbleby explained, 'he told us earlier today that this message of his was a personal one to the people gathered round him', but at 10.30 he came out again to deliver what was, strictly speaking, since the armistice became effective at midnight, the last of his wartime speeches. To his detective, still at his elbow, the Prime Minister had never sounded 'more impressive' although the speech was less a piece of oratory than a dialogue with the crowd, who laughed good humouredly at a slip of the tongue, 'You have had a day off tonight', and, to his bewilderment, gave 'great gusts of laughter' when he declared '"The lights went out" – and the floodlights went dim. He could not understand what had happened and looked to me for an explanation.'

'I shall always remember Mr Churchill as he was at that moment,' wrote his secretary, standing beside him, 'spick and span in black and white striped trousers, a flower in his buttonhole, his face smooth and pink, a man of medium height and somewhat round of figure. . . . That was Mr Churchill's hour. Whatever was to come, nothing could take it from him. As Mr Churchill emerged, the noise increased almost to deafening point. . . . He knew so well what to say':

One deadly foe has been cast on the ground and awaits our judgment and mercy but there is another foe who occupies large portions of the British Empire, a foe stained with cruelty and greed – the Japanese.

We were the first, in this ancient land, to draw the sword against Germany. After a while we were left alone against the most tremendous military power that has been seen. We were all alone for a whole year. There we stood. Did anyone want to give in? Were we downhearted?

The lights went out, and the bombs came down, but every man, woman and child in this country had no thought of quitting the struggle. London could take it. So we came back after long months, back from the jaws of death, out of the mouth of hell, while all the world wondered.

When shall the reputation and faith of this generation of English men and women fail? I say that in the long years to come not only the people of this island, but from all over the world, wherever the bird of freedom chirps in human hearts, they will look back to what we have done, and they will say, 'Don't despair, don't yield to violence and tyranny. March straight forward, and die, if need be, unconquered.'

The crowd had responded, at the appropriate moments, with loud booing, for the Japanese, and shouts of 'No' in response to any suggestion of surrendering, and finally with tremendous cheers. As they died away, Churchill himself struck up the first words of *Land of Hope and Glory* and the crowd enthusiastically joined in:

> Wider still and wider,
> Shall thy bounds be set,
> God who made thee mighty,
> Make thee mightier yet.

As the darkness settled over London, the bonfires came into their own. Although the worst of the bomb-damage had now been tidied up there was no lack of sites, with frequent gaps in every row of houses, and no shortage of raw material, for where broken timbers were scarce the doors and benches of air-raid shelters provided fuel. The glare of the thousands of small fires, reflected in the sky, cast an orange-red glow over the capital which irresistibly recalled the years of the bombs.

Similar thoughts were in the mind of the writer William Sansom, who had spent the war as an auxiliary fireman:

Pinpointed across the City [of Westminster] appeared the first urgent firebursts, ever growing, as though they were in fact spreading, as each bonfire reddened and cast its coppery glow on the house-rows, on glassy windows and the black blind spaces where windows had once been. Alleys lit up, streets took on the fireset glare – it seemed that in each dark declivity of houses there lurked the old fire. The ghost of wardens and fireguards and firemen were felt scurrying again down in the redness. Fireworks peppered the air with a parody of gunfire. The smell of burning wood charred the nostrils. And, gruesomely correct, some of the new street lights and fluorescent window lights . . . glowed fiercely bluish-white, bringing again the shrill memory of the old white thermite glare of the bursting incendiary.

VE Day in the North

Waiting for the fun to start in Leeds

Street party in full swing in Manchester. Note street air-raid shelter, complete with Union Jack and Churchill portrait in the background

VE Day in London

Soldiers and girls in Fleet Street

Crowds in Piccadilly

'*We want the King*'

The Royal Family (with Princess Elizabeth in ATS uniform) and Prime Minister, on the balcony of Buckingham Palace

Crowds outside the Palace, cheering the Royal Family

Victory tea party in Camberwell

Street bonfire in Leeds

Such memories no doubt explained why many people, standing round the bonfires, were quiet and thoughtful, like those who were attracted into the roofless ruins of St Clement Danes in the Strand by the unaccustomed glow from the windows. 'No one said anything,' recorded one of them. 'The crackling of the fire and the footsteps of the crowd outside alone broke the silence' and though some firemen appeared they decided 'it was as safe a place as any so they let it burn out'.

For once servicemen did not have to be back in their billets at the usual 2359 hours and dances in some service clubs continued until three in the morning. For many civilians, too, by choice or necessity, VE Day went on well into the small hours. One young shorthand-typist from Watford had, with a group of friends, spent the evening 'wandering around the town . . . feeling free and trying to realize that it was the end. . . . We . . . ended up at Waterloo Station about 3 am where we just sat down on the ground and leaned up against the bookstall until the first train about 6.30 am.' A few hardy souls even slept out in the parks, but soon discovered, what any ex-soldier could have told them, that a 'night under the stars' was a good deal less romantic, and less comfortable, than it sounded. Officially, however, VE Day, like the war itself, ended at midnight, and Stuart Hibberd reading the midnight news found himself deeply moved at its opening sentence: 'As these words are being spoken the official end of the war in Europe is taking place.'

As the historic moment approached many people made for Parliament Square, where the Houses of Parliament were floodlit and coloured lights were strung out along the famous terrace beside the river, with overhead a solitary Union Jack, picked out by searchlights, floating high in the air on the Victoria Tower. Across the river, wrote one woman to a friend next day, 'County Hall was lit in two colours and the training ship in the river strung with coloured lights.'

The crowd all faced Big Ben. It was absolutely silent. Just before the last stroke it had reached one minute past. A great cry went up and people clapped their hands. Something went off with a bang. . . . The tugs in the river gave the V sign.

So now it was VE+1. And, more important, it was peace.

6

BONFIRES OVER ENGLAND

'With a great "swoosh" everything burst into flame and there across the Downs for miles and miles was a great half circle of flaring beacons'

– Sussex housewife, recalling May 1945

All the way up in the train I looked out of the window. There was not a house in town or country without its flag flying. . . . Rural cottages, great Victorian villas, rows of railway-side tenements, however battered they or their surroundings, all had their flags.

This recollection of one woman, travelling up from Eastbourne, where she had heard Churchill's speech over the loudspeakers on the station, to London, on the afternoon of VE Day, could have been paralleled all over the country. Throughout the war the provinces had shared a widespread feeling that London was getting more than its share of the credit and the publicity, while often forgetting that it was also getting much more than its share of the bombs. VE Day provided an opportunity to show that when it came to patriotism the provinces were every bit as loyal as the capital. Croydon, which had suffered much from the bombs and even more from the 'doodlebugs', was probably typical of places near London and many others. Here, observed a local historian, the streets round the Town Hall were more crowded than on any time since Armistice Day 1918 and at 4 o'clock the mayor spoke from the balcony, then led the crowd in a service of thanksgiving. Later celebrations were concentrated in the residential districts. 'In many parts of the town there were bonfires, not always authorized, and at Balfour Road, South Norwood, a life-size effigy of Hitler was burned. Perhaps the climax of the celebrations was the appearance in North End towards midnight of pink and yellow neon lamps, which floodlit a great statue of peace over Kennards Store before which thousands of people danced.' In Luton, a typical medium-sized industrial town thirty miles from London, specializing in vehicle manufacure, there was a somewhat macabre ceremony, when 'in the Selborne Road district a scaffold was erected and the execution of Der Führer carried out, while an effigy of Göring' – who was in fact to cheat the hangman a year later – 'swung from a nearby lamp-post, lighted up by the rays of the lamp he had helped to keep extinguished so long. In other districts, Mussolini met a similar fate.' But the crowds who celebrated their enemies' downfall were orderly. Nineteen people were taken to hospital but none was seriously hurt and though early on many pubs were drunk dry, one sailor nobly toured the streets with a bucket of beer which he dispersed to all comers. A general feeling was abroad, here as everywhere, that it was one's duty to celebrate on VE Day, just as it had for a long time been one's duty to eat potatoes, or save paper, or search one's conscience before travelling by train. 'This is the sort of thing we want our children to remember, not the experiences they have undergone in the past five years,' explained the Chief Constable.

Throughout the war people attending race-meetings had come in for a good deal of criticism but on VE Day this again became a socially-acceptable activity. A large crowd watched the Thousand Guineas at Newmarket, and were, according to the BBC News, 'well pleased when the favourite, Lord Derby's Sun Stream, ridden by Harry Wragg, galloped home an easy winner by three lengths', easily beating 'Lord Rosebery's filly, Blue Smoke, and Mrs Feather. Many racegoers spent the night in the open on Newmarket Heath to be sure of seeing the Two Thousand Guineas the next day, when Lord Astor's colt Court Martial won by a neck from Dante.'

The university cities had been famous in peacetime for their rags, but the war, by robbing them of their young men, had also muted their former gaiety. The former Scientific Adviser to the Air Staff, Sir Henry Tizard, who had become President of Magdalen College, Oxford, two years before, wrote up his diary that evening in the shadow of its famous tower, which floodlit, he observed, 'looked beautiful. The night is clear and warm. Undergraduates are wandering over the roofs but are very quiet. . . . Nor is there much excitement in the streets.' Magdalen had celebrated victory with free port in Hall and 'a bonfire in the Meadows', but Tizard himself, like many people who had been close to the RAF, with its constant loss of young lives, did not 'feel elated', but 'rather sad'. The other ancient university was a little more joyous. 'Cambridge celebrated VE Day with a good deal of noise but . . . no serious disorder', reported Senior Tutor Gow of Trinity, to his ex-pupils in the Forces. 'The mayor lit a large bonfire on Midsummer Common . . . our undergraduates had a glass of champagne in Hall.'

Almost everywhere the mood of restraint, already visible in London, was clearly visible and sometimes the main event was a symbolic act, rather than a great outburst of festivity, as at Dover, which, apart from frequent air-raids, had been the target for 2200 cross-Channel shells in five years; the last had landed in October 1944. Here, apart from the customary service, a large flag was hoisted on the Town Hall; previously, it had been feared this might attract the enemy gunners.

All round the coast, still thinly populated due to wartime evacuation, the celebrating was milder and more modest than inland. Even in Brighton, famous for its pursuit of pleasure, 'a mood of thankfulness rather than joy' prevailed, felt the *Sussex Daily News*. The population was 'listless, with nothing to do', and the most unusual events the paper found to record were a cake baked at the Dudley Hotel, Hove, with coloured icing representing the United Nations, and a seafront bus festooned with flags. But one peacetime institution had already returned. 'Brighton's famous street musicians, Marc Antonio the harpist and his colleague Alexander the violinist,' noted a local historian, 'played all day long in West Street and in a few hours collected a sum of money that almost compensated for the lean war years.'

For most of the country a 'dim-out' had replaced the former 'blackout' as long ago as the previous September and in the same areas all restrictions on showing lights had been removed on Monday, 24 April. But this did not apply on the coast, or for five miles inland from it, for fear that lighted windows might still provide an illuminated backcloth for U Boat attack. On VE Day this ban caused much ill-feeling. 'How can there be any victory celebrations in Plymouth with the blackout still in force?' one speaker asked the local Chamber of Commerce that day. 'There was,' he thought, 'no case at all for the continuance of the blackout. . . . It had been retained by the Admiralty's request, but the ships in the Sound were lit.'

This was a fair point, and that day, all round the shores of Britain, the official order, which soon afterwards lapsed, was defied. In Plymouth, crowds thronged the Hoe all day, at first merely parading and dancing, then joining in community singing organized by the city's dynamic wartime Lady Mayoress, American-born Lady Astor, who on touring the waterfront had been 'distressed to find the crowds with nothing to do' and 'remained for three hours, until 10 pm' helping to liven things up. As darkness fell a monster bonfire was lit and eager hands collected up deckchairs and fed them to the flames, though a task force of thirty police rallied to the defence of a storage-hut full of those combustible but hard-to-replace items. Cheated of this source of fuel, 'sailors obviously determined that as far as they were concerned the war was over, threw their caps and even part of their uniforms into the bonfire to help stoke it up', no doubt regretting their high spirits next morning. Another sailor was in trouble after being caught trundling a cask of beer, valued at £6 3s 6d and stolen from the Avondale Arms Hotel, into the dockyard. 'A case of rolling out the barrel,' commented the magistrate indulgently next morning, dismissing the charge.

Curiously enough, as in many other towns, the local authority here seems to have done little to arrange more innocent celebrations. For the rest of the week the local paper was full of letters protesting at the 'meagreness of the official arrangements', described by one citizen as an 'absolute farce'. Where were the bands? asked another letter, complaining that the only music came from the Salvation Army. 'Never mind,' added its six signatories with heavy sarcasm, 'we can go to a cinema and see the really good time had by the inhabitants of London, New York, and Moscow and the north of England.'

In Hull, almost as badly bombed as Plymouth, matters were better managed. Here people had begun celebrating as long ago as the evening of 4 May, with the news of the first surrender to Montgomery, and the damage caused by their illicit bonfires then had still not been repaired when, on VE Day itself, as the *Hull Daily Mail* recorded, 'high carnival reigned in Queen's Gardens . . . festooned with multicoloured electric lights. After the band performance had come to a close on Tuesday night, the crowds left to their own devices staged a carnival which was joyously sustained until 2 am' with 'dancing to music relayed from the BBC'. The statue of Queen Victoria in City Square proved an irresistible attraction for climbers while other, even hardier, spirits, waded about in the fountain in Queen's Gardens 'getting soaked to the skin in the process'.

No single raid had caught the public imagination more than the devastation of Coventry in November 1940, especially the burning down of its ancient cathedral, whose ruins had long been a centre of pilgrimage. On VE Day people flocked into them continuously, especially at 11 am for a Thanksgiving Service, though this suffered from the great storm which, having moved on from London during the small hours, had by midday reached the Midlands. Because almost everyone in Coventry had suffered personally in some way from the bombing there was a more sombre note about the celebrations here than in larger cities. All day 'people who had lost relations in the war brought bunches of flowers and placed them in vases . . . provided in the sanctuary', which 'brought beauty to the tumbled masonry' of the cathedral and there was also 'a large pewter bowl in which Coventry people who had lost a relation' were 'invited to place the names of their dear ones'. The crowd which at 3 pm thronged Broadgate to hear the Prime Minister speak was a thoughtful one, though they stayed to hear, forty minutes later, the bells in the cathedral tower, which had survived the blitz, 'ring out to the world', via the BBC, along with those of such internationally famous churches as Westminster Abbey, St Paul's and York Minster. For this one day, as in November 1940, Coventry, normally a small, work-centred industrial city, was once again in the centre of the world stage.

In Canterbury, once the target for Göring's 'Baedeker' bombers, the cathedral was floodlit and there were 'hilarious processions in the streets'; in Norwich, also subjected to a 'Baedeker' raid in 1942 – so-called because the objectives were historic, architecturally-important cities – 'if it hadn't been for the Service visitors, there would have been little in the way of high-spirited demonstrations'. Here the great occasion, as in Plymouth, ended in recrimination, when a citizen wrote to the *Eastern Daily Press* to complain that – most unusually – the Prime Minister's speech had not been broadcast from the City Hall. If the Lord Mayor was under the illusion that 'the large crowd were admiring this imposing edifice or waiting for the appearance of himself and his councillors', pointed out 'One of the Crowd', he was mistaken. Before the next V Day, the council might, he suggested, consider spending some of the recent increase in rates on a public address system.

At Bristol the local press felt the celebrations had not been 'a patch' on Armistice Day 1918. In Liverpool, which had suffered so badly in the devastating 'Maytime Raids' of 1941 and had lost so many sailors and merchant seamen in 'The Battle of the Atlantic', the atmosphere, felt the *Liverpool Daily Post*, was one of 'joyous dignity', the cost of victory being recalled by a request to relatives to place slips of paper, bearing the names of the fallen, on a catafalque, surrounded by a guard of honour, placed in the nave of the new cathedral. After Churchill's broadcast the shipping in the Mersey 'produced a symphony' of hooters though one tugboat master, his siren drowned by the 'stentorian efforts of his larger neighbours', was forced to content 'himself with piping a victory V each time his competitors paused'. There had been the customary street parties – at one eighty-six children had sat down at a single table – but the paper also struck a sourer note. Telephone operators, it was said, had been sadly overworked, despite the appeal to the public not to make unnecessary calls, while many housewives had let victory go to their heads and bought up far more bread than they needed, so much would be wasted. As the unhappiest man in Liverpool on VE Day the local newspaper nominated a 'war reserve constable who spent the day on fatigue duty peeling mountains of potatoes to keep the canteens going for hosts of visiting police'. The most openly jubilant seems to have been a Jewish shopkeeper, who mockingly filled his windows with pictures of pre-war Nazi rallies.

The most dangerous place to be that day was Sunderland. Half an hour after Mr Churchill's speech some unknown ship in the River Wear fired a celebration burst of 20 mm live oerlikon shells, which came down in the surrounding streets. No one was hurt, though one elderly woman, sitting peacefully by the radio in the kitchen of her cottage in Osborne Street, Fulwell, had a narrow escape: a shell wedged itself in the ceiling above her head, but failed to explode.

To allow everyone to celebrate with an easy mind the government had ordered that both VE Day and VE+1 should be holidays with pay, by no means a common or universal practice at that time.

But two days' pay for no work was not enough for some industrial workers. In Bolton where the management of one mill run by Montagu Burton Ltd generously offered eight and a half hours' pay for each of the idle days, the workers demanded a full nine hours, plus bonus, leading to a dispute which led ten days later to a lightning strike and the calling in of the union.

The numbers attending church that day came as a surprise to many clergy. Britain was still largely in fact, as well as in name, a Christian country and in the Forces attendance at church parade was actually compulsory. In Birmingham, the *Birmingham Post* commented, 'while many waited for others to make the first move' in getting public celebrations going, 'others went to church'. The cathedral celebrated eight services, while worshippers arrived at one parish church, at Aston, in such numbers that the previously made plans were scrapped and a service was provided every hour on the hour, plus others, for those too busy to come earlier, at 7.30 and 10 pm.

But not everyone was equally pious. In Stephenson Place a 'leather lunged' American was observed 'selling newspapers and extracting kisses from female buyers', an odd combination of activities, but 'it was in the back streets and the suburbs that celebrations were most in evidence', especially in the district where 'some enterprising men had obtained a tar machine and set fire to it and pulled it through the streets'.

The cities of the north had the reputation of being less inhibited, closer-knit communities, than those of the softer south, but many suffered on VE Day from that notorious regional handicap, the climate. In Leeds it rained, so people sought the theatre and the cinemas, where long queues formed, the *Yorkshire Evening Post* reflecting (surely ironically) that the town was 'unusually lucky' to have 'Old Mother Riley and her daughter Kitty' (a female-impersonation act popular at that time) playing at the Empire Theatre, since this helped to create an appropriately hilarious atmosphere. A more solid contribution to the festivities seems to have been made by the city magistrates, who decided to be lenient to those accused who failed that day to turn up in the dock.

It was also a damp day in Manchester, though the *Manchester Guardian* did its best, describing the rain as 'soft and warm'. The day had begun, as in many places, confusingly because people were uncertain whether to turn up for work or not. There was, the same reporter observed, 'little music' and few bells to be heard and the official ceremony in Albert Square was 'lacking a little perhaps in spontaneity', with 'a sense of climax . . . missing. It was rather like watching a football match for which the score had already been pre-arranged.' After Churchill's speech, followed by one from the Lord Mayor, the Corporation laid on an impressive ceremony in which a fanfare of trumpets accompanied the ceremonial breaking out of a flag for each of the forty-four allied nations. Collecting all these must have given some official a victory headache and the unveiling did not go off quite as planned for though there were great cheers for the major allies and liberated countries, 'in the case of some of the more recent recruits to the United Nations' cause there was occasionally a slight air of bewilderment, as though the crowd had some difficulty in placing them on the world map'.

This was the public story, as the newspapers related it next day. But many people have more private recollections. One of the oddest is that of an Edinburgh family which had the shock of its life when on VE Day a large clock which had not functioned for years suddenly sprang into life, chimed its way through twenty-four hours, and then, according to family legend, 'dropped dead' and never again emitted a single tick. A Dorset woman remembers being woken by the sun, now streaming through the window in the early morning after years of blackout, and, finding it unendurable, she began the day by moving her bed. About the evening she remembers a 'Christmas' feel; strung round the garden were the fairy lights that normally decorated the Christmas tree. The display of lights remembered by a Perthshire woman was a good deal more noisy: the troops billeted in a local mill fired 'off all their Very lights and other signals'. One Wolverhampton widow remembers the most modest treat of all: 'a good cry', while a children's home in Northampton, as one woman then a young nurse there recalls with disgust, provided surely the meanest 'treat' of all: the staff nurse, as a great concession, allowed her juniors to listen to Winston Churchill on her wireless, and the children to have their tea on the verandah. The housewife working on a Midlands barge, mentioned earlier, remembers how it came to seem of desperate importance to hear the Prime Minister's speech in Stratford-on-Avon. She and her crew-mates just 'made it', after 'hitching' three lifts on the almost deserted roads, the last in an NFS lorry which had them 'rattling about in the back . . . like peas in a pod'. For evacuees who had settled down happily with foster-parents the impending separation overshadowed the prospect of reunion with their own families, but one such sufferer, at Harleston in Norfolk, remembers being somewhat consoled by the 'jolly Scotsman who paraded our streets with his bagpipes . . . playing the Conga. . . . We all followed on behind like the children following the Pied Piper of Hamelin.'

For parents, relief that their children were safe predominated. 'Walking to the shops with the children,' remembers a woman then living in Sunbury, 'it hardly seemed possible that at last we could breathe freely and look forward to a future for them. Everyone walked about with a smile and a cheery word. . . . Life was marvellous.' 'People who had hardly ever spoken to one another were joking together and patting each other on the back like old friends,' remembers another housewife, living in the staid surroundings of Leamington Spa. She could hardly believe her eyes when, in their 'respectable' residential road, 'some corrugated iron was placed in the middle of the road and a huge bonfire was set up' and that evening 'in the shopping centre' she found complete strangers, in their hundreds, 'doing something called the Hokey-Cokey'. This was the day, one Hounslow woman remembers, that, after delivering the milk all through the war, with a horse-drawn milk float, she struck a blow for female freedom and insisted on joining her brothers and her father in the public bar, 'which to us was taboo. We were supposed to go in the saloon. . . . The look on my dad's face was comical, he just said, "You can't come in here with all these men." "Why not?" I asked, "I've worked among men for five years, kept the home fires burning, earned my money, now we'll celebrate", which we did well and truly with *Bless 'em all.*'

About the fashionable colours that day there was no doubt. A Tunbridge Wells woman remembers a patriotic garden 'planted with red, white and blue flowers'. A woman living near Eastbourne made her 'little girls ready for the junketings on the village green by tying up their curls with red, white and blue ribbons'. Some unknown patriots in Belfast ventured out secretly to paint the kerbs and air-raid shelters in red, white and blue stripes. A Sheffield family even decked out their kitten in similarly coloured ribbons, but this was not a great success. He soon returned with his finery wet and bedraggled from the rain and 'somehow', remembers his owner, 'that brought home to me the terror of the war that had passed'.

Although the largest crowds were inevitably in the towns, there was a widespread feeling on VE Day that one was even closer to the real heart of the nation in the countryside. The account of victory celebrations in an unnamed Dorset village – in fact Piddle-trenthide – which the homely West Country accents of Ralph Wightman broadcast that night admirably reflects in its 'cosiness' and lyricism the atmosphere not merely of that night but of the whole era:

On Victory Night outside this village inn in Dorset, through the open window, you can hear the men of the village relaxing after six years of toil. I can see the bar through a thick haze of smoke. . . . The room looks very much as it does on a normal Saturday night when the week's work is over. Charles Battick is here – he's thatched most of the cottages in the village. His father was a thatcher before him and there are sons to follow him, though one has been missing since Arnhem. Trooper Clark is here – he is on sick leave from Germany. His father is the village haulage contractor. Then there are Tom Woodsford, a roadman, Charlie Briggs, a tractor driver, Jack Groves, a shepherd, and old Herb Clark, a professional rabbit catcher who may have done a bit of poaching before now.

Just opposite the inn a byroad climbs diagonally up the hillside until it reaches a little plateau on a cliff above the road and stream and valley. It is quiet up here. This is one of the places which come into my mind whenever I hear the name England. . . . From here you can see or hear or smell all the things which in their season are given to decorate our homes. Hedges of whitethorn, banks of primroses, sunshine through young leaves, bluebell woods, violets, primroses, honeycups, anemones, apple-blossom, woodsmoke in the evening, hoar frost on grass, the scent of hay, the dawn chorus of birds in the spring. Up in the valley you can see the church tower set against the woods of Morning Well. Below is the manor house, glimpsed through its horse chestnuts and elms and copper beech. . . .

A few lights are lit in the cobb-walled thatch-roofed cottages. These were the lights I missed. It was a hellish thing to have blackness over them all as if death has passed over. Of course death did pass over us. One bomb destroyed the butcher's shop, a shower of incendiaries fell at White Packington, a stick of HEs crashed across the meadows behind South House, and a landmine on Bellamy's farm shook the whole village. We had one German plane down in the Battle of Britain, but we'd no history to compare with Kent or Sussex. . . . We are a completely ordinary village.

Here by the stream you get an impression of things going onward forever the same. It is a very ordinary stream. It has seen every man in the village disguised in the uniform of the Home Guard or ARP or the NFS, which is like every other stream in every other village. This is the England for which a handful of us have worked in a way we never believed it was possible to work. This is the England we saw for the first time with open eyes in 1940. This is the England for which the most worthy of our handful have died.

Across the land that night the beacons of victory flared. One of the biggest was on top of Fern Hills in Trentham Park, Stafford, which could be seen for miles around. By a pleasing irony it had been built by German prisoners employed on timber felling in the neighbourhood, among them Rommel's former chauffeur, captured in Italy.

And even victory could not prevent one of those acrimonious disputes which so often enlivened local beauty contests. 'Controversy,' reported the *Staffordshire Advertiser*, 'has centred round an eighteen-year-old typist at a pottery factory, [living in] Scragg Street, Packmoor, Stoke-on-Trent, who, having been chosen to play the part of "The Spirit of Freedom" in a Burslem Victory Pageant has been replaced by another girl.' The reason, explained the chairman of the Pageant Committee, was that there had been 'objections to her playing the role on the grounds that she had a brother who was a conscientious objector'.

Some fires were not lighted until later that week, like the one which the wife of one Army officer 'living in rural Sussex, who had often read of the fires over England but never expected to see them', remembers attending 'three or four days after VE Day . . . on a hill above Fittleworth, near Petworth':

At about ten o'clock we walked up to the site. I gathered that the owners of the farm were 'newcomers' and had not even known that their field was a traditional site for part of the great bonfire chain which is always lit to bring news of victory in battle or foreign invasion. However, nobody seems to have asked their permission much. The really thrilling thing was to hear one of the younger farmers charged with the task of igniting the fire, call out 'There goes Arundel! Dunkery next! Now for Bury! Ah, there she goes! It's us next!'

The bonfire was as large as a two-storeyed house. With a great 'swoosh' everything burst into flame and there across the Downs for miles and miles was a great half circle of flaring beacons; all within minutes of each other. The hills seemed on fire and northwards they still kept calling out the names of the fires after ours. 'Horsham', 'Croydon', etc. . . . and away to London and the north the message went flaring that the twentieth-century Napoleon was defeated and England still free.

7

BLESS 'EM ALL

*'There were merry scenes at Pwllheli when hundreds of Dutch
sailors invaded the town, dancing and singing in the streets'*
– *The* Western Mail, *9 May 1945*

FOR the Germans 'England' had always meant the whole United
Kingdom; no sturdy paratroopers or airmen had ever sung *Wir
Fahren gegen Schottland* or *Bomben auf Wales*. But the residents
of those countries knew better and VE Day was a time for regional
as well as national rejoicing. A BBC commentator described the
scene in the ancient city of Caernarvon, with 'the sun shining
brilliantly on the great open space' filled with 'people from the
town and people from the villages of the Snowdonian valleys . . .
farmers and quarrymen, soldiers, sailors and airmen', crowded in
front of 'the old grey walls' of the castle built by Edward I and
swirling round 'the statue of David Lloyd George, the national
leader in the last war'.

Here, as everywhere in Wales, there was singing. In Cardiff, 'the
Civil Defence choir, under Mr Hubert Williams, sang the "Hallelujah chorus"' before the Lord Mayor's speech to a crowd of 25 000
in Cathays Park; on the lawn in front of the city-hall the 500 boys
and girls of the Cardiff Children's Choir, accompanied by the Cardiff
Transport Band, sang *Men of Harlech, Jerusalem* and *Hen Wlad Fy
Nhadau (Land of our fathers)*. The nature of the tunes roared out
by the 'singing American and British soldiers, sailors and railway
portresses' – services rarely linked together – from the jeep which
roamed the streets with 'every available inch of its roof and bonnet
occupied' were not recorded; they were, perhaps, not elevated
enough for the chaste pages of the *Western Mail*.

As in other places, it took a little time for people in Cardiff to
become accustomed to the idea that the war was really over. The
city had, felt the *Western Mail*, perhaps been 'a little too subdued'

in the morning, but with the civic formalities completed, in the late afternoon the atmosphere changed. 'The bells of St John's Church rang out; bands paraded and in their wake hundreds of joyous people, waving Union Jacks, marched with the spirit of a free people.' By evening 'the city throbbed with new life. It was gay, happy and alert, ablaze with merriment. In Kingsway American "doughboys" and British Jack Tars held an impromptu dance; pretty girls linked arms with strangers. . . . Five and a half years of war had taught us to be good neighbours.'

For this evening at least the traditional hostility between the allegedly 'overpaid, overfed and oversexed' American and British troops disappeared. 'GIs linked hands with Tommies in hospital blue, while ships' sirens and hooters added to the bedlam. . . . Detonators were placed on the tram lines. . . . For a period every tram that went by produced explosions and became partly hidden in clouds of smoke.'

One Cardiff mother who had spent the afternoon helping to organize 'the finest party' ever for the neighbourhood children, culminating in a fancy-dress parade by candlelight, later wandered into the city centre:

Outside the City Hall, thousands and thousands of people gathered, completely covering the gardens and lawns. A choir sat on a stone parapet and began to sing . . . what seemed to be a prepared programme, but the people, led by a policeman, outsang them with the old Welsh favourites, *Gwlad, Aberystwyth*, etc. To be there was to know real Welsh fervour and is another never-to-be-forgotten experience. Back in the suburb, fires were lit in the street, fed from the rubble of the bombed houses and aided by a door from the air-raid shelter that came too late.

In Llanelly 'four German prisoners of war were spotted in a car' and 'some of the crowd aimed fireworks at them, but only one was sufficiently well-directed to explode inside the car, which quickly drove off'. 'Swansea celebrated victory in a decorous manner', the main events being a drum-head service for the forces 'held in the morning in the forecourt of the Old Guildhall' and – unusual in Wales, where sectarian feeling ran high – an inter-denominational civilian service of thanksgiving in the evening. Amid the prevailing piety licence had little chance to raise its head; the most outrageous spectacle discovered by the *Western Mail* reporter was 'Siegfried

lines composed . . . of the more intimate objects of wearing apparel'
hanging up in some streets. In other Welsh towns the principal event
was also a service, though 'Haverfordwest had a victory dance' and
'there were merry scenes at Pwllheli when hundreds of Dutch
sailors invaded the town dancing and singing in the streets'. A
gloom was cast over rejoicings in the Rhondda because 'several
public-houses in the valley were closed' and despite licensing hours
being extended to midnight, 'the celebrations were', acknowledged
a local reporter, 'of a sober and restrained order'.

Scotland, as has been described, had begun to celebrate the
evening before and in some ways the scenes in the streets on VE − 1
were more joyful than on the day itself, when the weather was
unkind, though VE+1 was to prove a good deal better. In Edinburgh, as A. P. Herbert had discovered, victory had been ushered
in with a 'dry' day in the pubs, and much earnest debate took place
as to whether they should be allowed to open on VE Day, much
less get an extension of hours. In the event, as the *Scotsman* commented, 'the question . . . did not arise' as 'the large majority
closed between 7 and 8 o'clock because of the exhaustion of their
supplies'. In one respect, however, Edinburgh was much better off
than London. The City Transport undertaking not merely provided
a full weekday service of buses, but also ran extra buses for late-
night revellers.

The official celebrations in Edinburgh began at eleven when the
Town Council met to send a telegram to the King, offering 'their
heartfelt congratulations upon the triumphant victory achieved in
Europe' and expressing 'their warmest gratitude to Your Majesty's
Forces'. They then walked in procession to the Mercat Cross for a
formal announcement of victory by the Lord Provost.

Poor weather had discouraged the crowds earlier in the day but
by the afternoon the police were having to control 'thousands of
young people' who had gathered outside the American Red Cross
Club, where 'from the balcony and windows chewing-gum and
chocolate were showered upon them. Hats were tossed into the
street and a marine on the balcony, constituting himself conductor,
led community singing. *Roll out the Barrel*, *The Yanks are Coming*,
Tipperary and *Land of Hope and Glory* were among the choices.'
No one knew any Russian songs, but 'a Red Flag waved from the
balcony was cheered'. Another centre of activity was the Register

House, 'the focal point of which was Wellington's statue, which was climbed by several soldiers and sailors. For a time a British sailor stood perilously balanced on the mane of the horse and from this height, tried to catch caps which were thrown to him.'

In the evening every seat was filled for a civic thanksgiving service in St Giles' Cathedral but the public was more struck by a 'testimony meeting' of twenty young service men and women at the Mound, led by a private in the Pay Corps. On any other day this might have had the crowds mocking, but that night those who had come to jeer were soon joining in the singing. A good deal more typical, however, were the 'thirty young sailors', who had clearly managed somehow to overcome the drink shortage, and who, to the crowd's delight, gave a demonstration of drinking by numbers, after 'marching in solemn procession from the Leith Street direction. Each man had a pint glass of beer . . . and at a word from their leader stopped in regimental fashion and took a drink. Then, at another word of command, the party moved off down Princes Street – glasses raised high.' Another group of servicemen with more wholesale ambitions, were, however, repulsed. When, later in the evening, a lorry laden with barrels of beer was halted by sailors who 'surrounded it, unloaded some of the barrels and proceeded to roll them along the street, the police interfered and the barrels were returned to the lorry'. The police came off worst in another encounter, when 'at the West End . . . a number of sailors joined hands round a policeman on duty and started circling and singing . . . the signal for every naval man within hearing or sight to join in'.

In Princes Street Gardens the crowds danced to the music of the BBC, and near the Ross Fountain a piper provided the music for eightsome reels in which 'even mothers with babies in their arms joined'. Only one disappointment marred the festivities, the absence of floodlighting round the Castle, though the *Scotsman* consoled its readers with the somewhat curious thought that the noise from the crowds outside it compensated for the darkness.

Even in Glasgow, that tough and tempestuous city, VE Day was remarkably good natured. The reason, explained the *Glasgow Herald*, was that 'the whole scene was unspoiled by any sign of intemperance'. Even those pubs that did not shut early 'had been singularly lacking in spirits'. The day had begun in chaos with thousands of workers arriving at their factories as usual 'to find closed doors', it being widely assumed that VE Day would not begin until after the Prime Minister's broadcast, and many children had also had a wasted journey to school. Everyone admired the bus and tram crews, which had had 'a hundred per cent turn out' even for the 5 am shifts, though the police were rather less popular. There had been no serious disturbance, the Chief Constable told the *Glasgow Herald* at midnight, 'and, considering the occasion, the crowds were very well behaved indeed', but 'quite a number of youthful people had been arrested on charges of the theft of wood and other materials to feed the fires. In the Townhead district the crowd resented the intervention of two young officers and attacked them', leaving one with hand injuries and the other with 'a scalp wound which necessitated three stitches'. It was also a busy night for the famous Glasgow Fire Brigade, called to extinguish twenty-two bonfires.

One Mecca for the crowd as the evening wore on was Kemsley House in Hope Street, whose owners had provided music over loudspeakers, and there was 'hard reeling and jigging on the tram-lines for hours. Usually the dancers made way for the trams, buses and private vehicles good naturedly, but not when there was an eightsome in the air. Glasgow, especially Hope Street, belonged to them, so long as that music was on.'

An even bigger attraction was George Square 'garlanded with twinkling coloured fairy lights' and, as the *Glasgow Daily Record* described next day, 'packed with crowds such as it has never seen before':

100000 people jostled, sang, danced, shouted, leapt into passing buses, cars, taxicabs, tramcars, and formed human chains to guide them through the milling throng. Like a European city on the eve of liberation, Glasgow went daft with joy last night.

And those who had been cheated of making an early start to their celebrations were slow to end them. The city centre, reported the *Glasgow Herald*, 'at midnight had not emptied itself of roistering citizens. There were still women with babies in arms sitting on the seats under the foliage of lights. The Conga and the Goosestep and the Palais Glide were still going on with unabated energy and good humour.' But it was, everyone agreed, a singularly innocent occasion:

Seldom has a celebration been more bland in Glasgow – or even more infectiously gay in mood. . . . Noise, the sort of . . . gay, happy, carefree merrymaking, the sound of which has not been heard in Glasgow in the 40s came back to town. You could hear it a mile away. It was solid and heart-warming. . . . People assembled, friendly and relieved, with the war cares and threats thrown off . . . finding peace and freedom from anxiety an intoxication in itself.

Northern Ireland had always been detached in spirit, as well as by geography, from the rest of the United Kingdom. Although it had suffered its share of bombing and wartime restrictions it had escaped conscription, though many served in the Forces as volunteers. But on VE Night the province did not despise the transient fruits of victory. 'For the first time in years,' reported the *Belfast Newsletter*, 'the sky above the crowded streets glowed with the reflected lights of a thousand bonfires. . . . Long lines of revellers danced in and out among rows of tramcars immobilized by the crowds' and 'a tremendous cheer' greeted the switching on of the floodlights at 10.40 pm.

Just in case the unaccustomed gaiety should go to their heads the Lord Mayor of Belfast, 'addressing the citizens by loudspeaker', struck a stern note that even the grimmest Ulsterman must have approved. 'Let their happiness,' he told the crowds earlier, 'be tempered with the thought of what was still before them. Celebrate the victory and go back to work.'

In Londonderry, meanwhile, joy was unimpaired; 'a party of British sailors, linked arm in arm, paraded along Foyle Street singing *There'll Always be an England*' – a brave thing to do in many parts of Ireland in normal times; in Bangor 'VE' was picked out in lights on the Town Hall; in Armagh the band of the Royal Irish Fusiliers marched through the city and 'played a selection on the Mall'; in Omagh the 'YMCA provided free meals for soldiers' and the council gave the troops £10-worth of free cigarettes.

About the place in Northern Ireland which had the biggest bonfire there can be no argument; the honour belongs to a small fishing village in County Derry, where, just as the public bonfire on the street corner was dying down, there was an explosion in the building opposite, 'the largest and most modern bar and hotel for miles' due 'to be officially opened the next day'. This blew the doors right across the street and 'within minutes the whole building . . . was engulfed in flames'. By the time the fire brigade had arrived from Londonderry, eleven miles away, the whole building had burned to the ground and the firemen had their hands full trying to save the rest of the street. The cause of the fire was never discovered, though no one, in those comparatively peaceful days, suspected sabotage.

For the Forces neither VE Day nor VE+1 was automatically a holiday, although those not released from duty were promised two extra days' leave later. (I am still waiting for mine.) This was, in any case, essentially the civilians' day; the end of the war in Europe meant for many soldiers only the far worse prospect of service in the Far East. There *were* exceptions, like the aircrew of the RAF, suddenly reprieved from a likely death sentence, but on the whole neither in the British Isles nor overseas did VE Day mean very much to the average serviceman.

Undoubtedly, however, there was on VE Day a sudden upsurge of affection for the 'lads in khaki' as patriotic speakers liked to describe them. In South Shields one crowd spontaneously gave three cheers for the lads still fighting in Burma. In Brighton a shop-keeper wrote on a blackboard placed in his window: 'Men and women of the Forces, we thank you.' In Watford, a serviceman travelling to Uxbridge 'to see if I could find any of my old cronies in the *Eight Bells*' after being given a day off from his highly secret job at a branch of the Special Operations Executive, manufacturing radio sets and other equipment for British agents overseas, was deeply touched to be stopped by 'a dear old lady' who said 'I should like to thank you for all you have done. I think you have all been marvellous.' 'I accepted this tribute on behalf of HM Forces,' he remembers, 'with a smart salute and a bit of a lump in my throat, and did not spoil her day by saying I had not fired a shot for two years, and then only at a target.'

The overwhelming desire of most servicemen was to get home, or at least out of camp. 'We had to write out so many passes . . . that our hands were still shaking the next day', complained one corre-spondent in the Royal Engineers' journal *The Sapper*. For those left in camp, with the training battalion, 'VE celebrations naturally were more subdued than riotous', reported another. 'We had parades and inspections for some of our men who took part in neighbouring towns' celebrations'; the civilians who cheered such detachments rarely reflected that what was fun for them was work for the troops on parade.

Some units did their best to entertain their civilian neighbours in other ways like another in this camp which built 'a model Mustang produced to practically the correct size and suspended on an aerial ropeway on which a couple of kiddies could be whipped across the river at a smashing speed'. At Kitchener Barracks, 'most of the gang', observed another military scribe, 'were so excited that they couldn't wait for the official sports the next day; they organized their own races, from the "Square" to the Coy [company] Office, then Coy Office to the Railway Station. . . . Spr [sapper] Payne managed to equal his own record for the course.'

The Royal Army Ordnance Corps also managed to enjoy themselves, at 'The Humbers' camp:

As the orders came through from garrison . . . setting the machinery for VE Day in motion . . . the battalion . . . began to celebrate. . . . The sergeants' mess was the first reasonably organized jollification to get cracking, their singing, led by the doughty RQMS . . . whose voice did not falter for some six hours, resounding over the camp till it became infectious. . . . It became apparent that the sergeants' mess were, with the aid of a banjo, singing their own peculiar way round the whole of Humbers. Meanwhile a bright spark had, in complete defiance of the VE Day programme, lit the enormous bonfire.

The procession arrived at the bonfire and some whole-hearted singing was heard, still led by the RQMS . . . the selection including *There'll Always be an England* up to *Auld Lang Syne*. After a spontaneous gesture of singing *For He's a Jolly Good Fellow* and giving three cheers for the CO, the assembled company sang the National Anthem with considerable fervour and feeling. . . . The Day itself, VE Day . . . arrived. Just as the Sports Officer was speaking about his deep laid plans, the first part of the depression arrived. . . . Within ten minutes, however, an informal game of football was going. . . . The rainstorm went on for over five hours and the programme for the day had to be hurriedly rearranged, involving the cancellation of all outdoor sports and the substitution of housey-housey. . . . Lunch was the next event, enlivened by a pint of beer for each man, after which a fair amount of sleep was taken.

A mid-afternoon siesta that day was welcome in other places too. At Nescliffe Camp, the firing of guns on the early morning of VE Day provided an unwelcome 'reveille to those who had tottered wearily to bed in the early hours'. At the Command Ordnance

Depot, Sherborne, where the officers' mess invaded the neighbouring American mess on VE Night, 'the whole party returned to our own mess', the riotous celebrations continuing until 'well after dawn'.

Other regiments celebrated in various ways. The 'Buffs' (the Royal West Kents) mounted a three-day show in the regimental theatre in Canterbury, called Maytime Madness; the Essex Regiment at Warley had a church parade at 0900 hours, then took the day off; the Bedfordshire and Hertfordshire Regiment flowed into Bury St Emunds, with streamers in their caps, and returned for a democratic 'All Ranks Dance' in the evening, interrupted for the King's broadcast.

Women members of the Forces, with conscription likely to end at once and in no danger of being sent to Burma or Malaya, had more cause to celebrate than the men. One ATS girl in the Royal Signals at Stanmore remembers a bonfire being lit on which they threw all the Army forms and logbooks they could find, joyfully declaring – rather prematurely – that 'they wouldn't be wanting them any more'. By the light of the burning 'bumf', symbolizing, they hoped, the end of their military servitude, they danced until the small hours.

8

FLOWERS OVER EUROPE

*'By this time, we were all encrusted with flags and emblems
and bunches of flowers'*
– War correspondent Alan Moorehead in Oslo, 8 May 1945

BY 8 May most of the cities in Western Europe had enjoyed a dress
rehearsal for VE Day in celebrating their liberation, but that
Tuesday dawned with Oslo, the first capital to be occupied, still in
enemy hands.

On 7 May 1945, after all other German forces in north-west
Europe had surrendered, there was still not a single British soldier
in Norway and the allies were having trouble in contacting the
enemy commander, General Bohme. Eventually it was not a
fighting commander at all, but the General Officer Commanding,
Scottish Command, who got in touch with his opposite number in
Norway, through a message broadcast to him on the BBC's
European service. General Bohme was told that he was deemed to
have given in, and that a white-painted flying-boat would arrive
in Oslo Fjord shortly with emissaries to accept his surrender, but
in the event the brigadier concerned was beaten to the post by a
joy-riding party which 'hitched' a lift on an idle Dakota. The last
German stronghold in Western Europe succumbed not to the tough
fighting men of the 1st Airborne Division and the Norwegian
Parachute Company, earmarked for the job, who arrived two days
later, but to the less overwhelming strength of four war correspondents, three air force officers and two press photographers. Never,
surely, had the power of the press been more strikingly demon-
strated.

The story had begun that morning at the Hotel Angleterre in
Copenhagen where the correspondents 'fell in with two air commodores of the RAF Transport Command' who had a suitable
plane at their disposal, but no maps. This need was met unexpectedly

when a squadron of German fighters flew in from Latvia, escaping from the Russians, for one of the machines contained 'a schoolboy's atlas and a really good flying map showing the route to Oslo':

It was an odd and beautiful flight, northwards all the time. . . . The most uplifting scenery passed below us. Mile after mile of inlets and scattered waterways among the pines, a world of bright lakes and little beaches and gabled hamlets made of timber. Far ahead the eternal snow sat on the great backbone of the country. It seemed impossible among all those lakes and forests below that there could be a landing-ground but the third time round the city we saw it clearly. They flashed a red light warning us not to land, but the pilot decided to go ahead anyway. . . . Eventually we settled ourselves down in front of the hangars and bundled ourselves outside.

The little party now faced a whole German army, whose posses-sion of Norway had gone unchallenged for years:

It was a difficult moment. The Germans stood and stared. . . . While we waited . . . three RAF officers appeared beaming with delight. They had been shot down in the air battle of Norway, had broken out of their camp and had made their way to the airport. A German colonel now appeared, festooned with medals, followed by his officers, and made for our two air commodores. The colonel, a dark and muscular man, flung out his arm in a Nazi salute and offered his hand. This was rejected. . . . 'You are British,' the colonel said. 'Had you been Russians we would have re-sisted.' 'Resisted' was pretty good in the circumstances, since our force totalled a dozen men against at least a hundred thousand Germans in Norway.

After an argument with the senior German officer at the airport, who seemed to think that as 'the German capitulation did not take place until midnight . . . he should put us under arrest', 'three battered brown Wehrmacht cars', with Luftwaffe drivers, were provided to take the liberators into the capital, five miles away.

The man driving *The Times*'s correspondent, his passenger observed, 'was much amused by the wild cheers, which greeted us as we left the airport – something no German in Norway ever expected'. 'The German soldiers in the streets', Alan Moorehead who was also in the party noted, 'tried to keep the people from overwhelming the cars [and] some of the resistance lads pushed through to help . . . linking arms with their bitter enemies the

Germans', and so clearing a way 'to the Grand Hotel, the noted Quisling establishment of the town'.

By this time, we were all encrusted with flags and emblems and bunches of flowers and in this condition we were pushed out on to a balcony overlooking the central square. . . . The people flowed out beyond the square, up into the side-streets, a great pink carpet of upturned faces and waving red flags. They hung from the roofs and window-sills. They shouted across from the neighbouring buildings. . . .

Suddenly, under some common impulse, the shouting fell away and they began to sing their National Anthem, the men standing stiffly, the women in tears. Then the shouts again. The senior air commodore made a speech. Someone else made a speech. We all made speeches. . . . Then the National Anthem again, the German soldiers standing in the middle of the crowd. . . .

Then out of the hotel and through the crowds . . . back to . . . the airfield. . . . It was a quick take-off. Far down the fiord a Catalina and a Sunderland flying boat, both painted white, were heading past in the direction of Oslo. Norway was out of the war.

It was only in Norway that liberation and VE Day so happily coincided, but elsewhere, in Europe, too, it was a day for celebrations. In Belgium, crowds danced in the streets in Brussels in front of a huge picture of King Leopold, who was that day released from captivity in Germany by General Patton's 7th Army. In Holland even the windmills were flying flags and an RAF plane arriving at the Hague was mobbed by joyous crowds who showered the crew with tulips, while thousands of other blossoms spelt out the letters 'W', 'J', and 'B', for Wilhelmina, Juliana and Bernhardt, outside the Royal Palace.

Even neutral countries, with little reason to do so, joined in the rejoicings. In Lisbon 'vast crowds swept down the principal streets shouting the names of the allied leaders' and 'shop windows displaying German propaganda were smashed', while Switzerland at last climbed down off the international fence, by that day breaking off diplomatic relations with Germany.

In Paris the big event of the day was the broadcast by General de Gaulle. 'The war is won! Victory has come!' he told the French people. 'The victory of the United Nations and the victory of France.' Behind the scenes he had been busy ensuring that no one should overlook his country's contributions, especially during the conclusion of the cease fire at Rheims and in Berlin. 'Naturally,' he wrote in his *Memoirs*, 'I had arranged with our allies for the French to participate in the signing of these two documents', though the Russians had tried to exclude them on the grounds that all the Western allies were represented by Air-Chief-Marshal Tedder. The arrival of 'the representative of France' was also too much for Field-Marshal Keitel, who exclaimed 'What? The French too?' But de Gaulle stood no nonsense from either Russians or Germans and, 'on 9 May General de Lattre took his place alongside the military delegates of the major allied powers beneath a panoply in which the tricolour figured among the other flags'.

De Gaulle's own place on VE Day was clearly in Paris, from which at 3 pm he made his broadcast.

A little later, I went to the Place de l'Etoile; it was filled with a crowd which became enormous a few seconds after my arrival. No sooner had I paid my respects to the Tomb of the Unknown Soldier than the throng thundered its cheers as it pressed against the barricades. With difficulty, I extracted myself from the torrent.

This was no exaggeration, as one American woman present in Paris that day confirms:

In Paris the war ended the way it began – with marching. A frenzied spirit of enlistment seemed to take hold of the people of Paris the moment peace ceased being a rumour and became a fact. . . . They started marching on Tuesday afternoon at three o'clock, just after the voice of General de Gaulle announced the great news over the government's street loud-speaker system, and thousands were still marching at dawn the next morning. The crowds marched in the sunshine and on into the night with the collective, wandering rhythm of masses who are not going anywhere but are feeling something which their marching together expresses. VE Day here was like an occupation of Paris by Parisians. They streamed out onto their city's avenues and boulevards and took possession of them, filling them from kerb to kerb. They paved the Champs-Elysées with their moving, serried bodies. Around the Arc de Triomphe the marchers, pouring in from the spokes of the Etoile, solidified into a dangerous, living, sculptural mass which was swayed and pushed by its own weight until the marchers, limping and dishevelled, disengaged themselves to march back down the avenues and boulevards, in the dusty, beautiful spring heat. . . .

All anyone cared about was to keep moving, to keep shouting, to

keep singing snatches of the *Marseillaise*: '*Le jour de gloire est arrivé* . . .
marchons, marchons.'

The wife of an American diplomat observed the scene later that
day:

The Champs Elyseés was a wild sight and driving most hazardous due
to every jeep and Army vehicle in town being out with every possible
inch of it smothered in screaming boys and girls – there must have been
fifty over each jeep.

Flying Fortresses were buzzing up and down, just not hitting the Arc
de Triomphe, and the noise was terrific. . . .

I will never forget that evening – Arc de Triomphe, Opéra, Place de
la Concorde all lit up for the first time and the fountains on everywhere –
the Madeleine especially beautiful and flares and fireworks, and the Garde
Républicaine riding down the Rue Royale with their helmets gleaming,
and sweating police in their blue capes trying to make way for them, and
each member of the Guard having at least one girl riding behind him on
the horse, clinging to his Napoleonic uniform and screaming.

It was not a happy day at Supreme Headquarters at Rheims,
where victory was by now stale news and the correspondents 'out-
smarted' by Ed Kennedy were still thirsting for revenge. While a
few were generous enough to congratulate him on his enterprise,
fifty others assembled to denounce 'the most disgraceful, deliberate
and unethical double cross in the history of journalism' and, under
pressure from them, his accreditation to SHAEF was withdrawn
and he and his agency were for a time boycotted by the British
press.

Most of those who had borne the brunt of the notorious 'snafu'
of the previous day were in any case away, in Berlin, for the final
surrender to the Russians. Eisenhower was represented by Air-
Chief-Marshal Tedder and a US Air Force general 'Tooey' Spaatz,
but he sent his personal staff along, his secretary recorded, as 'a
happy VE Day present'. The occasion turned out, however, to be
more memorable than enjoyable. They made an early start, taking
off from Rheims at 8.25, but the French representative failed to turn
up – he caught a later plane – and at Stendal, where they were to
rendezvous with Russian fighters, there was no sign of them, a
serious matter, since only the day before a US plane had been shot
down over Berlin. The Russians finally arrived, an hour late – they
were operating on Central European Time, an hour behind

SHAEF time – and victors and vanquished travelled in the same convoy, with Keitel and his colleagues 'aloof, coldly and military correct' in one C-47, and the British and Americans in another.

Although the allied visitors were greeted politely, with a guard of honour and a band playing *God Save the King* and the *Star-spangled Banner*, and by 2.30 were being refreshed with 'sandwiches of thick, white bread, both black and pink caviare, ham and fish . . . good Rhine wine . . . and cognac', it was soon clear that this was very much a Russian affair. None of their hosts showed any interest in the broadcasts, at 2 pm Berlin time, by Churchill, Truman and de Gaulle making 'it plain that there was no VE Day till after their ceremony . . . Meanwhile', wrote Eisenhower's secretary, 'we sat . . . and sat . . . and sat . . . agreeing the Russians have about as much regard for time as a South Seas native.'

The rest of the afternoon ebbed away while the 'Anglo-American, French and Russian interpreters' argued 'over the meaning of the smallest phrases incorporated in the surrender documents', and, at a humbler level, those of the party who had 'come along for the ride' sought permission 'to return to the airfield for their hand luggage,' which, 'after an hour and a half of negotiation was per-mitted'. This was a great relief to the women in the party, who set out to smarten up, but found their bathroom 'incapable of use and upstairs a score of shouting Russians soldiers'. They were, however, agreeably conscious of their 'nylons and uniforms . . . creating something of a sensation . . . There were no wolf-calls, but a wolf-look is no different.'

By now it was clear that the whole party, who had expected to be back at Rheims by nightfall, 'would have to spend the night in Berlin'. 'The power failed just as darkness fell . . . Nana (General Eisenhower's chief stenographer) typed out some of the surrender documents while High Rankers held candles over the typewriter. The hours crept by in this flickering, impatient atmosphere.' But at last waiting was rewarded. 'About 10.30 we were summoned to the Surrender Hall, all our irritation and restlessness fading into sheer excitement at the ceremony about to take place.'

This was the long-awaited final German surrender. It was staged, like the earlier one at Rheims, in unimpressive surroundings, in this case a plain concrete-built, former German Army engineering college, at Karlshorst, a north-eastern suburb, where Marshal

Zhukov, the city's conqueror, had set up his headquarters. The room itself was, however, much larger, being 'about sixty feet long and forty feet wide, two storeys in height, with a small balcony along one side'. Eisenhower's naval aide, Captain Butcher, casting an experienced eye over his surroundings, decided that if the 'modest arrangements in our War Room looked like Hollywood, we were now looking at something that was super-Hollywood', a reaction shared by Eisenhower's secretary:

The huge room was banked with klieg lights, blinding as we stepped in from the dim hallway. Everything seemed to be set up for the sole convenience of the Russian press, who numbered close to a hundred and swarmed around in shouting bedlam. Movie cameras were ready in almost every conceivable spot. Microphones spouted from the floor, hung from the ceiling; they and the klieg lights created a veritable spider web of wires and cables.

A long table at one end of the room commanded all attention. . . . From it stretched three other long tables, for press and smaller fry. Set apart, under the balcony, was a short table apparently reserved for the surrendering Germans. . . . There was a momentary silence as Marshal Zhukov, a short, stubby officer with a stern expression, entered the room. Everyone stood up. . . . As we sat down, he called the conference to order.

I was surprised at the way a civilian, later identified as Andrei Vyshinsky (Deputy Commissar for Foreign Affairs), hovered over the entire proceedings, deferred to even by Zhukov. Even in this moment of Soviet military victory, the Kremlin was stepping in to take charge. . . . With final details arranged to everyone's satisfaction, the signal was given for the enemy's entrance. As a door opened just behind the empty table, a silence smothered the babble. Every pair of eyes in the room focused on a tall German officer in smart blue-grey field-marshal's uniform, his chest covered with decorations and medals, his head poised high. He stepped stiffly to the table, jerked up his silver-headed baton in a curt salute and sat down. The noise rose again. No one seemed to notice as the other two German principals took their places beside Keitel [who] . . . carefully pulled off one grey glove before taking the pen. He looked up contemptuously at the boisterous newsmen, then scribbled his signature . . . as though anxious to dispense with a dirty job. Some of the reporters and photographers climbed on tables to get a better view; two had a brief fist-fight; all yelled and pushed. [Admiral von] Friedeburg and [Luftwaffe Colonel-General] Stumpf signed hurriedly while Keitel glared without seeing, the incarnation of the traditional icy Prussian.

Zhukov and Tedder signed as representatives of the allies, followed by

General Spaatz and de Tassigny as witnesses. The Air-Chief-Marshal arose . . . and asked in an emotionless, high voice, 'Do you understand the terms you have just signed?' almost the exact question which General Eisenhower put to Jodl and von Friedeburg back in Rheims.

As the Germans nodded, Zhukov gave them the order of dismissal. The Nazis arose as at a parade-ground command. Keitel again jerked his baton in brief salute. They left the room with an exit . . . as dramatic as their entrance. . . . Now, even for the Russians, VE Day was official.

It was, by British and SHAEF time, almost midnight, and ninety minutes later the victors reassembled in the same room, now converted into a banqueting hall, complete with orchestra in the balcony, to celebrate their victory. The meal lasted four hours and one of the few participants to be sober at the end of it was Eisenhower's secretary, who drank mainly water.

By five o'clock in the morning, even the expert interpreter couldn't understand the toasts. The majority of the banquet guests were . . . good, old-fashioned drunk. Several Russians literally went under the table. Another in our party disappeared. Songs bubbled up in four languages, Russian predominating, closely followed by American. The orchestra, which had struck chords for each and every toast, began to sour as vodka penetrated to the balcony. . . . As the party broke up just before dawn [we women] agreed there had been between twenty-four and twenty-nine individual toasts, each requiring five to ten minutes for translation, plus the musical chord, and the final, deadly bottoms-up. We all agreed that we had been in on the VE party to end all VE parties.

The final gesture of Russian hospitality was to give their guests a conducted tour of the ruins of Berlin in the grey light of dawn, a depressing experience, made worse when one American woke from a drunken sleep and tried to strangle their driver, whereupon 'the other Russian pulled out a huge revolver'. Happily no one was hurt, but most of the party were glad to leave Tempelhof airfield at 7 am *en route* for Rheims. It was Wednesday, 9 May, VE+1 for the West, Victory Day itself for the Russians, whose official newsreel of the Berlin ceremony, which Eisenhower saw during a visit to Moscow several months later, made no mention of the part played by the allies or of the real surrender, at Rheims.

For the allied armies in Europe VE Day was an anti-climax. For most units it was a working day, like any other, indeed probably

harder than most, for everywhere there were prisoners to be disarmed or guarded, ammunition dumps to be made safe, order to be
imposed upon chaos. For the men 'at the front', reported one
British provincial newspaper that day, there had been no 'lie-in' and
no day off, only 6.30 reveille, as usual, and Army sausages for breakfast, though dinnertime had brought a surprise: a free pint of beer
for each man. 'VE Day came and went and . . . save for a parade of
remembrance on VE+1 passed almost unnoticed', testified the
historian of the Cheshire Regiment. 'There was no let-up in the
work of hoarding prisoners behind barbed wire.' Another writer,
in a Machine Gun Company of the same regiment, consoled himself
with the thought that 'knowledge of victory in the field at last was
reward enough'; any tendency to gaiety, he pointed out, was checked
by memories of dead friends and of the units' bitter campaign in
Italy. The 1st Battalion of the Herefordshire Regiment, stationed at
Segeburg, spent the day on the local sports field, but not playing
games: it 'was used as a collecting ground' to which 'thousand upon
thousand of the enemy came, often complete with transport and
heavy weapons. . . . The war was over [but] the task of clearing up
was on.'

Units not fully-stretched on such duties often had a more dis-
agreeable time as spit-and-polish-minded NCOs put into practice
that often-heard joke about getting back to real soldiering once
peace returned. An early victim was HQ Company of the 2nd
Battalion, King's Shropshire Light Infantry, roused from their
billets around Rethorn, near Bremen, on VE Day before it was
light. One sufferer wrote:

At approximately 0530 a good breakfast of biscuits and spam was eaten
by all [surely an ironical comment], haversack rations collected, a quick
look round made for undiscovered loot and away we went. Destination –
Friedewalde. . . . After a lot of swapping around, the company finally
settled down to what it hoped was a rest, but alas we were mistaken.
Sparks began to fly – not in the form of .88 shells or 'Moaning Minnies'
[i.e. mortar bombs], but in the form of blanco, drill, PT and last but
certainly not least DPs (Drill Parades) turning . . . mud-begrimed battle
veterans into a company of smart, clean-shaven and well-behaved men.

VE Day for three sergeants of the Glider Pilot Regiment was a
good deal more relaxed, if even more frustrating. Freed from their
prisoner of war camp by the Russians ten days before they had

enterprisingly 'acquired' an Opel saloon, driven 400 miles to an American unit in hope of 'hitching' a lift home and by 8 May were waiting near Mannheim for a spare place in a home-bound aircraft.

We were awakened by the sun streaming into our room and paraded for breakfast. Then a lazy couple of hours were spent reading until the morning parade for cigarettes [twenty], chocolate and gum was called, a razor blade per man being included on this particular morning [so] we were able to have a nice clean shave. Soon after hearing Churchill make his momentous speech we were ready to move out to Mannheim airfield. There we waited for our plane to Brussels, basking in the hot sunshine.

But they were out of luck. One pilot did land and ask cheerfully '"Anyone for England?" to which the reply was deafening' but this aircraft was soon packed out and their turn did not come for another two days.

Perhaps the best way for a soldier to spend VE Day was occupying newly-liberated territory amid the plaudits of its occupants, like the 1st Buckinghamshire Battalion, attached to the Canadian Army, and assigned to rounding up any Germans remaining in Rotterdam and Den Helder. This unit found itself 'brushing children off the bonnets' of its armoured cars 'every mile or so' as it drove forward and 'its progress . . . greatly hampered by the cheering crowds which smothered the armoured cars with flowers at every town and village'. At one town near Amsterdam, the military timetable forgotten, one convoy 'made a special diversion so as not to disappoint all the people drawn up outside the local school' and 'to complete the day Captain Eyles was presented at Alkmaar with an enormous bouquet of flowers which bore the inscription "With grateful thanks to our Canadian liberators"', a well-meant gesture, though the recipients were English.

The Guards Tank Brigade completed that day its 'wartime journey from Bayeux to the Baltic', at Kiel, for although 'the U Boat pens had gaping holes in their roofs, the pocket battleship *Admiral Scheer* was a capsized wreck and the cruiser *Admiral Hipper* completely gutted', the German Navy 'might have been contemplating any amount of nonsense and so a call had been sent to the 6th Guards Armoured Brigade to provide a display of armoured might':

The Coldstream had been chosen for the job and by 12 o'clock on VE Day they were lined up outside the shattered town, preparing to make a

Paris celebrates. Crowds in the Champs-Elysées

New York celebrates

Below left
Ticker-tape on Wall Street – plus a reminder the war isn't yet over

Below right
Crowds dancing in Times Square

Moscow celebrates

In Red Square on VE +1 (Russia celebrated a day later than the Western allies)

A British sergeant is tossed in a blanket

Prague welcomes the Russian troops

ATS girls enjoy a victory ride near Cairo

The last surrender

Top left
Germans and British aboard HMS *Bulldog* off the Channel Islands

Top right
Admiral 'Madman' Hüffmeier leaves his Guernsey headquarters, *en route* to captivity

Below
German troops wait to board landing craft off St Helier, to transport them to prisoner of war camps – a scene recalling the British leaving Dunkirk

triumphal entry. During the previous twenty-four hours Germans had been press-ganged into cleaning all the tanks for the drive and large gangs of prisoners had been made to fill in bomb craters and clear rubble along the route. The German police had been given instructions for traffic control. . . .

At 1.30 the leading vehicles started to enter Kiel. The tanks glistened in the sunshine and the colour fastened to the Commanding Officer's aerial fluttered in the breeze. Slowly and majestically the long column wended its way through the town, the German police saluting as the officers drove by. By 2 o'clock the procession had reached the northern end of the town and the expressions on the faces of the German civilians and sailors who were watching left no doubt that it had achieved its object. There would be no trouble in Kiel.

That day the Guards Infantry Brigade, having fought its way to the borders of Austria, where they joined those of Yugoslavia and Italy, was also advancing towards enemy territory:

The dawn was scarcely yet discernible when the Grenadiers set out from Cividale. For the first time in many weeks their lorries began to climb steeply. Above the drone of their engines they heard again the rush of a mountain torrent; they looked upwards towards the serrated knife-edge which formed the frontier between Italy and Yugoslavia, and downwards upon a thick blanket of grey mist covering the valley of the Isonzo. The villages were still asleep, the Red Star of Marshal Tito's Army swaying wetly from the wooden balconies. . . . The lorries climbed up and up round the hairpin bends of the Predil Gorge . . . and down into Tarvisio, the frontier town where Italian and Austrian notices hung side by side. It was now seven o'clock on the morning of 8 May. . . .

After a two-hour wait, while 'the commander of the 6th Armoured Division arranged with a German officer the final details of the British entry into the German Reich', the convoy set off again. It was a historic moment; after the long, hard-fought struggle up through the mountains of Italy and Yugoslavia they were at last setting foot on enemy soil:

The great striped pole which hung across the road was slowly raised to point into the sky, and the leading armoured cars of the 6th Armoured Division passed from Italy into Austria and continued driving eastwards hour after hour until they met the advanced elements of the Russian Army south of Graz. . . . German soldiers were still lounging against the customs house, watching with apparent indifference the passage of the unending convoy.

At one point two German tanks covered the road with empty, droop-
ing guns, and groups of uniformed figures stood at every farmhouse
door, outside every village inn. There was no overt hostility in their
faces; many of the civilians were even welcoming; bunches of lilac
were thrown into the passing lorries, lace handkerchiefs waved from
upper windows and an eager crowd of Austrian peasants would
gather round any vehicles halted at the wayside. Suddenly a group of
cheering and more familiar figures streamed across the road, clamouring
in English for news of home. They were our own prisoners, released that
morning by their Austrian guards. . . . The flag of the old Austrian
Republic, which was found floating from every building, was hauled
down on British orders and at a ceremony attended by the Corps Commander . . . the Grenadiers raised the Union Jack over the artillery
barracks . . . they had occupied. . . . At a dozen wireless sets scattered
through the camp small groups of guardsmen listened to Winston
Churchill's announcement of the end of the war with Germany. . . . There
was no time for celebrations.

The Navy's task too was not quite over, as German warships
surrendered on their return to port or popped up unexpectedly
from the depths of the ocean. On the morning people were supposed to return to work following the two-day holiday 'the first
German submarine surrendered in Weymouth Bay', after surfacing
fifty miles off the Lizard to be 'arrested' by two sloops from Plymouth, the *Amethyst* and *Magpie*. She was escorted into harbour
with the White Ensign flying above the German flag and that night
radio listeners heard a British naval commander accept the enemy
captain's surrender:

I'm now going to order the following general signals to be made: the
German ensign is to be hauled down at sunset tonight, Thursday, and
it is not to be re-hoisted. Chief, will you please make the following signal
to the Admiralty, repeated to the Commander-in-Chief, Portsmouth,
and Commander-in-Chief, Plymouth. 'The orders have been carried out.
U Boat 249 surrendered to the Royal Navy at Portland at 1100 today,
Thursday, 10 May.'

For American servicemen, the moment for rejoicing had come
several days earlier, when the fighting stopped. 'We celebrated more
when we pulled out of the line ten days ago, because we knew it was
over as far as we were concerned', some GIs of the US 9th Army
told the *New York Herald Tribune* reporter on VE Day. 'We've left

too many of our guys behind us to feel like raising hell today.' The men of the 3rd Infantry Division, whom VE Day found serving near Salzburg in Austria, having lived 'in constant apprehension of physical injury for the better portion of two and a half years', wrote their regimental historian, 'were almost sceptical, at first . . . that the war was indeed over. The ultimate goal of every soldier who had ever fought, the end had seemed like the pot of gold at the end of the rainbow. It had been wonderful to dwell upon, but it would never materialize. Then, suddenly, it was upon them all and the impact . . . failed to register . . . the full implication of it needed much time and serious consideration to sink in.'

The 243rd Field Artillery Battalion, stationed near Nuremberg, had a special reason for excitement as the end of the war approached, for some enterprising gamblers had launched two sweepstakes on the date of VE Day, one of them begun in far-away Brest in the 'too-optimistic days of last September'. The winner of both pools, the 'assistant battalion survey sergeant', had guessed 9 May and entered civilian life richer by 'a cool $1140'.

9

THE WONDERFUL 9th OF MAY

*'Nobody living in Jersey will ever forget that wonderful
9 May'*
– R. C. Maugham, Jersey under the Jackboot, *recalling
1945*

ONE part of Europe had not been able to join whole-heartedly in
the VE Day celebrations. The Channel Islands, abandoned by the
British government without a fight, had been occupied by the
enemy on 30 June 1940 and after five years of being cut off from the
British mainland were, by the beginning of May 1945, isolated and
starving. All the garrison, with one exception, were eager to surrender, but the exception, unfortunately, was their commandant,
Vice-Admiral Hüffmeier, a fanatical forty-six-year-old Nazi, whom
his own troops had nicknamed 'the Madman'; his announced
intention of fighting to the last man made, understandably, less
appeal to them than it did to him.

Until the very end, when his men were raking about in dungheaps
for edible turnip tops, he refused to acknowledge the possibilities
of defeat. On Saturday, 5 May, the Guernsey *Star*, under German
control, produced an issue which still firmly ignored the facts.
'U Boat Danger off Britain', 'Red Peril threatens Europe', 'Liberators bring hunger and chaos', ran the headlines. The death of
Hitler, 'at the head of the heroic defenders of the Reich capital', was
dismissed in a couple of column inches, but one did not need to
read between the lines of the war report which followed – 'American
tanks thrust forward . . . the Soviets drove a strong wedge in a
southerly direction' – to realize that the war was indeed lost for
Germany.

That week-end, ignoring their commander as far as they dared,
the Germans began to relax their hold on the islands. For five years
it had been a serious offence to display a British flag. Now, observed
one resident of Guernsey, 'wherever you went you saw people of

all ages, singly and in groups, carrying long sticks issuing from
paper coverings which quite failed to hide the unmistakable colours
of the Union Jack. Some carried them with no covers at all.'

But officially at least, the occupation was still in being. On
Monday, 7 May, as one Jersey man recorded in his diary, 'a German
official called at the office of the Department of Agriculture to
inform the authorities that the Germans were not at all satisfied
with the milk situation' and 'today new gun emplacements were
being made in various parts of the island'. There were, even here,
however, signs of the changing times. 'Four ounces of dried peas
were issued to everyone today and the bread ration has been increased to 6 lbs per head'; then, at 6 pm, thirty 'political prisoners',
i.e. people jailed for offences against German regulations, were
released. The authorities were, however, 'urging the population to
keep calm and dignified and refrain from any sort of demonstration', clearly fearing a bloodbath if the patriots who had already
been 'baiting Germans' went too far.

As news spread, from those with access to a radio, that the next
day would be V E Day excitement increased and 'there was keen
disappointment', the same observer noted, when 'it appeared early
this morning that nothing was going to happen.... Our spirits rose,
however, when it was learned the schoolchildren had been sent
home and that loudspeakers were being erected in various parts of
the town.' They soared still further when special editions of the
Evening Post on Jersey and the *Star* on Guernsey appeared around
midday.

This was their first 'free' edition for five years and the *Star* made
the most of it. 'The War is over for Guernsey' proclaimed a jubilant
headline of this 'Good News Issue'. 'German Officers inform
Bailiff of Surrender.' Two German delegates had, the paper
reported, 'called on the Bailiff of Guernsey at ... the Royal Court
House' at 10 am that morning to inform him 'that the war was over
in the Channel Islands as well as elsewhere'. The island's 'parliament', the States, readers were told, was to meet at noon, and, a sure
sign of the changing times, 'the German authorities had no objec-
tion to the hoisting of flags after the speech' by Mr Churchill due
at 3 pm.

This was the scene in St Helier that afternoon, but it could equally
well have been in St Peter Port, Guernsey:

The greatest crowd ... was in the Royal Square which, with the windows of surrounding houses, was packed with listeners. As the Town Church clock struck three a cheer went up at the announcement that Mr Churchill was to speak; his statement was punctuated by cheers, especially when he referred to 'our dear Channel Islands' and when, at the conclusion, the Bailiff hoisted the Union Jack and Jersey flag over the Courthouse ... many wept unashamedly. The Bailiff then ... made announcements about various services to be held, reminded them that the King was to speak at 9 pm and that there would be no further restrictions on the use of wireless in their homes. .... He then said that the Germans had told him that a British Commission was on the way, but the greatest cheer was raised when it was learned that units of the British Navy were approaching the Channel Islands. After appealing for good behaviour ... the Bailiff led the singing of the National Anthem, but emotion stifled many a voice.

For a native Channel Islander to hear this speech far from home was perhaps even more moving. Among them was a staff nurse in the children's ward of a London hospital, who had not seen her family, trapped on Guernsey, for five years. 'When Mr Churchill referred to "our dear Channel Islands",' noticed a colleague, 'her mouth quivered for a moment and her eyes were full of tears.'

So, too, were those of a Guernsey journalist with even more cause to hail the end of the war, for he had been sent to prison in Germany a year before for helping to run the Guernsey Underground News Service, which compiled an illegal daily news-sheet, entitled 'GUNS', from the BBC news. Five of the eleven Channel Islanders in his party had already 'died from malnutrition, dropsy and dysentery' and the survivors had endured frequent beatings and been forced to watch far worse atrocities, including one Frenchman being beaten and kicked to death for picking up a bone dropped by an Alsatian guard dog. Liberated by the Americans in April this man had been installed in the best hotel in the town, complete with 'white sheets' and 'a German maid to bring me my breakfast in bed', but he longed to get home, and Churchill's reference to the Islands left him, he confesses, 'entranced, speechless. .... As I sat there, a mere skeleton, I couldn't help wondering if my mother and friends had survived to greet the long-awaited day.' (Happily they had, as he discovered a little later, though his brother proved to have gone down with his ship in the Royal Navy.)

Churchill's promise that 'our dear Channel Islands are also to be freed today' was in fact premature, but the islanders, while they awaited their liberators, had plenty to celebrate. Soon, the diarist previously quoted noted, 'flags had been unfurled all over the island and church bells were ringing out for joy. Wireless sets had appeared from nowhere, their owners putting them in front windows to entertain passers-by . . . and one was soon dodging motor cars and motor cycles which had for five years been hidden away from the Germans.' One of the worst shortages had been of fuel but 'the Electricity Company turned up trumps and the light was on until very late, this being appreciated by owners of wireless sets and those who held parties or impromptu dances. It was funny to see young men coming out of jail carrying their beds, to hear people openly discussing the news, to ignore the curfew and forget the blackout.' As for the Germans, whose role had so dramatically changed, their discipline, this man conceded, 'remained excellent'. Most of them stayed out of sight, but 'at some of the Todt depots', built to house the island's slave labour force, 'large numbers of people were carting off furniture for firewood: wooden buildings were pulled down and those who had been left in charge were giving things away'. Even more remarkable, 'a notice published in today's paper . . . on German instructions, invites owners of wooden or corrugated iron bungalows or sheds which had been "physically removed" by the Germans to send in their claims.'

While, hardly daring to believe in it, the people of the Channel Islands awaited liberation, the negotiations that were to set them free had already begun. At 10 am that morning the chief British representative, Brigadier Snow, accompanied by a senior naval and RAF officer, had left Plymouth aboard HMS *Bulldog*, accompanied by another destroyer, HMS *Beagle*. Four hours later, as previously arranged by radio, they reached their rendezvous, four miles off Guernsey. On board was a British war correspondent:

A few moments later, looking ahead, we saw the German surrender ship . . . a dirty, battered minesweeper, her sides red with rust, the paint on her superstructure chipped and discoloured. . . . We watched . . . a small rubber dinghy . . . heaved over the side. Three Nazi sailors climbed into it, followed by a young naval officer . . . of not more than twenty-three or twenty-four . . . carrying an attaché case. He sat in the stern of the dinghy, his seat a few inches from the water and with the waves sweeping up and soaking him from the waist downwards. And so dripping, pale-faced . . . Captain-Lieutenant Arnim Zimmermann, of the 46th Mine-sweeping Flotilla, came to the *Bulldog* to be received by the click of saluting rifles and the shrill of the boatswains' whistles. . . . His hand shot out in the Nazi salute. . . . Then a young Birmingham lieutenant escorted him below to the wardroom.

Here the unfortunate lieutenant revealed that he had no powers to surrender, his mission being solely to carry back terms for a cease fire to his Admiral. He also, rather bravely in the circumstances, pointed out that the general armistice did not come into effect for another ten hours, and that he had been ordered to warn the British that 'your ships must move away immediately from these shores' and that their continued presence would be regarded as 'a provocative act'. Zimmermann learned, in his turn, like his predecessors at Lüneburg and Rheims, that the British were interested only in 'immediate surrender . . . not an armistice' and, with a further Nazi salute, withdrew to report back to his master.

The two destroyers – no match, had it come to a fight, for the heavy land-based guns ashore – then stood out to sea and patrolled up and down the Channel, until at midnight, just as the war in Europe was officially ending, there came another, even more dramatic meeting:

Out of the darkness came a German armed trawler . . . and, as we swept searchlights over the German vessel, there came into the rays a white eight-oared cutter. In her stern sat the same naval officer, but with him was a resplendent figure in light blue army greatcoat with great red lapels. He was Major-General Heine, of the German Army.

Heine, unlike Zimmermann, was authorized to act on behalf of Vice-Admiral Hüffmeier and he 'was immediately asked on going aboard if he accepted unconditional surrender on behalf of his Commander-in-Chief'. His reply was simple: 'Ja.' Two hours' discussion over the technicalities of the surrender followed, and then another five hours while the documents were prepared, Heine having been 'escorted to a cabin and told that he would be called upon to sign the necessary documents at dawn'; the British agreed that, because the German billets lacked electric light, the disarming of German troops would not begin until daylight.

At 7 am a table was placed on the little quarterdeck. Brigadier Snow took his place on one side of it and the other members of his staff grouped around him. The German general was summoned and, hesitating, almost tottering – he is a man in late middle age – he came to the table. Eight times he signed his name on copies for Britain, Russia and America. . . . The Brigadier signed and that was the end. . . . The time was 7.14 am.

Thirty minutes later the German trawler which had brought the Germans to the surrender ceremony reached St Peter Port, this time flying the White Ensign and bearing twenty men of the Royal Artillery. They were greeted by an 'unofficial reception party' of a police inspector and a sergeant, but words failed them as their countrymen stepped ashore and 'they were choking back their tears when, speechless, they grasped our hands'.

The tiny force formed up on the docks, fixed bayonets and marched towards the dock gates. There behind the gates was a seething, cheering, crying mob of men, women and children. Over them the church bells of St Peter Port were clanging tumultuously. . . . Then the crowd broke through the dock gates. In one second those gunners were marching like Guardsmen: in the next they were torn from the ranks, kissed, hugged, cheered. 'You have been so long coming.' 'We have waited so long for you.' 'British, they're British,' the Islanders cried. Somehow the soldiers re-formed. Two girls with great Union Jacks led them into the town. People rushed from their houses to join the crowd.

At the Old Court House the soldiers formed up on each side of the steps, at the top of which the officers of the landing party and Victor Carey, Guernsey Bailiff, stood. As a command rang out, a halyard was pulled and the Union Jack floated out in the soft, sunlit breeze. One could hear the sob from the crowd, then, rising to a great volume of sound they sang *God Save the King*. Then they stopped, looked up again and cheered – that to us all seemed the real moment of the liberation of Guernsey.

The arrival of the relieving forces had taken the island's 'Prime Minister', officially known as 'President of the Controlling Commission', unawares. He was in bed when the first two senior officers arrived and greeted them in his pyjamas and dressing-gown. But the proper formalities were duly observed later that day when the island's chief citizen, the Bailiff, handed in at the post office the first telegram to a British address since June 1940:

HIS MAJESTY THE KING, BUCKINGHAM PALACE, LONDON.

AFTER NEARLY FIVE YEARS OF GERMAN OCCUPATION THE PEOPLE OF YOUR BAILIWICK OF GUERNSEY RESPECTFULLY BEG

YOUR MAJESTY TO ACCEPT THEIR HUMBLE DUTY AND UNSHAKEN
LOYALTY.

  VICTOR G. CAREY, LIEUTENANT GOVERNOR AND BAILIFF.

Jersey had to wait a few hours longer to be liberated. Its Lieu-
tenant-Governor, Alexander Coutanche, the King's chief representative in the Channel Islands, learned that it was all over by a telephone
call from Guernsey, inviting him to collect the German Military
Commandant at midday and take him out to the *Beagle*, now on its
way to Jersey, to sign the formal surrender of the German troops
there. Afterwards he was invited to lunch in the wardroom and
enjoyed his first pink gin for years. He remarked on the luxury of
using real soap in the washroom, prompting an order rarely heard
on such occasions: 'Steward, a cake of soap all round.' Coutanche's
attempt to smoke some of the fearsome home-grown tobacco-
substitute produced during the occupation also led to the gift of
tins of the real thing. The party finally left with their pockets
bulging.

On the shore meanwhile expectation had been mounting all
morning, as one resident described:

From an early hour, dense crowds thronged the port and water-front,
every eye fixed on the direction whence the expected warship must make
her appearance. . . . At length there came a burst of cheering and loud
cries of 'There she is!' as, rounding Noirmont Point, the grey hull and
twin funnels of His Majesty's Flotilla Leader *Beagle* came steaming
majestically to her anchorage beyond Elizabeth Castle, the white ensign
of the Royal Navy flying out in the morning breeze. I think that that was
the moment . . . at which it came home to us that the long years of German domination were over.

The Army had been first ashore on Guernsey. On Jersey the
honour belonged to the Navy, in the shape of two lieutenants and
four ordinary seamen, but their reception was much the same:

Amidst roar after roar of delirious cheering, the welcome visitors at
length reached a waiting car and, as it crawled at a snail's pace through the
masses of excited people who pressed up to and even mounted the run-
ning-boards, the panting occupants were compelled to stand and shake
dozens of hands through the windows. Soon, however, the car was
forced to a standstill . . . and finally the two officers were plucked forcibly
from it and, showered with flowers, carried shoulder-high to the office

of the Harbour Master, where, appearing at one of the windows, they were greeted by more vociferous cheering and a thunderous rendering of the National Anthem.

Later that afternoon a detachment of the Hampshire Regiment and other troops disembarked and 'as new arrivals made their appearance, the crowds rushed to greet them'. The Germans were ordered to move into camp outside St Helier, and 'by nightfall . . . German uniforms, so long a loathsome eyesore to Jersey people, had completely disappeared from the streets'.

The reception of the first British troops to land on Alderney, third largest of the islands, was a good deal more restrained. Of its 12000 peacetime population only two families had been allowed to remain, but the head of one of them, a farmer who had stayed with his cattle, 'was waiting on the quay with a huge milk pail when the British troops arrived and offered them all glasses of milk as they came ashore'.

The smallest island was Sark, which even pre-war had had only 500 inhabitants, but its liberation proved most difficult of all. When telephoned from Guernsey on 9 May the Germans simply failed to answer, for a reason which became clear when a British detachment landed there next day from a naval tug: the gallant enemy had barricaded themselves in their headquarters and refused to come out. Eventually the island's ruler, the Dame of Sark, persuaded one trembling soldier to approach the door and, acting as interpreter, managed to convince the frightened Germans that they would not be harmed if they gave themselves up.

After five years of occupation the Channel Islands were in no hurry to get back to work. 'Everything was joyful,' wrote one Jersey man, 'from the unbroken May sunshine to the coloured flags.' It was marvellous when 'electricity and the telephone service were at once restored', wonderful when 'bread became abundant', deeply satisfying when 'everything German disappeared from their currency to their restrictions'. Apart from their genuine, patriotic delight at being freed from foreign thrall, the Channel Islanders hailed, too, an even more basic freedom, from hunger. 'A thirteen-day supply of food,' the Guernsey *Star* assured its readers almost incredulously on 9 May, 'would begin to arrive . . . on Saturday and . . . would include flour, meat, sugar, fats, tea, biscuits' and even 'chocolate . . . tobacco and soap. One thousand tons of gas and house coal are expected early next week . . . gas will probably be available to all consumers within a fortnight.'

Some British aircraft were seen that day, giving an unofficial victory display over Guernsey, but the first to land was an American pilot two days later who then delighted the crowds by taking off again and roaring so low over the heads of a fatigue party of German soldiers that they were forced to fling themselves flat 'like a row of ninepins'. Another sign of the times, which delighted all who witnessed it, was a haughty German major being put 'on the carpet' in the Royal Hotel, by a British colonel he had failed to salute.

But in spite of such scenes, freedom took a little getting used to. One schoolmaster, entering the office of the Jersey *Evening Post* the day after liberation, cautiously *whispered*, 'Have you heard the latest? They've got Göring', until reminded 'You needn't whisper now.' Nothing had annoyed the Germans more than being laughed at and years of frustration found joyous release in the cartoons displayed that week in the shop-windows of Beresford Street, St Helier. Farmer John Bull, with his shotgun, was seen chasing a cringing Hitler from the map of Europe and, even more gratifying, an unmistakable Churchill was holding up the Führer by the seat of his pants.

There was a darker side to the liberation. Although eventually not a single Channel Islander was even charged with collaboration, some loyal residents were determined that the notorious 'Jerrybags' who had openly associated with German soldiers should not escape unpunished. Some women, like similar offenders in France, had their hair roughly shaved off, and one at least, on 11 May, was 'cornered like a mad beast, dishevelled, torn and bleeding against the barbed-wire entrance to the pier' by a mob screaming 'Throw her into the harbour', until rescued by British troops. But such incidents were exceptional. The prevailing mood on Saturday, 12 May, which was proclaimed a public holiday to celebrate the liberation, was of joy, untainted by thoughts of revenge. It was, felt one Jersey man, 'a gala day in the true sense of the word . . . a real holiday with something to thrill one every minute'. Hitherto only token numbers of British troops and tiny amounts of supplies had arrived. Now 'Operation Nest-Egg', as the disarming of the

Germans and the restoration of normal life on the Channel Islands was, rather oddly, known, really got under way and both men and goods flowed in in full measure.

The diary of the Jersey man just quoted described the climax to the story:

Crowds watched the arrival of sailors and soldiers from assault-boats or 'Dukws', these coming from part of a convoy of over fifty ships which had been sent to the Channel Islands; on board this convoy were ten Channel Islands pilots and part of the headquarters staff travelled in the Great Western Railway cross-Channel steamer *St Helier*. Tank-landing craft came up right under the sea-wall of St Aubin's Bay, and these discharged all sorts of vehicles; so great was the enthusiasm of the on-lookers that even German prisoners who were working in the vicinity applauded excitedly.

An historic ceremony took place in the Royal Square at 6 pm: the States Banner headed a procession of the Assembly to a position near the statue, where a special dais had been erected from which Brigadier A. E. Snow, OBE, Military Commander of the Channel Islands, read the following Proclamation:

People of the Channel Islands: It having pleased His Majesty by Order in Council to vest in the officer commanding the armed forces in the Channel Islands all powers necessary for the success of our operation, the safety of our forces, and the safety and well-being of his subjects in the Islands, I, Alfred Ernest Snow, as the officer command-ing the forces, give you greeting on your liberation from the enemy.

I rely upon you all to work cheerfully and loyally to restore the normal life of your Islands. . . . It will be my firm purpose so to exer-cise my authority that your own government may rapidly be restored to your Islands and that you may enjoy in peace and prosperity your customary rights, laws and institutions.

GOD SAVE THE KING.

This was followed by a Message of Greeting from His Majesty the King:

To my most loyal people in the Channel Islands, I send my heartfelt greetings.

Ever since my armed forces had to be withdrawn you have, I know, looked forward with the same confidence as I have to the time of deliverance. We have never been divided in spirit. Our hopes and fears, anxieties and determination, have been the same, and we have been bound together by an unshakable conviction that the day would come when the Islands, the oldest possession of the Crown, would be liberated from enemy occupation. That day has now come, and, with all my Peoples, I cordially welcome you on your restoration to freedom and to your rightful place with the free nations of the world.

Later that day, Brigadier Snow presided at a similar ceremony on the steps of Elizabeth College in Guernsey.

On the following morning, Sunday, 13 May, there were thanksgiving services all over the Islands, and that evening the first Germans of the 30000-strong garrison, which had made the Channel Islands the most heavily-defended territory of their size in the world, left for captivity in England. As they travelled down to the docks to embark on the ships which had brought the liberating troops they were watched in hostile silence, though by a strange irony some passers-by mistook 'Madman' Hüffmeier, as he was driven to the harbour, for a British Admiral and cheered him.

With the Germans visibly departing the return to normality gathered pace though 'for days . . . there were dances in the narrow streets', one Guernsey schoolteacher remembers, and 'lights burned until late in the houses', unlimited electricity being still a great luxury. Getting used to what seemed equally unlimited amounts of food was even more difficult. 'The shopkeepers had expected to be overwhelmed in the rush,' the same observer recalls. 'Instead the people collected outside the bakers and the grocers, the butchers and fish shops, gazing in stupefied amazement.' She remembers 'rushing home breathlessly from school' one afternoon to tell a friend '"Come down to the town, there's bread there, shelves of it, all for sale."' The two women 'hurried into the town, to join the group standing outside the windows of the baker's shop, just staring at the loaves upon loaves of bread. In the streets the children had been tearing down the hated Nazi posters and scarlet-lettered *verboten* notices floated on the sea.'

10

POSTMAN'S KNOCK IN RED SQUARE

*'The . . . victory celebrations are popularly regarded as the
greatest moment in the history of this country since the
Revolution'*
– Manchester Guardian *correspondent describing events in
Moscow, Wednesday, 9 May 1945*

THE day the 63000 surviving inhabitants of the Channel Islands
welcomed their liberators was also the day on which the 180
million people of Russia celebrated the end of what they knew as
the Great Fatherland War. Most people in the West found puzzling,
or infuriating, the Russian insistence that peace could not begin
until the Germans had capitulated to them, as well as to the other
allies, and the demand for a second surrender in Berlin, but looked
at from Moscow the whole affair took on a totally different perspec-
tive. 'The one-day difference between VE Day in the West and
VE Day in the East made an unpleasant impression,' felt one highly
experienced foreign correspondent, Alexander Werth. 'While
Churchill was broadcasting the end of the war . . . Russian radio
was broadcasting its Children's Hour, a pleasant little story about
two rabbits and a bird.' Even someone as thoroughly British as
Mrs – later Lady – Churchill 'learned how different an event
seemed when you view it from Moscow instead of London or
Washington. On Victory Day I remember being struck with
astonishment that the Armistice was signed in Rheims and only, it
seemed, as an afterthought in Berlin. This was rather incomprehens-
ible to the Russians and, I confess . . . to me.'
  Mrs Churchill's presence in Russia seemed itself a good augury
for future friendship between the two countries. So vast was the
British public's admiration for the Russian armies and people at
that time that the British Red Cross Aid to Russia Fund she had
founded in October 1941 had within a year raised nearly £2 million
to buy clothes and medical supplies. Some of this was devoted to

equipping two hospitals in the devastated city of Rostov as a permanent memorial to the fund and Mrs Churchill, partly in the hope of restoring Anglo-Soviet relations, which at the official level were already becoming frayed, had accepted an invitation to pay a long visit to Russia to see how her fund's money had been spent.

7 May had thus found her in Moscow and though, as her biographer wrote, she 'longed to be with Winston in the hour of triumph', duty, in the shape of a promise to attend various ceremonies already arranged in her honour, kept her there. On VE Day itself her husband – although he added a dutiful postscript 'Much love, W' and also made a private telephone call – did his best to make use of his wife to further the cause of Anglo-Soviet relations. 'It would be a good thing,' he cabled Mrs Churchill, sending her a suggested script, 'if you broadcast to the Russian people, tomorrow, Wednesday, provided that were agreeable to the Kremlin.'

8 May was an ordinary working day in Moscow but the little British colony there, as everywhere, listened to the Prime Minister's broadcast. In the group who assembled at the British Embassy was the former French statesman, M. Edouard Herriot, recently liberated from German captivity. 'I am afraid,' he told Mrs Churchill, 'you may think it unmanly of me to weep, but I have just heard Mr Churchill's voice. The last time . . . was on that day in Tours in 1940 when he implored the French government to hold firm.'

That afternoon, too, Mrs Churchill spoke to correspondents at the Embassy on a highly topical theme. 'Unless,' she told them, 'the friendship that has been established between the Soviet Union and the English-speaking people during the war continues, increases and deepens, there will be very little happiness in the immediate future for the world; and . . . [in] the lives of our children, grandchildren and great-grandchildren. I hope that, in a small way, my visit will help.'

Also doing his best to promote the same cause was another British visitor to Moscow, Dr Hewlett Johnson of Canterbury Cathedral, better known to his countrymen, from his extreme left-wing opinions, as 'the Red Dean'. He was there on a separate tour from Mrs Churchill, but for a similar reason, having founded his own Anglo-Soviet Medical Aid Fund, which, after attempts to merge them had failed, co-existed harmoniously with hers and between these two very disparate personalities a deep mutual respect developed. Mrs Churchill, considered the Red Dean, had 'done excellent work for the Soviet Union and Russian friendship whilst in England' and 'crowned that work in Russia, winning the affection of all by her charm and unaffected manner'. Both were present at the main British event in Moscow to mark the end of the war, a thanksgiving service at the Embassy, on the morning of VE+1, conducted by the resident naval chaplain, in peacetime a Methodist minister. It was, thought Dr Hewlett Johnson, no mean judge, 'quiet, formal and impressive', while Mrs Churchill found it 'beautifully performed', and expressing 'perfectly the deepest feelings of thankfulness and dedication in our hearts that day'. The ambassador, rather bravely one must feel, had at Mrs Churchill's suggestion invited the 'Red Dean' to preach. He chose as his subject the death of President Roosevelt, and Mrs Churchill found it 'an inspiring address'.

The Russian people learned that the war was over from an announcement broadcast at 1.10 am, local time, on Wednesday, 9 May, by Uri Levitan, the combined 'John Snagge' and 'Stuart Hibberd' of Soviet broadcasting, whose 'Olympian voice', as a fellow broadcaster described it, was regularly employed to read out 'the Orders of the Day over Moscow Radio and the city's public address system'. He had even been the subject of one of Stalin's rare jokes. When asked when the war would be over the dictator had replied, 'Don't worry, Levitan will tell you.'

Even in well-disciplined, strictly-censored Russia it had been obvious that the end was approaching and the public had been waiting for several days for Levitan to tell them. 'As early as Monday night,' reported the same American correspondent, a 'group of . . . university students went to the Red Square and stood in the drizzling rain waiting for the voice of Levitan, but nothing happened. At dusk yesterday [Tuesday] I saw a group of people at a bus stop huddled around the evening paper which had just come out', and 'carried a Tass despatch from London dated Monday giving the full text of Admiral Dönitz's broadcast from German headquarters announcing the German surrender'. But only now, in the early hours of the day which everywhere else was known as VE+1, were the Russians allowed to know definitely that it was peace for them too.

After a brief report of the ceremony in Berlin an hour before,

Moscow Radio announced that 'in honour of the victorious conclusion of the great patriotic war' that day, 9 May, would be a
'festival of victory', with flags being hoisted on all public buildings,
and a general holiday. Then, a courtesy not observed by the other
allied countries after comparable announcements, the national
anthems of Britain, the United States and France were played as
well as the *Internationale.*

In spite of the hour 'the news', reported the correspondent of the
New York Herald Tribune, 'quickly spread, lights snapped on in
residences and people – many in night-clothes – tumbled out into
the streets, shouting and dancing. Some knelt on the ground and
prayed.' Russians making a telephone call instead of being greeted
by the Russian equivalent of 'Number, please?' were asked: 'Do
you know that today is Victory Day?'

Although it came a day later than everyone else's, Victory Day
in Moscow was to start earlier and last longer than in any other
capital. By six in the morning a BBC correspondent found Red
Square, 'the Trafalgar Square of Moscow', already filling with
crowds rapidly 'growing larger and larger and gayer and merrier',
many of them students from the Institute of Foreign Languages
'trying hard to think of a victory prank'. The day also gave them a
chance to try out their English and when they discovered 'a British
sergeant who turned out to see the fun . . . they pounced on him,
tossed him up in the air and shouted . . . *Victory! Victory!* Then
they asked for a song and he responded with *Tipperary.*' Before
long 'the sergeant and some others in British uniform were singing
and teaching the crowd *Pack up your troubles in your old kit bag*'.

The scale of the rejoicing also impressed the experienced correspondent of the London *Times*, surveying 'the whole stupendous
panorama of Moscow's victory celebration' from a strategically-
placed roof:

Hundreds of thousands of people since early morning have been streaming into the centre of Moscow. The crowds fill the broad street, two or
three times the width of Whitehall, that runs below the western walls of
the Kremlin past the university and the Lenin Library to the Moskva
River. They line the river bank below the terrace. They are packing the
Red Square. . . . Crowds sweep each side of St Basil's Church towards
the bridge over the Moskva River, away towards the theatre square,
where a bandstand has been erected for street dancing, and into the dark

streets of Chinatown. Wireless sets are broadcasting *Tipperary*, sung by a Red Army choir. It is a homely, democratic crowd, in which generals and soldiers, commissars and workers, mingle.

The number of people who had turned out, even on this bright and sunny day, amazed everyone. The Russians had always stressed loyalty to one's own factory and many groups on the street consisted of people who normally worked together, but there were also innumerable family parties: children, having at first gone to school as usual, had discovered that the holiday also applied to them. The resulting turnout was probably the biggest anywhere in the world that week. As the *Manchester Guardian* correspondent explained, 'The . . . victory celebrations are popularly regarded as the greatest moment in the history of this country since the Revolution. Never has Moscow seen such crowds, and never before during this war have the Soviet people shown their whole-hearted appreciation of allied help so freely and emphatically.'

This was perhaps the most noteworthy feature of the day, for the Russians had often been accused of being ungrateful for the sacrifices made on their behalf and determined to stay aloof from Western influences. But on Victory Day all was different. 'It was sufficient to look like a foreigner,' wrote the same reporter, 'to be kissed, hugged and generally fêted. In Red Square all foreign cars were stopped and the occupants dragged out, embraced and sometimes even tossed into the air.'

Among those to suffer this boisterous treatment, which had certainly never been accorded him in the cloistered calm of Canterbury, was the 'Red Dean', when he left the British Embassy after the victory service that morning:

A dense crowd, enthusiastic and genial, released at last from the long strain of war, blocked our road and engulfed us, cheering every Englishman or American. They seized General Younger, a British officer in full uniform and, tossing him in the air, caught him as gently as if he were a babe. My turn came next.

Other Britons that day experienced almost equally boisterous examples of the Russian desire to touch a British body, or hear a British voice. Usually a crowd gathering outside British premises abroad was cause for alarm, but not on Victory Day, where 'at the British Embassy a junior official was suddenly called upon to make a speech to a loudly applauding crowd which "stormed" the building. Outside a big hotel known to be tenanted by many British and Americans a large crowd waited to pounce on everyone leaving and demand a speech.' Carrying a Briton shoulder-high was another popular tribute, which even extended to a British-owned pet. 'In one of Moscow's main squares a British woman on the staff of the newspaper *Britansky Soyuznik* [British Ally] was walking with a dog when a mass of people waving Red banners and cheering wildly bore down on her. She and the dog were chaired all the way back to the hotel.'

The United States that day was equally popular, as the correspondent of the *New York Herald Tribune* discovered that afternoon when a crowd, thousands strong, 'assembled in front of the American Embassy shouting "Long live America! Long live Truman! Long live the memory of Roosevelt! Long live the American people!" American GIs danced over the ancient stones with pretty Russian factory girls. One American corporal, after an hour's celebrating, gasped: "Boy, oh boy. If I'd played post office every day until I got into the Army, I couldn't have been kissed as many times as I've been kissed today."'

That veteran newspaperman Alexander Werth also found 'the spontaneous joy of the two or three million people who thronged the Red Square that evening – and the Moscow River embankments, and Gorky Street, all the way up to the Belorussian Station – of a quality and a depth I had never seen in Moscow before. . . . The crowds . . . were so happy that they did not even have to get drunk.' He observed one odd sign that this was regarded as a special day, not noticed by other observers: 'Under the tolerant gaze of the militia, young men even urinated against the walls of the Moskva Hotel, flooding the wide pavement.'

Just as in other capitals, despite the anti-clericalism of the Soviet regime, people in Moscow that day were eager to worship, as Dr Hewlett Johnson discovered after a private visit to the Patriarch of the Russian Orthodox Church, the 'highest ecclesiastic in Russia', who presented his visitor with 'a magnificent jewelled enamelled crucifix suspended by a massive silver chain'.

After tea, we drove with the Patriarch in his own car to the cathedral, into which we had to force an entrance through crowds such as I have seldom seen before. Russian churches are chairless. People stand, and on that day so tight was the wedge of humanity that movement was well-nigh impossible. At length we reached the enclosure which shuts the altar off from the congregation, and were given a place of honour between screen and people. Near us sang the choir, men and women in everyday dress; the Cantor led the service with an immense voice which carried far down the huge building and boomed out to the crowds in the street.

While Dr Hewlett Johnson was doing his duty, at church, Mrs Churchill was faithfully carrying out her husband's instructions and broadcasting his message 'to Marshal Stalin, to the Red Army and to the Russian people':

From the British nation I send you heartfelt greetings on the splendid victories you have won in driving the invader from your soil and laying the Nazi tyrant low. It is my firm belief that on the friendship and under-standing between the British and Russian peoples depends the future of mankind. Here in our island home we are thinking today . . . about you all. We send you from the bottom of our hearts our wishes for your happiness and well-being and that, after all the sacrifices and sufferings of the Dark Valley through which we have marched together, we may also in loyal comradeship and sympathy walk in the sunshine of victo-rious peace.

Marshal Stalin, broadcasting that night, struck a sterner note. Alone among the allies he warned his listeners that the Germans were not to be trusted:

Comrades, fellow countrymen and women, the great day of victory over Germany has come. Fascist Germany has been forced to her knees by the Red Army and by the troops of our allies. . . . Being well aware of the subterfuges of the German leaders, who consider their treaties as mere scraps of paper, we have no reason to accept their word. Nevertheless, this morning the German troops . . . have begun to surrender their arms *en masse* to the Soviet troops. This is no longer a mere scrap of paper. It is actual capitulation of the armed forces of Germany. True, one group of German troops, in Czechoslovakia, is still trying to avoid capitulation. But we must believe that the Red Army will succeed in bringing it to its senses. . . . The age-old struggle of the Slav peoples for their existence and independence has ended in victory over the German invaders and German tyranny. . . . The great patriotic war has ended with our complete victory. . . . Glory to our heroic Red Army. . . . Glory to our great people. . . . Eternal glory to the heroes who fell in the struggle.

The Russians had ample experience of stage-managing great public events and on Victory Day it came into its own. The official celebrations in Moscow were on a far vaster scale than in any other capital. The 'artillery salute' fired by the Red Army sounded to the ears of at least one American 'tremendous', as well it might: 1000 guns, lined wheel to wheel along the river bank, fired off thirty salvoes. Earlier Red Air Force planes had 'swooped and circled over the gay scene, adding to the din of victory', and showering out 'multi-coloured flares'. Dr Hewlett Johnson, ending a busy day standing 'on the wide entrance steps' of Moscow's puppet theatre, where he had attended a gala performance, found the 'Victory firework display magnificent. The sky north, south, east and west blazed with coloured searchlight rays. A thousand feet overhead the searchlights played on a gigantic red banner held by invisible cords from invisible balloons.'

In London and Paris, by the early hours of VE+1, the bonfires were beginning to die down and the crowds to thin out – but not in Russia. Soviet planning saw to it that those who wanted to make a night of it could, and, as the *Herald Tribune* man observed – perhaps aware how half-hearted New York's rejoicing had been by contrast – 'more than a hundred bands and orchestras played in the squares and parks for the thousands who rollicked through the night'.

While the Russians were cheering their victorious troops, the Red Army was that day imposing peace upon the country whose annexation had set Europe on the final path to war. During 7 May the resistance movement in Prague had risen in revolt against the Germans, but though it described itself bravely as the Czechoslovak National Army, it was clear that it could not liberate the capital, let alone the country, unaided. Although at 1.30 am on the eighth the German High Command issued orders to all its units in the city to cease fighting, and began negotiations with the hitherto illegal Czech National Council for a full unconditional surrender, it was out of touch with many subordinate headquarters even inside Prague while elsewhere in the country, surrounded by vengeance-minded patriots and with the dreaded Russians approaching, most commanders refused to give in. At 4.54 pm on VE Day the Czechs, now in command of the radio stations, reported that the Germans were shelling the city and appealed for help from allied aircraft, while at 6 pm news reached London that 'five German divisions have been preparing an assault on Prague from the west'. Even worse, the Germans were treating as partisans and shooting out of hand 'Czechoslovak officers whom they capture' while, like another Lidice, 'the town of Konetopy . . . twenty-two miles north-east of Prague was burned down and the inhabitants murdered'.

The 4th US Armoured Division, part of the American 3rd Army, had been halted at 8 am on VE Day on its way to Prague. The Germans opposing it were only too eager to fall into American hands and, reported a correspondent, 'were driving themselves into the American lines in their own lorries and marching in columns with white flags'. On the Russian front it was different. A succession of Orders of the Day issued by Stalin revealed that, although Dresden had fallen, the advancing Russians from the north-west were still seventy miles from Prague and that it was only 'after stiff fighting' that other units had captured their most recent objective, 128 miles south-west of the city.

The campaign in Czechoslovakia ended in confusion, for units had begun to surrender piecemeal even before the general capitulation in Berlin and after it the Russians accused some troops of having violated its terms and resumed their attack. Czechoslovakia could be considered free again, at least officially, on 9 May when, after four days of street-fighting, 90000 SS troops abandoned their arms and marched out to the west to surrender to the Americans, while, from the east, the first Russian tanks were entering the city. They were draped with lilac blossoms by the cheering crowds, and their Russian crews, unused to being hailed as liberators, watched in amazement, reported an American correspondent, as pretty girls in Czech national costume climbed up to ride beside them.

I I

NEW LIGHT FOR MISS LIBERTY

*'The statue . . . blazed into victory splendour last night at
8.29 o'clock'*
– New York Herald Tribune, *9 May 1945*

It had begun as Europe's war; it ended as Europe's victory. In the
United States, as in the Soviet Union, 8 May was not even a
public holiday, though the decision probably matched the public
mood. As that invaluable barometer of public opinion, a taxi-driver,
told the correspondent of the London *Daily Telegraph*, 'I could not
celebrate today, I have a boy on Okinawa.' But the ordinary citizen,
it was reported, did not begrudge the British their two days off:
'"After five and a half years of blackout and bombs they have
earned it", was the general comment.'

In Washington it was an ordinary, quiet, working day and the
flags still flew, dispiritingly, at half mast, in honour of the dead
President Roosevelt. In San Francisco it was worse than a normal
working day. 'The only form of celebration,' noted Sir Alexander
Cadogan, 'is the closing of all bars for twenty-four hours.' This was
a heavy blow to the British contingent which he and Anthony Eden
were leading at the United Nations conference, for they 'had taken
the bar at the top of this building, on the 19th floor, a rather marvellous place with glass walls all round and wonderful views', to
'hear the King's broadcast, which was at noon by our local time. . . .
The speech came over very well', but 'we couldn't drink his health'.

Even in New York the celebrations were, in the judgement of the
New York Times, only 'a pale imitation' of those which had greeted
the unofficial announcement of the news the day before. Thirty
thousand citizens began the day by assembling in Times Square to
hear President Truman's victory proclamation, at 9 am New York
time, but were disappointed; no one had bothered to arrange for
the loudspeakers to carry it. Even to those New Yorkers who did

hear it, however, at home or on car radios, it was hardly calculated to trigger off an explosion of rejoicing:

If I could give you a single watchword for the coming months that word is 'Work, Work, Work'. . . . We must work to finish the war. Our victory is but half won. The West is free but the East is still in bondage to the treacherous tyranny of the Japanese. When the last Japanese has surrendered unconditionally then only will our fighting job be done.

The news that the European war was truly over reached the waiting thousands 'in the form of a hoarse and ever-growing chorus from craft in the Hudson, in the East River and in the Bay', when 'there broke loose', reported the New York newspapers, 'a bedlam of marine and factory whistles, auto horns and bells that could be heard all over the city'. As the din was at its height 2600 German prisoners of war disembarked, staring around them in 'awe and wonderment', perhaps assuming that the noise was some curious expression of hostility, or else a permanent feature of life in America. On the Stock Exchange, however, on Wall Street there was briefly silence, when staff and brokers stood unspeaking for two minutes in memory of the fallen.

In Times Square the response to the distant uproar was immediate:

Factory workers and office workers, chiefly women, joined the crowds. They linked arms and moved up and down Times Square in high-kicking formations. . . . They ran back and forth squealing and breathless, trying to get within range of all the newsreel cameras and news photographers.

Then rain began to fall, putting a stop to the proceedings, which were not resumed until the evening:

The second [celebration] broke spontaneously after 9 pm, inspired by the restoration of much of the lighting on the Great White Way [i.e. Broadway]. The nocturnal revel had everything that was missing from the daytime jamboree. In noise-making uproar, high jinks and real enthusiasm it almost duplicated a peace-time New Year's Eve.

Fife and drum corps marched into the square from the north, the west and the south, and cheering throngs of servicemen and civilians tramped behind them blowing horns, clanging cowbells. Police broke these formations as fast as they could . . . only to have them reorganize a block farther north, or a block further south. Servicemen of all the allied nations formed dancing rings and sang victory melodies. They roared verses of *God Bless America* in front of the Astor Hotel, *The Caissons go Rolling Along* in front of the Palace Theater.

All thirty-three Broadway theatres were open that night and the brightly lighted façades proved a big attraction. 'Boy,' was the general comment, 'New York looks like home again.' The replacement of darkness by light was also the theme of a ceremony on the waterfront that evening, when the floodlights were switched on around the Statue of Liberty, 'whose war-dimmed torch', the *Herald Tribune* recalled, 'alone had marked its presence in the harbour at night since 7 December 1941, except for fifteen minutes of full light on D Day'. Now at 8.29 pm the wife of the statue's custodian 'threw the master switch' and Miss Liberty shone forth across the gateway to the New World in all her old splendour, indeed in more than her old splendour, for new bulbs were used 'to give the torch the bluish characteristic of living flame'.

New York finished its celebrations early, even in Times Square.

At midnight . . . mounted men cantered into the square and gently herded the crowds off the pavement. Police sound-trucks boomed the warning: 'All pedestrians back on the sidewalks!' Grudgingly the crowds obeyed. Still blowing, singing and cheering, but that was the end. VE Day was over.

Across the border, in Canada, which had been at war ever since 1939, it *was* a holiday and Churchill's speech was relayed throughout the country at 9 am Eastern time. The main event in Ottawa was an 'official service of praise and thanksgiving' on the steps of the City Hall; the real force and fervour of rejoicing had, as in New York, been spent on the previous day. But Canada could claim one distinction on VE Day, the only serious disorder to take place anywhere in the world. Eight thousand sailors and merchant seamen roared through the streets of Halifax, looting and wrecking, allegedly as 'a protest, a vengeance for the way the city had treated them' and especially 'lack of accommodation and high prices'. In these complaints there may have been some substance. As one local politician commented: 'Drunkenness alone is not sufficient to start a riot. There must be deep-seated basic grievances.' Whatever the cause – and the frightened citizens blamed the Canadian Navy for simultaneously releasing some 8000 sailors from duty – the results were only too visible and the cost of repairing the damage was estimated at five million dollars.

What started the notorious Halifax Riots is still not clear, but the report which appeared in next day's Canadian newspapers told its own story. 'Two are dead, shops looted, liquor stolen', ran one headline. By nightfall on VE Day, when a curfew was enforced, 'thousands of Victory rioters had smashed and looted virtually every store in the downtown business section' and 'one entire ward at the Canadian Royal Navy Hospital was filled with riot casualties', many of them drunks who had fallen 'on to broken glass in the streets and came up bleeding from many cuts'. If the Navy had started the trouble the civilians were not slow to join in:

Men and women walked calmly down the street carrying armloads of shoes, clothing and with their pockets filled. . . . The streets were soon littered with . . . groceries and articles of a dozen kinds thrown carefully around. A sailor grabbed a mannequin [i.e. display dummy] from a store, tossed away his cap, and put on the wig of the mannequin. He smashed the head of the mannequin against a window and then moved along to other stores and repeated the performance. Five swings, and thousands of dollars of damage went crashing to the sidewalk. . . .

One store remained untouched because the brave woman owner stood for fifteen long and tiresome hours outside diplomatically talking at least a dozen people out of breaking her window. 'This store has been here for fifty-six years. It wasn't even broken in the Halifax explosion of 1917.'

At the height of the turbulence men and women reeled through the streets, carrying cases of beer . . . whisky or rum, or . . . walked with hands full of bottles. The parks were turned into beer gardens as couples and groups sprawled on the grass with a case of whisky – an entire year's ration – beside them. It was a vicious celebration, the worst incident of the war in Halifax.

If Halifax, Nova Scotia, was the noisiest place in the Empire that VE Day, the quietest was Melbourne, its citizens being preoccupied with the continuing threat from Japan. According to the *Yorkshire Evening Post*, Australia was 'the gloomiest country in the world apart from Germany', for, though 9 May was a public holiday, all hotels and places of entertainment were closed by law. VE Day itself passed quietly, for Churchill's broadcast was not until 11 pm Australian time.

In South Africa, curiously enough, the one dominion which had been somewhat half-hearted about joining in the war against Germany in 1939, though it had eventually sent a contingent of troops to the Middle East, the rejoicing was far more fervent. In Cape Town, Churchill's broadcast was 'punctuated by the sound of a victory salute of twenty-one guns from Lion Battery', followed by 'a peal of bells from St George's Cathedral'. Then, according to the *Cape Argus*, 'Cape Town went slightly mad':

The first sirens sounded, more bells began to chime, scattered cheers merged into a continuous roar, train whistles and car hooters joined in the chorus and in a few moments Adderley Street was filled with excited, laughing people. Utter strangers shook hands or clapped one another excitedly on the back. . . . Traffic came to a standstill, no one having either the nerve or the desire to drive through Bedlam.

On the ninth it was a different story, for, even worse off than London, Cape Town had no buses or trains at all, the absence of public transport contributing to 'the quietest public holiday . . . since the war began'.

The 'New York' of South Africa had always been Johannesburg, a noisy, bustling city, which on VE Day fully lived up to its reputation. Crowds surged through the streets, arms linked, 'waving flags of the allied nations . . . the scream of sirens and the whistle of mine hooters heralded the official announcement . . . in a city gay with thousands of fluttering flags. . . . Crowds of thousands . . . gathered behind the gun positions . . . on the heights of the Berea' as 'a salute to victory crashed out . . . from a battery of 25-pounders' and 'a snowdrift of white ticker-tape and scraps of office paper swirled down from skyscrapers in Commissioner Street between Sauer and Harrison Streets'.

Another display later that day revealed the deep piety never far below the surface of the Afrikaner heart:

A symbol of the principles that inspired the war . . . appeared high on the kopjies surrounding the city last night. Five crosses, forty feet high, were illuminated on the higher points on hills on Northcliff, Kensington, Cyrildene, Yeoville and Linksfield at the moment when, after a short talk by the mayor's chaplain . . . a choir began the first lines of *When I survey the wondrous cross*.

Although this had essentially been the white man's war, the African population also made a distinctive contribution to victory with a specially composed song of *Praises for the Fighting Forces of the Allies*, delivered by a Zulu chieftain to his warriors. Even in translation, as broadcast by the BBC, it was not quite what listeners to Geraldo and his orchestra were used to:

Heroes of the King Emperor, swimmers in the deep pool of crocodiles, the crocodiles of Germany and Italy, they've tried hard to grab you but you destroyed them with the grindstones of the grinders. You mighty young men of the United Nations, conquerors of our enemies at the height of their power, it was you who danced last . . . heroes of our lion. Then the lion roared, the weapons of Hitler and Mussolini fell and he devoured them. Hail, hail, great elephants!

VE Day was a big occasion for British colonies and expatriates everywhere. In Kenya 'masses of all races from outside areas congregated in the centre' of Nairobi, 'which was thick with flags'. An open-air united thanksgiving service outside the Law Court was attended by the Governor and there was a march past of soldiers, and in the evening 'a big torchlight procession through the main streets ended at a huge bonfire opposite Nairobi Cathedral'.

In Cairo the staff of GHQ Middle East Forces flocked to a traditional holiday event, the Donkey Derby at the Gezira Sporting Club. But even in victory distinctions of rank remained. One race, the High Command Stakes, was for mounts belonging only to lieutenant-colonels and above.

In India, largest of British possessions, there was a novel, and among those affected no doubt popular, tribute to victory, in the shape of a remission of sentence for many prisoners in jail, though, for old-guard British residents, the reflection, voiced by *The Times*, that 'all shades of opinion hope that it has brought nearer the day of India's independence', must have cast its shadow of foreboding.

In Poona, the much-joked-about home of the British Army in India, the celebrations were equally traditional, with a two-day cricket match, covering both VE Days, between a combined services and a local eleven, but to allow time for the celebrations to be properly organized most celebrations in India were postponed until 14 May, which was proclaimed a public holiday. A Victory Parade in Bombay attracted 50000 holiday-makers and in the capital, New Delhi, there was a brave display of 'tens of thousands of earthen lamps supplied free . . . by the municipality'. Here there was no rain to mar the celebrations; crowds flocked through the streets far into the night, despite the blazing heat, which earlier had reached 107 degrees.

Here, as in Europe, it was the civilians who did most of the cheering. One Army medical officer, then stationed with a unit at Cocanada, north of Madras, remembers how, as not infrequently happened in the Army, the authorities had somehow lost track of his men, who were supposed to be preparing to receive casualties from Malaya, prior to moving there themselves. With no orders from above, and nothing to do except await this unwelcome posting, those manning this 'forgotten outpost' of the 'forgotten army' devoted themselves to a celebration party of two and a half days.

Nearer the front there was not even much drinking. In Rangoon, the capital of Burma, only recaptured from the Japanese a few days before, the first deepwater ships arrived that day, but everyone knew that the monsoon was due to begin in only twelve days, so that the troops faced another miserable summer floundering through the worst fighting country in the world. The war correspondents made no pretence that the average soldier in the Far East was much excited by the news from Europe. 'The thought uppermost in the minds of the senior commanders is equipment,' reported *The Times* correspondent. Although proud of having 'fought and won the Burma campaign on a shoe-string' they hoped that unlimited stocks of the stores and weapons they had lacked would now become available. As for their men, 'the thought uppermost in the minds of the British soldier is repatriation. At last he hopes it will be possible to reduce the term of overseas service.' Many men, the *Manchester Guardian* reporter found, were unaware even that the war in Europe was over; few in Rangoon had heard Churchill's broadcast and there were no official celebrations, though 'some unit commanders celebrated . . . by making an issue of extra rations'. The reaction in the 14th Army, the writer considered, 'was best summarized by a senior commander who . . . remarked "The war is over. Let us get on with the war."'

For 80000 British prisoners in Japanese hands the war had already been over for three years, only to be replaced by a far more bitter struggle for mere survival. Although most camps had a clandestine wireless, it did not do to be too well informed since this aroused Japanese suspicions and exposed one to the risk of torture.

One former lance-corporal in the Sherwood Foresters, then in Changi Jail on Singapore Island, remembers that rumours did begin to circulate that the Germans had surrendered, but they were not believed: the camp was always full of some sensational story or other. When the news was accepted, after appearing in a local Japanese-sponsored newspaper, the prisoners' feelings were mixed. The Japs, they feared, might avenge their defeated allies by butchering some of their British prisoners.

For the Americans in the Pacific this, not the comparative side-show in Europe, had always been the real war, but on embattled Okinawa, scene of some of the bloodiest fighting of the whole campaign, where the Japanese were holding out 'in battered caves and pillboxes', one tribute was paid to that far-off surrender. 'Exactly at noon' on 9 May, reported the *New York Herald Tribune*, 'every gun of the artillery massed behind the American 10th Army positions and every gun of the fleet offshore cut loose in a single simultaneous round in recognition of the United Nations Victory in Europe . . . probably the largest single salvo ever fired . . . a blast which must have sounded like a crack of doom to the enemy'.

12

BURMA LOOMS AHEAD

'Those of age and service group 27 and over . . . had been warned that "Burma Looms Ahead" was the real significance of the initials BLA'
– History of the 1st Buckinghamshire Battalion, *recalling July 1945.*

WHILE the British forces in the Far East were preparing for their next, and probably most costly, offensive those in Europe had other preoccupations. The task of getting Germany back on to its feet again seemed enormous, and many units soon found themselves having to move on from the areas where the cease fire had found them, as forces were redeployed to cover the whole of the conquered territories, which were now shared out between the four major allies, as agreed at the Yalta conference in February. The Russians held the eastern part of Germany almost to the Elbe, the rest being divided roughly in two, with the British in the north, the Americans in the south and the French holding a smaller area along their own frontiers. Austria was shared, roughly half and half, between the British and the Russians, though Vienna and Berlin were both inside the Russian zone. Berlin itself was controlled by a joint four-nation commission, which took it in turns to exercise some overall control, though the city was also divided into four separate zones. The intention was that, after the intermediate stage of military government, through officers specially assigned to the job, the British zone of Germany would increasingly be run by the civilian Control Commission for Germany already waiting in London to cross the Channel, and a similar organization set up the Americans, in parallel with the normal military machine. The restoration of a normal elected civilian government seemed in 1945 almost impossibly remote, and it was not achieved, with the granting of full sovereignty to the new West German state, centred on Bonn, until 1955.

The price of defeat

The Dönitz government is rounded up by British troops

Captured U-boat in the Thames. It had heeled over at low tide, but was in perfect condition

Election meeting in Abingdon, 1945. The Conservative candidate was elected here, but over the country as a whole there was a Labour landslide

The new Prime Minister. Clement Attlee addresses his supporters after the announcement of the result of the General Election

Bread queue in Manchester. Bread, unrationed throughout the war, was to be rationed for the first time in peacetime

'Bowler-hatted.' Demobilized officers being measured for civilian suits at the clothing depot in Olympia

Homecoming. Gunner Murdoch, a former prisoner of war of the Japanese, returns to Tulse Hill. The house is a prefab which has replaced his bombed home. His son had been six months old when his father last saw him

At first the whole job fell on the Army. On VE Day Eisenhower commanded sixty-one American divisions, more than three million men, and Montgomery had under him almost as many British troops. Within the British zone there were, needing immediate attention, some one million wounded German soldiers, another million displaced persons, drawn from all over Europe, and about one and a half million able-bodied prisoners, who had to be rounded up, disarmed, looked after and finally got home again. It was hard, as I saw myself, travelling by road from Ostend to Copenhagen and right across northern Germany in the week after the war ended, not to feel sorry for these long lines of sad-faced men shuffling along the roadside towards captivity, grimed by the dust of every passing allied convoy, or dumped in makeshift 'cages' of barbed-wire enclosed fields, often without shelter. The film-actor David Niven, then serving in the British Army, clearly felt the same after passing 'one hastily erected prisoner-of-war cage in the open country between Hanover and Osnabruck. . . . There must have been a hundred thousand men already inside. The first warming rays of the sun were just touching the prisoners. It had rained heavily during the night and now a cloud of steam was rising from this dejected field-grey mass of humanity.'

It was even harder to feel indignation against individuals. 'On a country road near Brunswick' Niven soon afterwards came upon a German general, who had escaped from Berlin, and, driving a horse-drawn wagon, disguised as a farmer, with a sack over his shoulders, but still wearing his officer's field boots, was only a kilometre from home and safety. 'I had never seen such utter weariness, such blank despair on a human face before. . . . We stared at each other . . . for a long time. Then I said, "Go ahead, sir" and added ridiculously, "please cover up your bloody boots".' Easier to deal with were the German officers still driving about in style, like the 'two SS officers and a storm-trooper' in a 'smart Mercedes-Benz', accompanied by a van full of baggage 'and a woman', who were stopped at a bridge checkpoint on the Kiel Canal. A passing BBC war correspondent, only released a few weeks before after three years as a prisoner of war, readily agreed to act as interpreter:

The senior SS officer told me he had given his word as an officer that he had no more pistols. With Buchenwald fresh in my mind . . . I told the

SS officer that word of honour or not we were going to carry out a routine search of some of his baggage. In the very first bag which we opened we found another automatic. After that those British troops . . . went through those SS men's baggage in a way which would have done credit to the toughest customs officer. The SS showed signs of being somewhat restive in the course of this ordeal, but they soon quieted down when . . . a heavy machine-gun, manned by a very determined-looking Scotsman, was pointed at them. In the end four more automatics came to light. As well as this we found five brand new pairs of field-glasses . . . a radio, a number of bottles of schnapps and brandy and about twenty thousand cigarettes. While . . . the SS were grinding their teeth in silent and impotent rage, a large party of displaced persons came by . . . Frenchmen, Hollanders and Russians. Our troops handed over all the drinks and cigarettes to them and I confess I took considerable pleasure in explaining to the SS officers that this seemed only fair after the kind of things they have done to . . . foreign workers when the boot was on the other foot.

Although on 6 May, before the general surrender, Montgomery had reminded his men that 'looting by individuals or bodies of individuals was . . . forbidden' and punishable by court martial this was one order that was widely ignored. The fashionable verb that spring was 'to swan', which meant going on some allegedly military errand that was really a sightseeing trip, to enjoy the countryside and to gather what booty one could. The official orders about handing over captured goods were universally ignored. Clocks and pictures, furniture and carpets, even an occasional piano, might be seen in Army lorries, and crates of wine were too commonplace to attract attention. But mostly it was the smaller, more portable, objects that were 'liberated'. It was a fortunate German soldier who reached home still in possession of his wrist watch, a rare officer whose binoculars were not 'won' from him. (Later 'attractive stores' as they were known, were officially collected and sold to the troops; my ex-German binoculars cost me several weeks' pay.) The more senior the officer the more substantial his acquisitions. Most captains soon possessed at least a Volkswagen, and every colonel had his Mercedes. The goods so acquired were regarded by their new owners as the legitimate 'perks' of victory, and one war correspondent noted that May a British Army lorry bearing the engaging notice, PRIORITY: LOOT. The American Military Police, said to be especially skilled at 'shaking down' their prisoners, earned at the same time a new nickname, 'The Lootwaffe'.

Everyone was anxious to bring home to the Germans that they had been utterly beaten but it proved an uphill task. 'With few exceptions,' complained one Grenadier Guards officer, responsible for a prisoner-of-war 'cage' near Villach in Austria, 'they seemed to regard the capitulation as a mere transference of authority. In their dealings with the British they would venture thin jokes and offer limp cigarettes: there would be appeals to "honour among soldiers". In talking of the future they were most concerned about the date of their own demobilization, as though the teams could disperse now that the game was ended.' In areas like this where there was no damage to be made good by working parties the prisoners had an easy life. 'They would lie about all day, idling and sunbathing,' protested this officer, 'their attitude to their British guards being one of servility more than of hostility or shame. Their officers would come for orders and advice on matters which were well within their own powers and capacities to solve.'

A classic example of the same syndrome was experienced by the British colonel in charge of the captured airfield at Flensburg and its former Luftwaffe garrison of 3000 men, who had hardly taken over when the German commandant arrived with two requests: 'Have I permission to shoot one of my officers for cowardice?' and 'Have I your permission to have a woman in my room tonight?', both questions being accompanied by salutes and heel-clicking. The British officer's answer was a model. He replied to the first 'My dear fellow . . . you are in charge until tomorrow morning and as far as I am concerned you can shoot all of them' and to the second, concerning the woman, 'As long as she doesn't mind, I don't!'

The discovery of the concentration camps, and the scarcely less appalling barracks full of slave workers – Belsen, for example, was not, strictly speaking, an 'extermination camp' at all, but one for working prisoners – made everyone eager to punish the civilians who now professed ignorance of the crimes committed in their midst. In the provinces of Lüneburg and Westphalia one of the first orders issued by the British military government was that every civilian must provide a complete suit of clothing for the former camp inmates. People living in towns like Hamburg needed no reminder that it was unwise to start a war but others, like the residents of the

6th Tank Brigade's area, who had 'not experienced the soul-destroying sensation of cringing in their cellars while a battle raged above them', would benefit, it was felt, from a timely display of strength. Here Churchill tanks were sent 'through every village and along every passable road' and there were wholesale searches of the houses of former Nazis and frequent scrutiny of identity documents.

Nazi officials above a certain rank were at this time on the 'automatic arrest' list, though those not wanted for war crimes were released after their backgrounds had been investigated. Some who had been prominent in the old days, however, proved slow to realize that their former glory had departed. In Hamburg the Gauleiter, or Nazi 'commissar' for the area, who was at first kept under house arrest in a single room, arrogantly protested at his treatment, suggesting to his captors that he was valuable to them as he alone had authority to dissolve the Nazi Party in the area. He was rapidly informed, none too politely, that he was under a misapprehension. But many of his subordinates also seemed to consider themselves indispensable. When the British Intelligence Corps officer responsible for security in the city ordered the Bürgermeister to call a meeting of all the senior Nazi officials there they responded readily, the ten-man delegation from each of the six surviving *Kreise*, or districts – four more had been virtually obliterated by allied bombing – tidily lining up behind its leader in strict order of rank, all apparently expecting to be invited to take over the local administration under British direction. They were hurt, as well as amazed, at instead being led out to board a waiting bus, *en route* to a detention 'cage' for potential trouble-makers.

In dealing with 'ordinary' Germans, military government officers everywhere were urged to take a tough, but not inhumane, line and did their best to comply, like this Town Major in the little town of Bentheim, who took up his duties with ringing in his ears advice of which he proved the truth over and over again: 'In Germany you must rule or be ruled':

We drove north . . . through one devastated town after another, often with not one house standing. Both my driver and I were very silent. You can say 'serves the Germans right', if you like, but you cannot be unaffected nor avoid a feeling of awe and depression. . . . On arrival I sent for the Burgermeister. I told him 'I want these two houses in forty-eight hours. The owners and occupants will be out by 1400 hours the day after tomorrow. They may take their personal belongings only, clothes, food, jewelry, but they will leave all furniture and will leave the houses in a thoroughly inhabitable condition.' ...

At the stated time, two days later, I returned to find the houses stripped of everything, even carpets, and the owners had started on the flowers in the garden. I turned to my Dutch interpreter and said 'Send for the Burgermeister! ... Tell him that I give him five minutes or he ceases to be Burgermeister.' In four and a half minutes he arrived breathless and I gave him my ultimatum. It was then 1430 hours. I would allow until 1800 hours to get the houses back *exactly* as they were when I first saw them. Failure would mean that I would requisition all houses on both sides of the street, but this time there would be no warning. ...

In a matter of minutes Germans arrived from every direction with furniture. It was rather like a Walt Disney film. Pictures were being put up, carpets laid, beds made and by 1800 I moved in, but not before I had a final word with the Burgermeister. 'Tell the people of the *Kreis*,' I said, 'they will find it much easier to obey my orders the first time. If they do not this sort of thing will happen every time, except that as time goes on, and the more my orders are disobeyed, the shorter my temper will become.'

To be in charge of a German town or district at this time bore many resemblances to being a District Officer in some far-flung outpost of the Empire, surrounded by alien and sometimes hostile natives. A major in the Buffs, who had taken over in mid-April responsibility for the 30000 inhabitants of Hamelin, of Pied Piper fame, with the help of four officers and six Other Ranks, wrote in July for the regimental magazine this account of his experiences:

If there are still any vacancies in MG [Military Government] when this article appears I should strongly recommend the job to anyone who wants a complete change of work and environment. One has enormous power for one's rank ... there is a never ending stream of visitors of all ranks and nationalities ... mostly wanting something. The Reichsbank wants a cool five million to enable it to stave off a run on the bank; a DP camp of several thousand is looting and demanding more rations; there is an outbreak of meningitis ... a Nazi leader is reported holding meetings in a house at X; the gas works must have five hundred tons of coal or it will close down; so it goes on all day. 'Never a dull moment', as the theatre handbills say. On the other hand the job has its compensations. ... One lives well. ... There is bathing and riding, wild boar shooting and fishing for those who can spare the time. We each have a civilian car.

(Mine is an eight-cylinder sports 'Horch'.) There is a steamer, a small paddle-boat, which we have taken over and done up. With our AMG flag at the bow, a Union Jack on the stern and the name *Belinda* on the paddle-box she makes a fine sight as she steams up the Weser on Saturday afternoons. . . . Tea is served aboard and an Italian DP orchestra plays light music.

A favourite saying of the time was that, when the occupation zones were shared out, the Americans acquired the scenery, the Russians were given the agriculture and the British got the ruins. There *was* some truth in this, for the British zone included the worst-bombed parts, like Hamburg and Kiel, and the area over which there had been the fiercest fighting in the west, but the British zone of Austria had escaped such damage and life that summer, for the Grenadier Guards who had moved into it on VE Day, was as tranquil as any soldiers' could be:

With time to look around them they discovered that they were in a part of Europe which had much to offer to tired and victorious campaigners. A chain of long lakes sparkled at the bottom of each valley and on their shores there were villas, chalets, hotels and bathing spas which before the war had been the summer resorts of the Viennese and were now requisitioned by the Eighth Army as billets for their men. Never in Africa or Italy had they seen better. It was not only that their accommodation was comfortable, the countryside pleasant and almost untouched by the war; they also found waiting for them the apparatus of a vast adult playground. On the lakes there were speed-boats and small yachts, water-skis, surf-boards, racing eights; and on land there were golf courses, tennis courts, the pick of the German army horses on which to ride through the woods, fishing, climbing and shooting. The Grenadiers, the bulk of whom were billeted on the shores of the largest lake, the Wörther See, were so happy that even the offer of a free holiday on the Lido at Venice could tempt few away from Austria.

But over this idyllic scene, as over the whole occupation, there hung a dark shadow, that of the non-fraternization rule, which made it a military crime to have any unofficial contact whatever with any German or Austrian. The troops just described, admitted their officer, disliked having to turn 'obedient cold shoulders to the blandishments of a friendly and decorative population', and the Town Major of Bentheim pointed out the absurdity of having 'to rely entirely upon German clerks, typists, cooks, cleaners and interpreters', while required to 'treat them entirely as machines' and 'to turn a deaf ear if the woman secretary with whom you worked all day gave you a formal greeting'. Off duty with no other British troops in the town, 'I and my British staff were condemned entirely to our own company. In the evenings I never spoke to anyone at all.' The eleven members of the military government team at Hamelin also found this the worst feature of their otherwise agreeable daily lives:

The only thing missing ... a very big one, is human company other than our own. ... No one amongst us is likely to forget the Germans' guilt but there will come a time when the stony stare must give place to a reasonably human glance and the hand to be shaken in politeness if not in friendship. Most of us are looking forward to that day if only to be able to tell the Germans what we have been thinking of them all this time.

Unpopular with those who obeyed it, ridiculed by the far larger number, especially of allied troops, who did not – the current euphemism for a German mistress was 'my little bit of frat' – the non-fraternization policy already lay in ruins when Field-Marshal Montgomery issued, on 10 June and in his own inimitable style, an explanatory letter *To the Population of the British Area in Germany.*

You have wondered, no doubt, why our soldiers do not smile when you wave your hands, or say 'Good morning' in the streets, or play with the children. It is because our soldiers are obeying orders. You do not like it. Nor do our soldiers. We are naturally friendly and forgiving people. But the orders were necessary; and I will tell you why.

In the last war of 1914, which your rulers began, your army was defeated; your generals surrendered; and in the Peace Treaty of Versailles your rulers admitted that the guilt of beginning the war was Germany's. But ... the war never came to your country; your cities were not damaged, like the cities of France and Belgium; and your armies marched home in good order. Then your rulers began to spread the story that Germany was neither guilty nor defeated and because the war had not come to your country, many of you believed it, and you cheered when your rulers began another war.

Again, after years of waste and slaughter and misery, your armies have been defeated. This time the allies were determined that you should learn your lesson – not only that you have been defeated, which you must know by now, but that you, your nation, were again guilty of beginning the war. For if that is not made clear to you and your children, you may again allow yourselves to be deceived by your rulers, and led into another war. . . . You are to read this to your children, if they are old enough, and see that they understand.

Two days later the ban on speaking to children (already universally ignored, as I saw for myself in Germany that May) was lifted, and in July conversations with Germans, though not visits to their homes, became permitted. All restrictions, except on marrying Germans, were lifted in September, in line with a similar relaxation of the rules in the American zone.

The results were at first less striking than had been expected. In the summer of 1945 hatred of all things German went deep, and the Town Major of Bentheim, aware of the 'tense feelings of strain' previously existing, was 'amazed how very few soldiers made friends with German girls. . . . Even at dances . . . the soldiers in most cases left the girl immediately the dance was over. . . . They could not forget that Germans are, after all, Germans.' But, he concluded, with a tolerance rare at the time, 'Do not say they are *all* bad. There are a *few* decent ones' and 'many can be led in the right direction if we take the trouble.'

Within a few days of the war ending most leading Nazis had been accounted for. Apart from Martin Bormann, the most wanted member of Hitler's inner circle to remain at liberty was Heinrich Himmler, formerly, as Minister of the Interior, overlord of the Gestapo and creator and administrator of the concentration and extermination camps. Himmler had celebrated VE Day by shaving off his moustache, prior to leaving the Flensburg area two days later disguised like a pirate with a patch over one eye, and bearing the papers of a man long since executed by a Nazi court. Himmler had reduced his usual vast entourage to four cars and a handful of SS officers and for several days they drove rather aimlessly about Schleswig, sleeping in station waiting rooms and farms, before splitting up and taking to the roads. Himmler was detained, on suspicion, at a checkpoint at Bremervörde at 2 o'clock on the afternoon of 23 May and around 8 pm, after being identified, managed to bite a hidden poison capsule. Fifteen minutes later, after a struggle to save him, he was dead, 'and when he died' related the British sergeant-major present in a classic BBC interview next day, 'we threw a blanket over him and left him'. Two days later Himmler was buried in an unmarked spot near Lüneburg, his body wrapped in camouflage netting bound with barbed wire. The soldier who dug his grave was in civil life a dustman.

Five days later on 28 May, 'Lord Haw Haw' was captured, his famous voice giving him away when, quite unnecessarily, he spoke to two British officers while walking near the village where he was hiding. One, suspecting he was reaching for a gun as he put his hand in his pocket for his identity papers, shot him in the thigh, but William Joyce survived to stand his trial for treason in London, where he was hanged on 3 January 1946.

One of the last members of Hitler's entourage to be captured, on 14 June, was Germany's recent Foreign Secretary, Joachim von Ribbentrop, whom Hitler had flatteringly described as a 'second Bismarck', though his final appearance on the diplomatic stage was to display a striking lack of realism. After arriving in Flensburg from Berlin, von Ribbentrop at first tried to persuade Admiral Dönitz to submit to the allies a plan for the creation of an independent German government in Schleswig-Holstein, which, he privately predicted, could provide the foundation for a new 'national Socialist Germany'. Dönitz wisely refused to have anything to do with this plan and von Ribbentrop then went into hiding in Hamburg, awaiting the time when British hostility to Germany could die down and he could fulfil the last mission entrusted to him by the Führer, namely to convince the British government of the need for Anglo-German friendship – the same task which, as German ambassador in London, he had carried out with some success in the years before Munich. Soon after reaching Hamburg, however, he was betrayed by the son of an old acquaintance in the wine trade – von Ribbentrop had once sold champagne for a living – from whom he had sought help, and after being arrested in bed, was identified beyond all doubt by his sister, with whom he was suddenly confronted, to the great satisfaction of the Field Security Section responsible: another unit elsewhere had claimed the credit for capturing the former Nazi Foreign Secretary, but had clearly got the wrong man. The real von Ribbentrop was dispatched to captivity, and ultimately to the gallows, after being relieved of his last diplomatic message, a letter in his own hand addressed to 'Field Marshal Montgommery', pleading for an interview with 'Mr Vincent Churchill'. The 'second Bismarck' and ex-Ambassador had, curiously enough, got both names wrong.

While the search for wanted war criminals was going on a more tragic quest was in progress by families split up by the war trying desperately to find loved ones who had simply disappeared. At railway stations all over Europe one saw displayed pathetic snapshots with notices begging for news from anyone who had seen the person shown. The Germans suffered with their conquerors, as parents waited for news of sons last heard of fighting in Russia or demobilized soldiers came home to find their homes in ruins and their families gone. An advertisement in *Le Monde* at this time was typical of thousands published that summer:

Any persons having known Mmes Marie-Louise Roure and Adriene Baumer, deported for the camp at Compiègne in June 1944, are begged to furnish their information to Monsieur Remy Roure.

While the tragic consequences of Nazi rule were still being felt throughout Europe, in Flensburg the Dönitz government, formed primarily to end the war, was waiting to be put out of its misery. Dönitz himself, the surrender signed, had become essentially a mere figure-head. The nearest Germany possessed to a Prime Minister was Count Schwerin von Krosigk, who was both Foreign Secretary and Finance Minister and also presided over the meetings of the Council of Ministers, or Cabinet. Von Krosigk had been a successful civil servant, and then a minister before the Nazis came to power and had a reputation, so a BBC correspondent who interviewed him remarked, as 'the foremost financial expert in Germany . . . a slightly built man in his fifties, with thin, grey hair, he looked as if he might have been the manager of an unimportant branch of a bank. "As far as I am concerned personally,"' he told his visitor from behind his cheap deal table in his ministerial office, 'a small room with the plainest of office furniture, "I should be only too glad to retire, but my colleagues and I feel that we cannot abandon the German people in the hour of their need and we feel that we are the men best qualified to . . . assist the allied . . . powers!"'

Even though it possessed no real authority the new government could at least act as if it did, and Albert Speer, occupying his old job as Minister of Production, later wrote in prison a humorous account of this curious episode in German history. The government, he observed, set up an 'information service': an old radio set in one of the classrooms. A Minister of Food was appointed, though his only responsibility was to fetch the whisky with which meetings were enlivened. Official pictures were taken of the new government at work and the Grand Admiral, as it was agreed the new Chief of State should be addressed, was provided with a Mercedes to carry him in style the 500 yards from his home. The ministers wrote memoranda to each other and, on the insistence of the new Foreign Minister, 'every morning at ten a Cabinet meeting took place in the so-called Cabinet Room, a former school-room. It looked as if,' wrote Speer, 'Schwerin-Krosigk was trying to make up for all the cabinet meetings that had not been held during the past twelve years.'

We used a painted table and chairs collected from around the school. We ... discussed how to reshuffle the cabinet to bring it into line with the changing times. A hot debate arose over the question of adding a Minister for Churches to the cabinet. A well-known theologian was proposed for the post, while others regarded Pastor Niemöller [imprisoned by the Nazis] as the best candidate. . . . My tart suggestion that a few leading Social Democrats and Liberals be brought forth to take over the functions went unnoticed.

The Dönitz government finally came to an end on 22 May, when the allies, quite unnecessarily, sent a task force of several hundred soldiers to round up its members. They were herded into a court-yard by British troops to find machine guns pointing at them from every window, and made to stand with hands on their heads for half an hour facing a 'firing squad' of photographers and newsreel men. The fallen ministers, who, after all, had undertaken the thankless job of winding up a lost war with the minimum of bloodshed, held their last cabinet meeting, as Speer noted, 'in a room that resembled a waiting room' at Flensburg airport, 'surrounded by suitcases' and then faced an uncomfortable flight, seated on crates and their luggage, to Luxemburg where they were reunited with Göring and other prominent prisoners. The journey ended for almost all of them in the dock at Nuremberg, where in October 1946 Speer and his colleagues were sentenced to long terms of imprisonment or death.

However agreeable life was in conquered Germany that summer, two prospects, one intensely feared, one eagerly desired, dominated the mind of every wartime-only soldier, British or American – the prospect of being sent to the Far East, and 'demob'. As early as 11 May the *Stars and Stripes* warned its readers, the US forces in Europe, that 'for a couple of million men from the ETO [European Theatre of Operations] going to the Pacific it is going to be a long war yet – a year and a half to two years at the minimum, by all official estimates, and maybe longer'.

The future for the British troops on the continent seemed equally bleak. In the last two weeks of June two battalions of the Guards were sent back from Austria to the United Kingdom to prepare for service against Japan and by the following month the catchphrase in the 1st Buckinghamshire Battalion, stationed in Westphalia, was that the letters BLA no longer stood for 'British Liberation Army', the official name of the British forces in Germany, soon to be renamed 'British Army of the Rhine', but 'Burma Looms Ahead'.

In the American Army the more 'demobilization points' one had the better; in the British the lower one's 'Age and Service Group' the sooner one would be out, each man's date of release being decided by the month and year in which he had been born and the date he had enlisted. The key number was 27, for men in this and lower groups were safe from being sent to the Far East, though they faced a long delay before returning to civilian life either in Great Britain or in the occupation zones in Germany.

Among the first out were the 'Militiamen', who six years before, in July 1939, had been called up for six months' military training, only to be overtaken by the outbreak of war. Back in 1939 when Britain's first peacetime conscripts had joined up the papers and newsreels had shown them improbably cheerful, being 'kitted out' with Army uniform. Now it was as though the film had been reversed. The 'Demob Centre' provided a universally popular subject for the journalists and photographers – and was even more popular with the men who passed through it in an increasing number from June 1945 onwards. Entering a large room at one end the soldier was passed from desk to desk, a new rubber stamp being added to his documents at each, until he emerged at the other a civilian, and then passed into the stores where he acquired in rapid succession the gifts of a grateful government: one suit three piece; one raincoat or overcoat; one hat; one shirt, with two collars; two pairs socks; one tie; one pair shoes walking. Other largesse followed: a civilian clothing book and ninety clothing coupons; a

National Insurance Card; a railway warrant home and a Post Office Savings Book containing his pay during his 'demob leave' and his gratuity, strictly related to rank. But one concession was made to the democratic temper of the times. The government decided not to ask Parliament to vote large cash rewards for the victorious commanders, such as had been showered upon earlier generals from Marlborough to Haig. These 'top brass' and others – mainly officers – who elected to stay in the Army, did not even receive a 'demob suit'.

13

OUTLOOK: 'DRY'

'Beer: Outlook continues "Dry"'
– Evening Standard *headline, Monday, 28 May 1945*

FOR the civilians, the victory party really finished on Sunday, 13 May. That morning services of national thanksgiving were held throughout the country, including one attended by the royal family and the Prime Minister in St Paul's Cathedral.

That evening Winston Churchill broadcast his last major review of the war. He had planned to deliver the speech earlier but, the papers explained, had been too 'busy . . . to prepare his broadcast' and had acquired 'a slight hoarseness' due to all the impromptu oratory of the past few days. He also felt, it was suggested, 'that the public, after two days of rather exhausting celebrations, will be in a more receptive mood on Sunday'.

The Prime Minister struck in fact an unexpectedly sombre note:

I wish I could tell you tonight that all our toils and troubles were over. Then indeed I could end my five years' service happily, and if you thought that I ought to be put out to grass I would take it with the best of grace. But, on the contrary, I must warn you . . . that there is still a lot to do, and that you must be prepared for further efforts of mind and body. . . .

On the continent of Europe we have yet to make sure that the simple and honourable purposes for which we entered the war are not brushed aside or overlooked in the months following our success, and that the words 'freedom' and 'liberation' are not distorted from their true meaning as we have understood them. There would be little use in punishing the Hitlerites for their crimes if law and justice did not rule and if totalitarian or police governments were to take the place of the German invaders. . . .

We must never forget that beyond all lurks Japan, harassed and failing, but still a people of a hundred millions, for whose warriors death has few terrors. . . . We are bound by the ties of honour and fraternal loyalty to the United States to fight the great war at the other end of the world at their side. . . . I should be unworthy of your confidence and generosity if I did not still cry: Forward, unflinching, unswerving, indomitable, till the whole task is done and the whole world is safe and clean.

Few can have missed the thinly veiled references to the Russians, but what attracted even more attention at the time were Churchill's remarks about Eire, which, he pointed out, had done nothing to help Britain when her supply routes were in danger of 'strangulation':

Owing to the action of Mr De Valera, so much at variance with the temper and instinct of thousands of Southern Irishmen, who hastened to the battlefront to prove their ancient valour, approaches which the Southern Irish ports and airfields could so easily have guarded were closed by hostile aircraft and U Boats. This was indeed a deadly moment in our life and if it had not been for the loyalty and friendship of Northern Ireland, we should have been forced to come to close quarters with Mr De Valera or perish for ever from the earth.

The Irish Prime Minister did not take kindly to this public reproof and the following Wednesday broadcast a long reply, in which he blamed Churchill's criticism on 'the first exuberance of his victory', and argued that Ireland had only exercised the right of every small nation 'to go its own way in peace'. The *Irish Times* was more clear-sighted. 'Ireland has lost by virtue of her neutrality', it admitted candidly on 15 May, and a suggestion for a thanks-giving service for those Southern Irishmen who had fought in the British forces – and incidentally won seven VCs and 314 other decorations – came to nothing. Those who had deserted from the Irish Army to fight Hitler were actually court-martialled when they came home. It was to be a long time before the country lived down its wartime record and the fact that apart from Portugal it had been the only nation in the world to send official condolences to the German government at the news of Hitler's death. 'Eire felt the cold breath of international disapproval in the aftermath of the war', admitted the Irish writer Conor Cruise O'Brien, and it was not until 1955 that she had 'worked her passage' back to inter-national respectability sufficiently to be admitted to the United Nations.

If the war was far from over for the four million men and women in the Forces it was clearly finished for the forty-five million civi-lians in the United Kingdom. On their first day back after the two-day victory holiday, Wednesday, 10 May, the House of Commons cheered Herbert Morrison's announcement that a long list of Defence Regulations had been revoked, including one making it an offence to spread alarm and despondency, and it now ceased to be illegal to foment a strike which would disrupt an essential service. More fortunate than the loyal citizens in the Army, who still faced indefinite detention in uniform, fifty potential traitors detained under Regulation 18B were to be released. The Prime Minister was cheered even louder when he announced that the petrol ration for 'inessential' private motoring would be restored in a month's time. It came back in fact on 2 June, when cars up to eight horse-power received four gallons a month, and those from ten to thirteen hp only five. There was, too, good news for yachtsmen and gardeners: even petrol motor-boats and driven lawn-mowers would receive an allowance. From midnight on 10 May or VE+2, according to one's calendar, the citizens of places like Whitby and Worthing were also permitted to tear down their blackout shutters, for, the Admiralty announced, all lighting restrictions in coastal areas would now be lifted.

The first peacetime Bank Holiday since August 1939 was cele-brated on Whit Monday, 21 May. Although there was a rush to the seaside the occasion was only a shadow of its pre-war self, except in the rain which sent everyone back into the shelters on the prome-nade, though many lacked glass and badly needed a coat of paint. 'Brighton tried to be its old gay self,' felt the *Daily Mail*, 'but with most of the shops, cafés, amusements, public houses and hotels closed, it was impossible. . . . Even the beach was rationed. Most of it was closed because of mines.' These were a problem everywhere. A sobering note in the *Evening Standard* two days later revealed that in the past eighteen months between the Wash and Chichester alone sixty men had died in making the beaches safe again, though 100000 mines had been safely removed or exploded. It was not until July, recalls a local historian, that the shores at Brighton were safe again, 'after bulldozers had raked deeply up and down along the . . . shingle'. Another pre-war pleasure returned at the same time with the arrival of 'a new *Skylark*, replacing the one which had given five years' service in the Navy during the war'. The tradi-tional week-end at Brighton became easier to enjoy with the re-opening of the Hotel Metropole, but a stroll out to sea was not so easy; both Brighton's piers had had large gaps blown in them and were not to be reopened for another year. But even with crowded trains – no extra Bank Holiday services were run – and when you got to the seaside, buckets and spades being hired by the shops, instead of offered for sale, since none had been made for five years, no one was disposed to grumble. The scenes at Seaburne on the north-east coast, where a small section of the beach was opened that Whit Monday for two hours, witnessed by a local resident, were typical:

The population of the whole of that part of County Durham converged on that section, or so it seemed. To paddle in the shallow water it was necessary to find an empty space and defend it against all comers. Yet, such is the discipline of the British people, that when the allotted time for the beach to be closed once more came along, the police and military authorities were able to get the day-trippers back on to the promenade in less than fifteen minutes.

By now the 'holidays at home' habit was deeply ingrained and London offered more recreations than it had done for years. The Tower of London was still closed, but Horse Guards Arch was open again and much used, by sightseers enjoying the novelty of a short-cut into Whitehall.

That week-end the children's zoo at the Zoo in Regent's Park reopened with, according to the *Manchester Guardian*, 'a frolicsome air'. Richmond Park, closed to walkers since December 1940, also unbarred its gates that week-end, as did the glasshouses at Kew Gardens, closed during the flying bomb period due to the hazard they presented if hit by blast. But, it was reported, 'London's hotels are crammed', and so, too, were the buses and tubes, where there were many complaints about the continuing presence of the anti-splinter netting on the windows. London Transport's attempts to discourage people from removing this, through admonitory rhymed couplets delivered by 'Billy Brown of London Town', had provoked ripostes from amateur poets throughout the war, and 'Londoner's Diary' in the *Evening Standard* printed a final salvo against poor Billy on 25 May:

> Remove this stuff! Procrastination
> Still makes us miss our proper station.

London Transport effectively replied, in similar vein, on the following day:

> 'Tis gone from many a bus and train,
> But labour problems still remain.

If Bank Holiday had provided everyone with a much-needed breather, the weeks which followed brought many reminders that peace had its shortages no less than war. Two headlines in the *Evening Standard* on Monday, 28 May, told their own melancholy tale: 'London has its worst cigarette famine' and 'Beer: Outlook continues "dry"'. For the first, explained a Tobacco Control spokesman, victory itself was to blame: 'The factories were idle for at least four days, people were in carefree mood, they smoked more, and the workers from the closed factories went to the shops for their cigarettes instead of their canteens.' As for the lack of beer, the reasons were also cheerful: 'Hotter weather . . . is on the way' and 'the average man is drinking more beer because, although he is earning nearly twice as much money as he did pre-war, he has far fewer outlets on which to spend it.' Little improvement seemed likely until demobilization brought more men back to the breweries, and to make more casks and more delivery lorries.

No one liked the beer shortage, but food rationing, with its guarantee of 'fair shares', had actually been popular, something many better-off politicians, unable to realize that millions of people had fed better during the war than ever before, already found hard to grasp.

The idea of sacrifice for the sake of others, also implicit in the rationing system with its favoured 'priority' users, exerted powerful appeal and there was little adverse reaction when on 22 May, the day on which people went back to work after the Bank Holiday, the Minister of Food, Colonel Llewellin, announced a whole range of reductions in the rations to take effect the following Sunday. The cooking fats ration was to be halved, to a single ounce, and the bacon ration cut from four ounces to three, while there would be a reduction of the number of 'points' which were needed to buy tinned food and semi-luxuries like biscuits, in the next four weeks from twenty-four to twenty. The soap ration, except for small children with a 'green ration book', would be reduced by an eighth from sixteen ounces a month to fourteen, there was 'no

prospect of rice for civilian consumption this year', and though the
meat ration was being maintained people would still have to take at
least one-seventh in corned beef. Ice-cream, just again becoming
available, would 'probably be in shorter supply', even less fat would
be available for biscuit manufacture, the allowance of milk to non-
priority customers (i.e. all those except expectant mothers and small
children) would probably suffer its usual seasonal cut earlier this
year than last and, making home-baking more difficult, even
shredded suet would 'have to be brought into the rationing scheme'.
The cheese ration, already down to two ounces a week, was in
danger, but the Minister hoped to maintain it at its present level,
as he did the sugar ration, though he gave an early warning that
there was no hope of a 'Christmas box' of an extra half pound per
head this year. The savings were needed, explained Colonel
Llewellin, to help 'find food for the liberated countries' and he
believed they would be made 'with good spirit', the more so
because 'in view of the world shortage of food the rations of
German prisoners would be reduced'.

The President of the Board of Trade, Hugh Dalton, also made
his contribution that day to damping down any lingering feeling
that it was now all over bar the shouting. Owing to the run-down
of stocks, which had cushioned the impact of the reduction in the
output of clothes and footwear over the past four years, he announced, 'the public must be prepared for some time . . . for a
ration at a rate which cannot be higher than that of the current
period'. The next clothes rationing period would begin, as planned,
on 1 September, but it was too early yet to say how long the twenty-
four new coupons that would become usable then would have to
last. (It was, in fact, to be eight months not six as at first intended.)
The Minister hoped, however, that 'during the next twelve months
there will be an improvement in the supply of clothing, household
textiles and footwear' and, as a modest beginning, children would
'receive a further issue of coupons on 1 August'.

Far more annoying to most people, who had become used to
them, than these major limitations on their spending, were the
minor shortages – a notorious one was of alarm clocks – which
could exert an effect on one's life out of all proportion to their
economic importance, and any concession in other directions made
such inconveniences seem even more intolerable. One lady, *Over*

Seventy, wrote to *The Times*, 'I believe I shall voice the feeling of a very large section of the public by asking the government to give us rubber hot-water bottles, before they allow tyres to be made for private motoring.' 'Is someone soon going to tell my wife what she is to do with her civilian gasmask?' asked a major from Berkshire. 'My local authority has informed me that it is not collecting my warden's respirators and tin hats and they are therefore filling the rubbish bins. . . . The rubber facepiece of a gasmask weighs nearly one ounce, and my wife wants to know why the government . . . cannot make use of her and my warden's gasmasks to provide her with . . . hot-water bottles, suspenders etc.'

The major was far from alone in his reactions. Salvage had given to many citizens a deep satisfaction and much ingenuity was now used in finding peacetime uses for wartime necessities. Many Anderson shelters had a new lease of life as garden sheds and already wardens' uniforms and Home Guard boots were becoming standard working wear on millions of allotments. Housewives eagerly pressed their discarded blackout curtains into other domestic service. One Thames Ditton housewife made gardening aprons from them for herself and a gollywog for her small son, while other blackout curtains faced a more glamorous future: 'The Arts Theatre Club,' reported the *Evening Standard*, 'is asking members to give their blackout curtains for use as lining for theatre costumes.' A week later there came a reminder of another continuing shortage, fuel. The floodlighting of government buildings had ceased on 14 May and now *The Times* announced 'the Minister of Fuel and Power has decided that because of the need for continued fuel economy all outdoor decoration and display lighting should now cease'.

It was hard that summer to be sure whether, as some people grumbled, things were worse than they had been during the war, especially as one no longer had victory to look forward to, or whether, as everyone wanted to believe, normality was returning, albeit a little uncertainly.

In June there were queues for bread, which had suddenly become scarce after being plentiful and unrationed throughout the war, but in July there was the first Henley Regatta for six years, and at Ascot, enjoying its first post-war meeting, 'lobster mayonnaise', the *Sunday Express* reported, was 'to be had . . . by the early arrivals' and 'champagne for those who could afford it'. Austerity had, however, left its mark sartorially, for there were 'few smart Ascot frocks' and only 'a solitary grey topper in the Royal Enclosure, worn as a joke by an American soldier in uniform'. More impressive was the 'first non-austerity fashion show since the government restrictions came into force', with 'a dress of shaded chiffon containing thirty-three yards of material, an unheard of amount in England for years', though the explanation was simple: the goods on show were 'for export only', a phrase to be heard increasingly in the next few months.

But the euphoria of victory had not yet quite worn off. One could send a letter with a victory stamp, and, by courtesy of London Transport, enjoy a victory poster which bore, with a suitable illustration, an extract from a speech made by Winston Churchill in 1940, 'The day will come when the joy bells will ring again throughout Europe.'

London that summer made much of the victorious commanders. General Eisenhower arrived unexpectedly on a private visit in May, the Customs authorities at Northolt turning a blind eye to eighteen bottles of champagne brought for his 'VE party', and after a celebration lunch at Telegraph Cottage and a buffet supper in General Bradley's suite at the Dorchester 'Ike' and his party went to see a cheerful revue, 'Strike a Light', at the Prince of Wales Theatre where, as his secretary saw, 'the entire audience rose to its feet and almost shouted the roof off with un-English abandon. They cheered, whistled, stamped and applauded' until the Supreme Commander, in response to cries of 'Speech!' made one of the brief, impromptu replies at which he always excelled: 'It's nice to be back in a country where I can *almost* speak the language!' Cheering crowds mobbed the Supreme Commander's car as he took his party on to supper at Ciro's, where he danced impartially with all the women in turn and asked the band to play *One Dozen Roses*, 'a heartfelt tribute to Mrs Eisenhower'.

It was already being whispered at SHAEF that Eisenhower had more than a boss's normal attachment to his secretary Kay Summersby, and was planning to leave his wife and marry her. The rumours were in fact true but Eisenhower was persuaded to change his mind by the US Chief of Staff, General Marshall. No word of all this, however, reached the general public, whose affection and respect for 'Ike' that summer was boundless. When he returned to London on 12 June to accept the Freedom of the City of London he received a tremendous ovation. His formal speech, at the Guildhall, led the press to compare his powers as an orator to those of Churchill and when the two men appeared together on the balcony outside the Mansion House, home of the Lord Mayor, they received the biggest cheer heard anywhere since VE Day. There was probably real sadness in Britain, as there certainly was among British members of SHAEF, when on 14 July this famous headquarters, which had already moved from Rheims and Paris to the former I. G. Farben building in Frankfurt, by far the most luxurious of all its homes, was formally dissolved.

The armies SHAEF had led to victory were now returned to their separate national commanders and this meant, for the British, Field-Marshal Montgomery, a more abrasive figure than the idolized 'Ike' and one less universally loved, especially by the Americans with whom he had worked in harness rather than harmony. 'Monty' appeared in London on 23 May to great applause wherever he was seen, and made an even more successful visit to Paris two days later, watched by the British MP, A. P. Herbert. At the Invalides, recorded Herbert, 'small, clambering boys sat on the arms and shoulders of the great Napoleon to see the British general who, after all, had gone as far and fared better. He looked more like a shy schoolboy himself waiting for the headmaster than a conqueror. . . . The tall de Gaulle came, at last, and embraced him right and left, and invested him with the *Grande Croix* of the *Légion d'Honneur*. The band played and we all felt like embracing somebody. . . . In the streets Napoleon himself could hardly have had a more rapturous . . . reception than the Parisians gave "Montee".' The Field-Marshal, like 'Ike' no linguist, heroically delivered a speech, in what he himself described as 'schoolboy French', from the balcony of the British Embassy, when the crowd refused to disperse, ending it *'Et maintenant – allez-vous en'*, which delighted the crowd despite its apparent rudeness – it means, in fact, 'Now, clear off!' – and the speaker. 'They tell me I said the wrong thing,' he remarked afterwards, but 'that means "Go away" doesn't it' and 'that's what . . . they did. I think my French must be pretty good.'

Although, mercifully one may feel, Montgomery resisted all suggestions that he should 'go into politics', the British public was soon to have its fill of speeches. By VE Day no election had been held for ten years and, unless Parliament again extended its own life, one was bound to be held by November, but everyone realized how unrepresentative the House had become, especially due to the electoral truce, under which none of the main parties contested vacant seats previously held by others. It was clear from the successes gained by a number of independents and newcomers, like Common Wealth, how massively public opinion had shifted since 1935 and as early as 10 May the Prime Minister was asked in the House of Commons about the prospect of an early dissolution. 'Though some people think it near to treason to be talking of an election at all,' commented the *Manchester Guardian*, 'that does not alter the fact that the politicians are talking of little else.' Churchill himself had declared in October 1944 'that it would be wrong to continue this Parliament beyond the period of the German war . . . unless all political parties resolve to maintain the present coalition until the Japanese are defeated', but now that the prospect had actually arrived, he was much less enthusiastic about it. On 18 May he invited the Labour Party 'to carry on with us until a decisive victory had been gained over Japan', possibly after 'taking the nation's opinion, for example, through a referendum, on the issue whether . . . the life of Parliament should be further prolonged'. This suggestion the Labour Party's National Executive, supported later by a special Party Conference, firmly rejected. Labour, Mr Attlee wrote on 20 May, would certainly support the war against Japan, whether in government or opposition, but did not 'think it right or possible to obtain from Parliament another prolongation of its life' or to allow 'the introduction into our national life of a device so alien to our traditions as the referendum'. It was clear that already the unity of the coalition was splitting up, for Mr Attlee went on to suggest that the Prime Minister's 'reasons for rejecting an autumn election', which the law required, and which Labour favoured, 'seem to be based not on national interest, but on considerations of party expediency. It appears to me that you are departing from the position of a national leader by yielding to the pressure of the Conservative Party, which is anxious to exploit your own great service to the nation in its own interests.'

This suspicion lay indeed at the heart of Labour's preference for the autumn, when, it hoped, the nation's judgement would not be obscured by a wave of emotional gratitude to Churchill personally for the victory in Europe, or for the subsequent defeat of Japan. It dreaded a 'snap' election, in which the distinction between Churchill the war-winner and Churchill the party leader might be forgotten, and, even more, a 'coupon' election, like that of 1918, when, irrespective of merit and almost of party, anyone able to produce a certificate of support from Lloyd George had been virtually guaranteed a seat in the House. The 'coupon' election had, incidentally, completed the ruin of the Liberal Party, which in 1945 tried to compromise: it would, said Sir Archibald Sinclair, prefer an autumn election but would stay in the coalition if the other two parties decided to continue it.

But it was Labour's attitude which was decisive. With neither side really wanting an election at that moment, and with each blaming the other for having forced it upon the country, on 23 May Churchill resigned as head of the coalition and formed a new, all-Conservative 'caretaker' government. On 4 June, he delivered his first election broadcast and the campaign began in earnest, though it was not until 15 June that Parliament was dissolved and not until the twenty-fifth that the 1683 candidates handed in their nomination papers.

The General Election of 1945 was one of the most bitterly fought of the century. During it all the frustrations and resentments which had accumulated during five years of political truce boiled over and I recall an American remarking to me that he had thought his country second to none in fighting a 'dirty' election, but this time he had to give the British best. Churchill struck the keynote in his first broadcast when he declared that the Labour Party could not establish the socialist system set out in its manifesto without having 'to fall back on some sort of Gestapo, no doubt very humanely directed in the first instance'. This fantastic charge, said to have been made under the influence of Churchill's evil genius, Lord Beaverbrook, rebounded disastrously on the Conservatives. On its effect abroad and on the Forces I can speak from personal experience. To the recently liberated Danes, who knew what a Gestapo-supported regime actually meant, it seemed ludicrous. To the Forces, the suggestion that they had fought to establish at home the very tyranny they had been acclaimed by Churchill for destroying abroad, seemed a monstrous insult.

Attlee, in his mild but effective way, made a devastating riposte on the following evening. After recalling that the dominions of Australia and New Zealand had had socialist governments for years he commented dryly that the Prime Minister had 'evidently wanted the electors to understand how great was the difference between Winston Churchill, the great leader in war of a united nation, and Mr Churchill, the party leader of the Conservatives'.

The branding of Churchill at the very start of the election as a mere party politician, prepared to stoop to any lie to discredit his opponents – whom he had, until recently, been happy to have in his own government – was all the more disastrous for the Conservatives because their whole campaign revolved round the slogan 'Send him back to finish the job', and he delivered four of the ten Conservative broadcasts. He also involved himself in the other great Conservative scare, rapidly labelled – and depicted by the cartoonists as – a 'red herring', which built up the Labour Party chairman Harold Laski into a sinister, near-Communist figure, likely to influence Labour policy in a pro-Bolshevist direction. Laski's real attraction, from the Conservative point of view, was his foreign-sounding name, but the British electorate had matured since the days when this might have done its owner harm: everyone had recently met GIs with far more bizarre surnames. Here, too, the cartoonists rallied to the Labour cause, with a picture of a giant Conservative-operated gramophone blaring out incessantly 'Laski', while a bewildered elector asked quietly, 'Yes, but what's your policy?'

The campaign of calumny launched against leading Labour candidates – without, it must be said, any encouragement from their own Conservative opponents – also did its authors no good. Hugh Dalton, until recently President of the Board of Trade, found himself accused of having harmed the children, by having refused them extra clothing coupons. Herbert Morrison, Churchill's choice as Home Secretary for four years, heard even darker whispers that he was personally responsible for the deaths in some major bombing incidents because of a change in the warning system. Dalton increased his majority. Morrison chose to fight a seat previously held by a Conservative and turned his predecessor's majority of 6000 into a Labour one two and a half times as large.

By polling day, on Thursday, 5 July – though it was postponed in twenty-three constituencies for up to a fortnight due to local holidays – the signs were clear to all except those blinded by false optimism. Wherever Mr Churchill had gone – and he had toured most of the country during the campaign – he had had a tremendous reception, but the car-loads of local Conservative candidates, following behind, had often been greeted by boos. Mr Attlee, meanwhile, arriving modestly in his own small car, driven by his wife, made a deep impression of a different kind, and one admirably calculated to silence the remaining echoes of the 'Gestapo' charge.

The Conservative manifesto seemed, however, designed to revive it, for in his 'Declaration of policy to electors' Mr Churchill qualified his promises of 'food, work and homes' with solemn warnings against 'a permanent system of bureaucratic control, reeking of totalitarianism'. The Labour programme, 'Let us face the future', better matched the forward-looking and unselfish mood of the time, as did its slogan, 'Vote for Them', whether one interpreted it to refer to the servicemen or one's children or to those who had given their lives for victory.

After polling day the nation settled down to wait, while the postal votes from the Forces overseas came in. On Wednesday, 26 July, Mr Churchill, who had been attending the Potsdam Conference in Berlin, where, with President Truman and Marshal Stalin he was struggling with the problems of finishing the war against Japan and the resettlement of war-torn Europe, flew back from Berlin. In another aircraft travelled Mr Attlee, no longer Deputy Prime Minister but Leader of the Opposition, whom the Prime Minister had, very honourably, invited to accompany him to ensure continuity if, as he clearly did not expect, the electorate rejected his leadership.

Shrewder than the experts of 'Conservative Central Office', whose 'latest view . . . was that we should retain a substantial majority', Churchill for once found it hard to sleep that night and 'just before dawn . . . woke suddenly with a sharp stab of almost physical pain. A hitherto subconscious conviction that we were beaten broke forth and dominated my mind.' He then slept again until 9 o'clock and soon afterwards went into his wartime Map Room where the results were being displayed for him.

All over the country people were now waiting by their radios just as they had done on VE – 1 and the news they heard made all the more impact because, unlike a normal election, all the figures were announced within a few hours. The very first result at South Salford showed a Labour gain, setting the pattern for what was to come. 'By noon,' wrote Churchill, 'it was clear that the Socialists would have a majority. At luncheon my wife said to me, "It may well be a blessing in disguise." I replied, "At the moment it seems quite effectively disguised."'

The roll-call of Labour gains continued all day, until and including the last declaration, at Hornchurch, that evening, when the magnitude of the Labour victory became fully apparent. A Conservative majority of 183 over all parties combined in the old House, with a total strength, including regular supporters, of 393, had been transformed into an overall Labour majority of 146, with a Labour voting strength, including assured allies like Common Wealth, of 414. The figures of votes cast were almost as emphatic: 48·6 per cent of the electors had chosen Labour and only 39·8 per cent had voted Conservative. It was not merely an anti-Conservative vote but a pro-Labour one. The Liberals now had only twelve MPs instead of eighteen and even their leader, Sir Archibald Sinclair, had lost his seat. So, too, had thirty-one members of the government, including five Cabinet Ministers, the most popular defeat, received with acclaim throughout the Army, being that of the Secretary of State for War, who was never known to have done anything whatever for a single soldier. An even greater sensation was the size of the vote cast against the Prime Minister himself. The Labour Party had not contested his seat, but an unknown eccentric, who was brave enough to do so, had collected 10000 votes; if an official opposition candidate had fought Churchill he might well have won.

The Forces' vote was believed to have been overwhelmingly Labour and in my own unit this was certainly true; if there was any Other Rank who voted Conservative he never dared own up to doing so, and I remember a friend, who had betted a week's pay on a Conservative victory, handing it over with a beaming face, delighted to have lost. By early afternoon as news that Labour had already gained a clear majority spread through the building, the noise of jubilation rose with it until the brigadier in charge was reported to have gone home early in disgust. It was by far the most cheerful day I ever witnessed in the Army: VE Day had been the civilians' moment, a time of hope and fresh beginnings; this was ours.

At 7 o'clock that evening Churchill resigned, issuing a dignified farewell message explaining that in accordance with 'the decision of the British people . . . I have . . . laid down the charge which was placed upon me in darker times'. A little later Clement Attlee, addressing a rapturously happy Labour victory rally, announced, almost apologetically, 'I have this evening accepted His Majesty's commission.' He was already Prime Minister of the first Labour government in British history to possess real power.

The new government's majority might have been even greater had those who voted Conservative so that Churchill could 'finish the job' foreseen how soon the war in the Far East would be over. Only ten days after the new ministers had taken office, on the evening of Monday, 6 August, the first August Bank Holiday of peacetime – enlivened in the traditional way by 'strong winds and torrential rain' in most seaside resorts and 'hailstones as big as marbles' at Lords – the British public learned of the dropping of the first atomic bomb. At midnight, on Tuesday, 14 August, the Prime Minister broadcast the announcement of Japan's surrender.

Two days of celebration followed, though the rejoicing was, by comparison with VE Day, half-hearted and spirits were further dampened by bad weather. For most British civilians Germany had always been the major enemy and their war had finished three months before. Although there was wild revelry in the United States, especially in San Francisco, the part of the United States nearest to the distant Japanese enemy, in the capitals of Europe final victory went almost unnoticed. In Moscow, though Russia had belatedly declared war on Japan a few days before, it was ignored, though the formal signing of the armistice agreement on 2 September was marked by a holiday. Everywhere it was the servicemen who rejoiced most, rescued almost miraculously, it seemed, from the prospects of years of servitude, or a painful death in some distant jungle. The Germans on VJ Day were already pre-occupied with their own grim problems but were not allowed to forget their late ally's defeat. The ceremony carried out by one Anti-Tank Regiment of the Argyll and Sutherland Highlanders was typical of many:

On that day 146 Battery were accorded the supreme honour of firing a
royal salute of one hundred and one guns in the main square, before the
Town Hall of the city of Kiel. Our twelve M.10s, drawn up in line and
gleaming in new paint, thundered at solemn ten-second intervals before
a huge crowd of silent Germans. On that morning, at the hour, guns were
thundering wherever the armies of Britain stood upon captured soil. We
fired on the day of triumph not only as a battery; we fired as well in
memory of our comrades lying at rest beneath their white crosses,
scattered from Normandy to the Baltic, for our comrades sick and
wounded still in hospital . . . for Scotland, for Britain, for victory, and,
we hoped, as we thought of our children, for the end of war.

Thirty years later, looking back, it is clear that these high hopes,
idealistic though they seemed even then, were not wholly unjusti-
fied. War has clearly not been banished for ever, for there have been
a succession of minor conflicts in many parts of the world, some
long drawn out and immensely costly for the nations involved.
British troops have been in action since 1945 in Korea, Malaya and
many other parts of the world, just as they were in the frontier wars
of Queen Victoria's 'peaceful' reign, but Great Britain has not been
involved in a major war, and, unlike many other countries, has been
able to revert to an all-volunteer army. Here at least is cause for
satisfaction.

The First World War was supposed to make the world safe for
democracy and to prevent Germany starting yet another war. It
failed to do either. The Second World War, by contrast, though
not without some sad exceptions in Eastern Europe, has succeeded
in doing both. The 'glorious Russian ally' of 1945 had within a
year become 'the menace in the East'. In 1946 Churchill referred to
the Iron Curtain which had descended across Europe, and it was
soon clear that Poland, to protect which the allies had gone to war
in 1939, and Czechoslovakia, for which they had failed to fight in
1938, had exchanged one tyranny for another. But Communist
rule, however intolerable by Western standards, is surely preferable
to German occupation, and the Second World War, whatever
tragic headlines it left behind, has already given Europe peace for

more than thirty years, a period half as long again as the uneasy truce achieved after 1918.

Ever since 1945 warnings of impending world catastrophe have been issued by those who (by a somewhat puzzling process of logic) argue that peace would be best assured by the West leaving Russia in sole possession of the atomic bomb. In fact, despite their proliferation, not a single nuclear weapon has been used since the attack on Nagasaki in August 1945. All the destruction and death of the last thirty years has been caused by conventional weapons and, formidable though it is in terms of human suffering, the number of people killed and injured and families broken up amounts to infinitely less than in the preceding six. The so-called balance of terror has proved a force for peace.

For those, a steadily dwindling number, who remember VE or VJ Day, perhaps the most astonishing development of all in the world scene since 1945 has been the re-acceptance of Germany and Japan as independent powers. That the Germans should not merely be permitted to have a large conscript army but actively be encouraged to do so, that Japanese businessmen should openly walk the streets of British cities and freely compete with British industry, would have seemed inconceivable in 1945. Here at least the cynics have been proved right. They predicted at the end of the war that once again the nations which had caused it would somehow evade the long-term consequences, and so indeed they have.

Hardly less surprising than the re-emergence of Germany and Japan has been the creation of a host of newly independent nations from the former British Empire. Exactly two years after VJ Day India became self-governing; ten years later the retreat from benevolent colonialism began in earnest, with the ending of British rule in Ghana, the forerunner of a whole series of new African states, and in Malaya, for which fewer than twenty years before so much British blood had been shed. Now there is hardly a corner of the globe still ruled from London, though whether the substitution of self-government for 'imperial' government has promoted the happiness of the ordinary citizens in all these countries is a matter of opinion. What is indisputable is that almost everywhere the British hand-over of power has been dignified and peaceful. Britain may have had its Suez; it has avoided the long-drawn-out humiliation of an Algeria or a Vietnam.

Nearer home the picture is, at first sight, less reassuring. The national mood today is very different from that of VE Day and the months that preceded and followed it. Patriotism has become unfashionable, self-interest makes more appeal to many than self-sacrifice, the prevailing temper is one of resignation rather than hopeful expectation. Much of the explanation must lie in the debilitating effects of a constantly depreciating currency, in striking contrast to the success of wartime governments in holding down prices in spite of the classic conditions for inflation. But the roots of the malaise go deeper. Although the wartime Parliament was unrepresentative of public opinion on many issues, as became clear in 1945, there existed a basic accord between rulers and ruled which has since vanished, a confident trust that sacrifices called for were necessary and that changes were introduced to win the war, not to silence or satisfy some vocal sectional pressure group. Today, in spite of regular elections, the prevailing mood is one of frustration and impotence, induced by the fear that, contrary to the known wishes of the vast majority of electors, long-established national traditions are being destroyed to please those who favour innovation for its own sake or to conform to foreign practice, and the whole character of what Churchill called 'the island race' is being threatened without even the pretence of consultation with those involved.

But if there is cause for foreboding in looking towards the future there is also much cause for satisfaction in looking at the recent past and the present to which it has led. Blemishes, even major inequalities, remain, but the more just society to which everyone in 1945 professed dedication has largely been achieved. Although unemployment is at the time of writing again a serious problem, mass, long-term unemployment on the pre-war scale, regarded before 1945 as a permanent feature of peacetime life, has not materialized. 'Equality of opportunity', again with many obvious exceptions, has. The Beveridge Report was regarded in 1942 as at once idealistic and revolutionary. Today its principles have been universally accepted and all its recommendations have been implemented, or surpassed. Examples of poverty, misfortune, even tragedy, can still be found; but no one who can remember the nineteen-thirties is likely to dispute that for the overwhelming majority of the population life today is fuller, richer, more comfort-

able and more secure than it was then. Hard though it may sometimes be to accept the fact, the better world so often promised in
wartime speeches and in the newspaper cartoons of 1945 has
arrived.

Yet it is an illusion to suppose that the war was waged, as was so
often implied at the time, for a brighter future and a fairer society.
It was fought for one purpose only: national survival. There was, as
Churchill so often repeated, only one war aim: victory. We fought
because we had to, and, having to fight, we won. There could have
been no better reason; and, without consequences almost too fearful
to contemplate, no other conclusion.

A NOTE ON SOURCES

My principal sources have been eye-witness accounts in contemporary newspapers, but I have also made extensive use of autobiographies and biographies and, a source hitherto much neglected, regimental magazines and histories. On the civilian side I have also drawn on my own archive of unpublished reminiscences supplied by contributors to my *How We Lived Then* (Hutchinson 1971 and Arrow Books 1973) and *The GIs* (Hutchinson 1975), but I have not used here any material that has appeared in them. The place of publication of the books listed is London unless otherwise stated and I have given full particulars only the first time a book is mentioned. Thus, for example, 'Chapter 3' after an author's name means that fuller details appear in the sources listed under that chapter. Where the origin of a quotation is obvious from the context I have not identified it here.

Every author will know how easily errors creep into print, especially in the case of dates, but the euphoria of victory seems to have affected many of those mentioned below to a quite extraordinary degree. Thus two writers listed here place VE Day on 8 *June* and a third, having described 7 May as a Monday and 9 May as a Wednesday unaccountably refers to 8 May as a Thursday. One observer present on the balcony with Churchill claims to have heard him deliver on 8 May a speech not in fact made until the following day, while a collection of Churchill's speeches attributes another speech to VE Day which was clearly delivered on VE+1. Even more surprising, one of the small group of correspondents present at the liberation of Oslo places it on 9 May, when the others date it correctly on the previous day. This accumulation of errors means that, so far as dates are concerned, many of the books listed here should be treated with caution, and this is even more true of the times to which the various events are assigned, since, thanks to summer-time, a bewildering variety of time-scales were in use in various parts of the globe in May 1945.

GENERAL BACKGROUND

Major L. R. Ellis and A. E. Warhurst, *Victory in the West*, Volume II, *The Defeat of Germany* (HMSO 1968); S. Woodburn Kirby and others, *The War against Japan* (HMSO 1965 and 1969), IV and V; Chester Wilmot, *The Struggle for Europe* (Collins 1952); Alan Moorehead, *Eclipse* (Hamish Hamilton 1945), and the excellent illustrated abridgement by Lucy Moorehead (Hamish Hamilton 1967); Winston S. Churchill, *The Second World War*, Volume VI, *Triumph and Tragedy* (Cassell 1954); *The Post-War World* (Part-work, Marshall Cavendish 1975), I and II; Angus Calder, *The People's War* (Cape 1969); Mass-Observation, *Peace and the Public* (Mass-Observation 1947); Desmond Flower and James Reeves (eds.), *The War, 1939–45* (Cassell 1960); Joseph Macleod, *A Job at the BBC* (William Maclellan, Glasgow 1947); Stuart Hibberd, *This is London* (Macdonald and Evans 1950); *How Britain was fed in Wartime* (HMSO 1946); T. H. O'Brien, *Civil Defence* (HMSO 1955); A. S. M. Gow, *Letters from Cambridge* (Cape 1945); Nigel Nicolson (ed.), *Harold Nicolson: Diaries and Letters 1939–45* (Collins 1967); Robert Rhodes James (ed.), *Chips, The Diaries of Sir Henry Channon* (Weidenfeld and Nicolson 1967); Anthony Weymouth (pseud.), *Journal of the War Years and One Year Later* (Littlebury and Co, Worcester 1948), II.

Chapter 1

Hitler Kaput

My principal sources were H. E. Trevor-Roper, *The Last Days of Hitler* (Macmillan 1947); Alan Bullock, *Hitler, A Study in Tyranny* (Penguin Books edition 1962); Albert Speer, *Inside the*

Third Reich (Weidenfeld and Nicolson 1970); R. Manvell and H. Fraenkel, *Joseph Goebbels* (Heinemann 1960), *Heinrich Himmler* (Heinemann 1965); Omar N. Bradley, *A Soldier's Story* (Eyre and Spottiswoode 1951); Ralph Ingersoll, *Top Secret* (Partridge 1946); and Lt-Colonel F. F. Laugher, *History of the 6th Battalion Royal Welch Fusiliers* (G. Evans and Son, Caernarvon 1946). On William Joyce's last broadcast I used J. A. Cole, *William Joyce, Lord Haw Haw* (Faber 1964), and on the spy whose suitcase was safe J. C. Masterman, *The Double Cross System* (Sphere Books 1973). Eisenhower's views on VE Day appear in Harry C. Butcher, *Three Years with Eisenhower* (Heinemann 1946), and the account of the liberation of the *Prominente* is in Giles Romilly and Michael Alexander, *The Privileged Nightmare* (Weidenfeld and Nicolson 1954).

Chapter 2

Chaos or signature

On events at Lüneburg I used Moorehead and *The Memoirs of Field-Marshal Montgomery* (Collins 1958); on the surrender in Holland J. L. Hodson, *The Sea and the Land* (Gollancz 1951); and on what happened at Rheims, before and during the final capitulation, Butcher; Dwight D. Eisenhower, *Crusade in Europe* (Heinemann 1948); and Kay Summersby, *Eisenhower was my Boss* (Werner Laurie 1949). Reaction in Copenhagen came from private information.

Chapter 3

Waiting for Victory

On Ed Kennedy see *Newsweek* (New York), 14 May 1945; on events at Rheims and in Berlin see Butcher (Chapter 1) and Summersby (Chapter 2). I also consulted Cicely Courtneidge, *Cicely* (Hutchinson 1953); Janet Flanner, *Paris Journal 1945–66* (Gollancz 1966), the 'Paris resident' referred to; Nigel Nicolson, *Harold Nicolson*; Verily Anderson, *Spam Tomorrow* (Hart-Davis 1956), the resident of St John's Wood; Susan Woolfit, *Idle Women* (Benn 1947), the boating housewife; Macleod; Paul Hollister and Robert Strunsky (eds.), *From D Day through Victory in Europe* (Columbia Broadcasting System, New York 1945); and private information.

Chapter 4

The German war is therefore at an end

My sources were Hibberd, Channon and Nicolson; A. P. Herbert, *Independent Member* (Howard Baker 1950); and the following: Elizabeth Nel, *Mr Churchill's Secretary* (Hodder and Stoughton 1958); Jane Gordon, *Married to Charles* (Heinemann 1950), the volunteer nurse referred to; Tom Driberg, *Colonnade 1937–1947* (Pilot Press 1949); and John Lehmann, *I am my Brother* (Longmans 1960).

Chapter 5

'We want the King'

Among the books I used most were: W. H. Thompson, *I was Churchill's Shadow* (Christopher Johnson 1951); Hugh Dalton, *The Fateful Years, Memoirs 1931–45* (Frederick Muller 1957); John W. Wheeler-Bennett, *King George VI, His Life and Reign* (Macmillan 1958); Hodson (Chapter 2), the journalist who commented on the King's broadcast; Humphrey Lyttleton, *I Play as I Please* (Pilot Press 1949); Derek Lambert, *The Sheltered Days* (Andre Deutsch 1965), the schoolboy from Banstead; Verily Anderson (Chapter 3), who saw the dancing in Soho; and William Sansom, *Westminster at War* (Faber 1947). The fire at St Clement Danes was described in the *Manchester Guardian*.

The text of Churchill's speeches, in this and later chapters, is taken from a number of sources, including *The Times*, *Keesing's Contemporary Archives* and the following: Guy Boas (ed.), *Winston Churchill, Selection of Speeches* (Macmillan 1952); Charles Eade (ed.), *Winston Churchill, Victory, War Speeches, 1945* (Cassell 1946); and *Winston Churchill, War Speeches, 1940–45* (Cassell 1946), I also consulted Lord Moran, *Winston Churchill, The Struggle for Survival* (Constable 1966), and Lewis Broad, *Winston Churchill, 1874–1951* (Hutchinson 1951).

Chapter 6

Bonfires over England

The woman travelling up from Eastbourne was Verity Anderson and the boating housewife Susan Woolfit (both Chapter 3).

On Cambridge I quoted from Gow. I also consulted: W. C. Berwick Sayers (ed.), *Croydon and the Second World War* (Croydon Corporation 1949); *Luton at War* (Home Counties Newspapers, Luton 1947); Ronald Clark, *Tizard* (Methuen 1965); Clifford Musgrave, *Life in Brighton* (Faber 1970); and the script of BBC *Victory Report No. 1*. A private informant described the Fittleworth bonfire.

Chapter 7

Bless 'em all

On the Forces I consulted: *The Sapper*, Journal of the Corps of Royal Engineers, July 1945; *The Royal Army Ordnance Corps Gazette*, June 1945; *The Dragon* (Regimental Journal of 'The Buffs'), August 1945; *The Eagle* (Journal of the Essex Regiment), September 1945; *The Wasp* (Journal of the 16th Foot, the Bedfordshire and Hertfordshire Regiment), June 1945. The serviceman in Watford, the Cardiff mother and the ATS girl at Stanmore were private informants.

Chapter 8

Flowers over Europe

The surrender in Norway is described by F. S. V. Donnison, *Civil Affairs and Military Government, North-West Europe* (HMSO 1966) and the liberation of Oslo by Moorehead. On Holland I consulted Lt.-Colonel Sir J. E. H. Neville (ed.) *War Chronicle of the Oxfordshire and Buckinghamshire Light Infantry. 1944–5.* (Gale and Polden, Aldershot 1954), Volume IV, Captain J. D. Bicknell and M. Flower, *The 1st Buckinghamshire Battalion, Narrative 1 January – 30 June 1945,* and on Paris, Charles de Gaulle, *Memoirs*, Volume III, *Salvation* (Weidenfeld and Nicolson 1960); Janet Flanner ('one American woman', Chapter 2) and Susan Mary Alsop, *Letters to Marietta* (Weidenfeld and Nicolson 1975), 'the wife of an American diplomat'. *Newsweek* (Chapter 3) reported the vote of censure on Ed Kennedy, and Kay Summersby and Harry Butcher (Chapter 1) described events in Berlin. The lack of a 'lie-in' for British forces was mentioned by the *South Wales Evening Post*. Other material on the Forces came from: *The Oak Tree* (the Journal of the 22nd Cheshire Regiment), Autumn 1945; *The King's Shrop-shire Light Infantry and Herefordshire Regimental Journal*, October 1945; and *The Eagle* (Journal of the Glider Pilot Regiment), 1954, Volume 2, No 9, Patrick Forbes, *The 6th Guards Tank Brigade* (Sampson Low n.d. [1946]); Patrick Forbes and Nigel Nicolson, *The Grenadier Guards in the War of 1939–1945*, vol. II (by Nigel Nicolson), *The Mediterranean Campaigns* (Gale and Polden, Aldershot, 1949). The surrender of the U Boat at Weymouth was described by the *Manchester Guardian*, 11 May, and in *Victory Report*, No 3. On American units I referred to: Donald G. Taggart (ed.), *History of the 3rd Infantry Division* (Infantry Journal Press, Washington DC 1947) and Frank Smith (ed.), *Battle Diary, The Story of the 243rd Field Artillery Battalion in Combat* (Hobson Book Press, New York 1946).

Chapter 9

The wonderful 9th of May

My sources were: R. C. F. Maugham, *Jersey under the Jackboot* (W. H. Allen 1946); Frank Falla, *The Silent War* (Leslie Frewin 1967), the 'Guernsey journalist' imprisoned in Germany; L. P. Sinel, *The German Occupation of Jersey* (the *Evening Post*, Jersey 1956), identified as a 'Jersey diarist' and 'resident'; Jane Gordon, the 'staff nurse in a London hospital' (Chapter 3); the correspondent of the *Scotsman*, who witnessed the surrender and liberation of Guernsey; Carel Toms, *Hitler's Fortress Islands* (New English Library 1967); Alan and Mary Wood, *Islands in Danger* (Evans 1955), on the surrender of Jersey; and Ernest-Vivian Coltman, *Birds of the Storm* (Frederick Muller 1963) on the 'shelves of bread' incident.

Chapter 10

Postman's knock in Red Square

I quoted from: Alexander Werth, *Russia at War 1941–1945* (Barrie and Rockcliffe 1964); Jack Fishman, *My Darling Clementine* (W. H. Allen 1963); Clementine Churchill, *My Visit to Russia* (Hutchinson 1945); The Very Rev. Hewlett Johnson, *Searching for*

Light (Michael Joseph 1968); the *Cape Argus* (Cape Town) on the 'Number, please' story; Churchill Volume VI (General Bibliography) on the text of Mrs Churchill's broadcast; and, on events in Czechoslovakia, the *Scotsman* and the *Manchester Guardian* for 9 May. I also consulted Adam B. Ulam, *Stalin, The Man and his Era* (Allen Lane 1973).

Chapter 11

New light for Miss Liberty

This chapter is based on press reports and, for events at Cocanada and in Changi Jail, on private information. The 'great elephants' appeared in BBC *Victory Report No 2* and the Donkey Derby in Cairo in the Army magazine *Parade*, for 19 May 1945.

Chapter 12

Burma Looms Ahead

The title quotation is from Bicknell and Flower (Chapter 8); Montgomery (Chapter 2) describes conditions in the British zone and quotes his letter on fraternization; David Niven recorded his experiences in *The Moon's a Balloon* (Hamish Hamilton 1971). The BBC war correspondent quoted was Edward Ward, *Give Me Air* (John Lane, The Bodley Head 1946). J. L. Hodson (Chapter 2) observed the sign Priority: Loot, Nigel Nicolson (Chapter 8) the German prisoners at Villach, Patrick Forbes (Chapter 8) the display of strength by the 6th Tank Brigade. The Town Major of Bentheim was Major C. W. Kidwell, 'A Point of View upon Germany', in *The Oak Tree* (Chapter 8), summer and autumn 1946, and of Hamelin, Major P. T. E. Lyndon-Bell, *The Dragon* (Chapter 7), August 1945. Manvell and Fraenkel (Chapter 1) described Himmler's fate and L. A. Cole (Chapter 1) that of Lord Haw Haw. The advertisement in *Le Monde* was noticed by Janet Flanner (Chapter 3). Speer (Chapter 1) observed the closing days of the Dönitz government. On demobilization I consulted *Regulations for Release from the Army* (War Office, HMSO February 1945) and *Demobilization, Questions and Answers* (Ministry of Labour, HMSO November 1945).

Chapter 13

Outlook: 'Dry'

The *Scotsman*, 11 May, reported Churchill's hoarseness and Churchill Volume VI carries the text of his broadcast and of his comment on his electoral defeat. Reaction in Dublin appears in the *Irish Times*, 14 and 15 May, and the *Daily Express*, 14 May, and Conor Cruise O'Brien's view appears in his *States of Ireland* (Hutchinson 1972). Musgrave (Chapter 6) described Brighton's return to normal, Kay Summersby (Chapter 2) Eisenhower's London visit; *The Times House of Commons, 1945* (Times Newspapers 1945) the election campaign; Dalton (Chapter 5), the 'children's clothes' incident, and Bernard Donoghue and G. W. Jones, *Herbert Morrison* (Weidenfeld and Nicolson 1973) the references to the air-raid warning system. The description of VJ Day in Kiel is from Desmond Flower, *History of the Argyll and Sutherland Highlanders. 5th Battalion, 91st Tank Regiment, 1939–45* (Nelson 1950). A private informant described the scene at Seaburne. While the present book was in the press, new light was thrown on the relationship between General Eisenhower and his secretary in the posthumously published: Kay Summersby Morgan, *Past Forgetting: My Love Affair with Dwight D. Eisenhower* (Collins, 1976).

Newspapers and Magazines Consulted

The Times; the *Daily Telegraph*; the *Daily Express*; the *Daily Mail*; the *News Chronicle*; the *Evening Standard* (London); the *Sunday Express*; the *Daily Worker*; the *Manchester Guardian*; the *Birmingham Post*; the *Liverpool Daily Post*; the *Newcastle Journal*; the *Yorkshire Evening Post*; the *Coventry Evening Telegraph*; the *Sussex Daily News* (Brighton); the *Western Daily Press* (Bristol); the *Eastern Daily Press* (Norwich); the *Western Mail* (Cardiff); the *South Wales Evening Post* (Cardiff); the *South Wales Echo* (Cardiff); the *Herald of Wales* (Cardiff); the *Scotsman* (Edinburgh); the *Glasgow Herald*; the *Glasgow Daily Record*; the *Belfast Telegraph*; the *Belfast Newsletter*; the *Irish Times* (Dublin); the *Sunday Independent* (Dublin); the *Illustrated London News*; the *Guernsey Star*; the *Jersey Evening Post*; the *Stars and Stripes* (US Forces in Europe); *Parade* (British Army magazine); the *New York Times*;

the *New York Herald Tribune*; *Newsweek* (United States); *Life* (United States); the *Globe and Mail* (Toronto); the *Cape Argus* (Cape Town); the *Times of India*.

Other Books and Periodicals Consulted

The Historical Committee (eds.), *The King's Royal Rifle Corps Chronicle* (Warren and Son, Winchester 1946); Hilary St George Saunders, *The Red Beret, The Story of the Parachute Regiment at War* (White Lion Publishers 1950); Major G. R. Hartwell and others, *The Story of the 5th Battalion, the Dorsetshire Regiment in North-West Europe, 23rd June 1944 to 5th May 1945* (Henry Ling, Dorchester n.d. [1946]); A. J. Evans, *Escape and Liberation 1940–1945* (Hodder and Stoughton 1945); Group-Captain Johnnie Johnson, *Wing Leader* (Chatto and Windus 1956).

Regimental Journals

Roundel, Volume 13, No 2, March 1961, on RAF prisoners; *The Journal of the Honourable Artillery Company*, August–September 1945; *Firm*, the magazine of the Worcester Regiment, November 1945; the Journal of the Queen's Royal Regiment; the *Journal* of the East Surrey Regiment; the *Faugh-a-Ballagh*, the Regimental Gazette of the Royal Irish Fusiliers; the *Royal Military College Magazine*.

GENERAL INDEX

Compiled by Gordon Robinson

Alexander, General Harold (later 1st
Earl Alexander of Tunis), 29
Alexander, Michael, 23–4
Anderson, Sir John, 67, 79
Anglo-Soviet Medical Aid Fund, 128
Antonio, Marc, 84
Armed Forces victory celebrations,
100–2, 114–15
Armistice Day (1918), 78, 82, 87
Army, British: Airborne Division (1st),
103; Argyll and Sutherland High-
landers, 172–3; Army in India, 141–2;
Auxiliary Territorial Service (ATS),
102; Bedfordshire and Hertfordshire
Regiment, 102; British Liberation
Army (BLA), 144, 156; 1st
Buckinghamshire Battalion, Oxford
and Buckinghamshire Light Infantry,
112, 144, 156; Cheshire Regiment,
111; Coldstream Guards, 112; Essex
Regiment, 102; 14th Army, 63, 100,
142, 144; Glider Pilot Regiment, 111;
Grenadier Guards, 113, 114, 147,
150; Guards Brigades: 6th Armoured,
112–13, 148, Infantry, 113;
Hampshire Regiment, 123;
Herefordshire Regiment, 111;
Intelligence Corps, 148; Irish
Guards, 69; King's Shropshire
Light Infantry, 111; Middle East
Forces, GHQ Cairo, 141; Royal
Army Ordnance Corps, 101–2;
Royal Artillery, 121; Royal
Engineers, 100; Royal Horse Guards,
65; Royal Irish Fusiliers, 99; Royal
Signals, 102; Royal Welch Fusiliers,
16; Royal West Kents (the 'Buffs'),
102, 149; 21st Army Group, 20, 25,
28; victory celebrations, 100–2, 111
Army, United States: 1st Army, 20, 21;

2nd Army, 39; 3rd Army, 135; 3rd
Infantry Division, 115; 4th Armoured
Division, 135; 6th Army Group, 20;
7th Army, 105; 9th Army, 21, 114;
12th Army Group, 20; 53rd Division,
23; 243rd Field Artillery Battalion,
115; Military Police, 77, 146–7
Astor, Lord, 83
Astor, Nancy, Lady, 85
Attlee, Clement (later 1st Earl), 167,
169, 170, 172
Attlee, Mrs (later Lady), 170

Baedeker raids, 86
bands, 55, 94, 141
Battick, Charles, 91
Battle of the Atlantic, 87
Baumer, Adriene, 154
Beaverbrook, Lord, 168
Bernhard, Prince, 36
Beveridge Report, 175
Bevin, Ernest, 79
blackout, 72, 84, 89, 160
Bland, Peter, 68
Blasowitz, General, 36–7
Bohme, General, 103
bonfires, 58, 80–5, 90, 92–3, 95, 98,
99–100, 101
Bormann, Martin, 17, 152
Bradley, General Omar, 20–1, 22, 28,
55, 165
Briggs, Charlie, 91
British Broadcasting Corporation
(BBC), 15, 17, 62, 72, 75–6;
announces Hitler's death, 15;
Churchill's broadcasts, 65, 82, 86, 87,
114, 127, 128, 139, 140, 142, 158–9;
King's broadcast, 74–5; 'Monday;
Night at Eight', 55; 'Music While
You Work', 15; news-flash of

German capitulation, 32, 33; *Radio Times*, 54; Religious Broadcasting Department, 61–2; VE Day announcement, 55–6; 'Victory Report', 52, 54; 'War Report', 54
British Red Cross Aid to Russia Fund, 127–8
Busch, Field-Marshal Ernst, 17–18
Butcher, Captain Harry, 33, 37, 38, 39–40, 41, 42, 43, 44, 45, 109

Cadogan, Sir Alexander (later Lord), 136
Canadian Navy, 138–9
Carey, Victor, 121–2
Chamberlain, Neville, 65
Channon, 'Chips', 32, 63–4, 67, 74
Churchill, Clementine (later Lady), 127, 128–9, 133
Churchill, Winston (later Sir), 32, 33, 37, 39, 43, 45, 53, 55, 60, 63, 64, 65–9, 71–2, 74, 78, 79–80, 82, 86, 87, 89, 98, 108, 112, 114, 117, 118–19, 127, 128, 138, 139, 140, 142, 153, 158–9, 160, 165, 166, 167, 168–72, 173, 175, 176, 177
Clarke, Herb, 91
Clarke, Trooper, 91
clubs, 56, 57, 64, 69, 78, 96, 164
collaborators, fate of, 124
Columbia Broadcasting System (CBS), 43, 49
concentration camps, 23, 147
Cooke, Alistair, 46, 47, 48
Courtneidge, Cicely, 50
Coutanche, Alexander, 122

Dalton, Hugh, 72, 163, 169
De Gaulle, General, 105–6, 108, 166
De Lattre, General, 106
De Tassigny, General, 110
De Valera, Eamon, 159
demobilization, 156–7
Derby, Lord, 83
Devers, General, 20
Dewing, General, 34
Dimbleby, Richard, 78, 79
Dönitz, Admiral Karl, 15–16, 17–19, 25, 26, 35, 38, 39, 40, 51, 129, 153, 154–5
Driberg, Tom, 68, 73

Eden, Anthony (later Lord Avon), 37, 62, 136
Eisenhower, General Dwight, 22, 23, 25, 28, 30, 32–3, 37, 38, 39, 40, 41, 42, 43, 44, 45, 62, 107, 108, 109, 110, 145, 165–6

Eisenhower, Mamie, 165
Elizabeth, Princess (now Queen), 71, 75
Elizabeth, Queen (now the Queen Mother), 54, 71, 75
Entertainments National Service Association (ENSA), 50
evacuees, 90
Ewart, Colonel, 29
Eyles, Captain, 112

Ffoulkes, General, 36, 37
Frank, Anne, 35
Frankfurt, 166
fraternization ban in Germany, 150–2
Friedeburg, Admiral von, 26–7, 28, 29, 30, 38–9, 40, 109, 110
Friedel, Major, 26, 28, 30

George VI, 54, 55, 62, 71, 74–5, 76, 96, 102, 121–2, 125–6
German Navy, 16, 26; *Admiral Hipper*, 112; *Admiral Scheer*, 112; *Nürnberg*, 35; *Prinz Eugen*, 35; surrender of, 75, 114
German surrender: Berlin, 106, 107–10, 127, 129, 135; Denmark, 34; Channel Islands, 119–21; Holland, 36–7; Italy, 29 37, Lüneberg Heath, 26–32, 120; Navy, 75, 114; Norway, 75, 103–5; Rheims, 41–2, 106, 108, 110, 120, 127
Gillard, Frank, 55
Goebbels, Dr Joseph, 16, 17, 19
Göring, Hermann Wilhelm, 16–17, 21, 83, 124, 155
Gow (Senior Tutor, Trinity College, Cambridge), 84
Greenwood, Arthur, 67
Groves, Jack, 91

Heine, Major-General, 120
Henley Regatta, 164
Herbert, A. P. (later Sir Alan), 57, 67, 96, 166
Herriot, Edouard, 128
Hibberd, Stuart, 60, 62, 81
Himmler, Heinrich, 16, 17, 18–19, 152–3
Hitler, Adolf, 15–17, 18, 19, 21, 23, 25, 26, 66, 72, 82, 83, 116, 141, 153, 159
Hodson, J. L., 36–7, 61, 69
hotels, 32, 51, 64, 84, 85, 103, 105, 132, 160, 165
Hüffmeier, Vice-Admiral, 116, 120, 126

Irish neutrality, 159
Iron Curtain, 173

Japanese war, 62, 63, 65, 70, 137, 142–3, 156, 158–9, 167, 170, 172, 174; atomic bomb, 172, 174; VJ Day, 172–3
Jodl, General, 18, 25, 40, 41–2, 65, 110
Johnson, Dr Hewlett, 128–9, 131, 132–3, 134
Joyce, William, 19, 153
Juliana, Princess (later Queen), 36

Keitel, Field-Marshal, 18, 28, 30, 38, 61, 106, 108, 109, 110
Kennedy, Ed, 44, 45–6, 47, 107
Kinzel, General, 26, 30
Konev, Marshal, 20
Krosigk, Schwerin von, 51–2, 154, 155

La Guardia, Mayor, 48–9
Laski, Harold, 169
Lehmann, John, 70
Leopold, King, 62, 105
Levitan, Uri, 129
Llewellin, Colonel, 162, 163
Lloyd George, David (later 1st Earl), 94, 168
looting by Allies in Germany, 146–7
Luftwaffe, 17, 26, 104, 147
Lyttleton, Humphrey, 76

Macleod, Joseph, 54
Margaret, Princess, 71, 75
Marshall, General, 165
Maugham, R. C., 116
Molotov, V. M., 62
Montagu Burton Ltd, Bolton, 88
Montgomery, Field-Marshal Bernard (later 1st Viscount Montgomery of Alamein), 20, 22, 26–33, 36, 85, 145, 146, 151, 153, 166
Moorehead, Alan, 29–30, 33–5, 103, 104–5
Morrison, Herbert (later Lord Morrison of Lambeth), 79, 160, 169
Mussolini, Benito, 78, 83, 141

National Fire Service, Glasgow, 58
Nel, Elizabeth, 64
neutral rejoicings, 105
newpapers, 62–3; Belfast Newsletter, 99; Birmingham Post, 88; Britansky Soyuznik, 132; Cape Argus, 140; Daily Express, 53; Daily Mail, 53, 56, 62, 160; Daily Mirror, 63; Daily Telegraph, 53, 136; Daily Worker, 62; Eastern Daily Press, 86; Evening Standard, 158, 161, 162, 164; Glasgow Daily Record, 98; Glasgow Herald, 58, 97–9; Guernsey Star, 116,
117, 123–4; Hull Daily Mail, 85; Irish Times, 159; Jersey Evening Post, 117, 124; Le Monde, 154; Liverpool Daily Post, 56, 87; Manchester Guardian, 46, 48, 54–5, 63, 69, 88–9, 127, 131, 142, 161, 167; New York Herald Tribune, 47, 49, 114, 130, 132, 134, 136, 138, 143; New York Times, 47–9, 136–7; News Chronicle, 15; Scotsman, The, 57–8, 68–9, 96, 97; Staffordshire Advertiser, 92; Stars and Stripes, 62, 156; Sunday Express, 164–5; Sussex Daily News, 84; Times, The, 50, 53, 56, 62, 104, 130–1, 142, 164; Western Mail, 94, 95; Yorkshire Evening Post, 139
Nicolson, Harold, 52, 64, 65, 67, 68, 74
Niemöller, Pastor, 155
Niven, David, 145
Norwegian Parachute Company, 103

O'Brien, Conor Cruise, 159
Occupation Forces in Germany, 144–56
Operation Eclipse, 20, 25
Operation Overlord, 20

parliamentary election (1945), 167–72
Patton, General George, 21, 22, 105
Poleck, Colonel, 30, 38
premature celebrations, 45–55
prisoners of war: Allied, 23–4, 75, 142–3; German, 126, 145–7

race-meetings: Ascot, 164–5; Newmarket, 83
Rechelt (German Chief-of-Staff in Holland), 37
Red Army, 21, 22, 113, 131, 133, 134; 1st Ukranian Army Group, 20
restaurants, 51, 71, 73, 165
Ribbentrop, Joachim von, 74, 153
Roosevelt, Franklin Delano, 129, 132, 136
Rosebery, Lord, 83
Rosenberg, Alfred, 18
Roure, Marie-Louise, 154
Roure, Remy, 154
Royal Air Force, 75, 83–4, 103–5
Royal Navy, 114, 118, 119, 122; Amethyst, HMS, 114; Beagle, HMS, 119, 122; Bulldog, HMS, 119, 120; Magpie, HMS, 114

Salvation Army, 85
Sansom, William, 80
Sark, Dame of, 123
Sevez, General, 41
Seyss-Inquart, Arthur, 35–6, 75

shortages and rationing, 162–5
Sinclair, Sir Archibald, 168, 171
Smith, Lieutenant-General Bedell, 38, 39, 40, 41, 44
Snagge, John, 32
Snow, Brigadier Alfred Ernest, 119, 120–1, 126
songs, hymns and anthems, 49, 50, 51, 61–2, 69, 73, 76, 79, 80, 90, 94, 95, 96, 99, 101, 107, 108, 121, 130, 131, 138, 141
Spaatz, General, 107, 110
Special Operations Executive, 100
Speer, Albert, 18, 154–5
SS, 145–6
Stalin, Joseph, 53, 54, 55, 129, 133, 134, 170
street parties, 87, 95
Strong, General, 40, 41
Stumpf, Colonel-General, 109
Summersby, Kay, 32–3, 37–8, 40–1, 44–5, 109–10, 165
Supreme Headquarters, Allied Expeditionary Force (SHAEF), 21, 25; Bushy Park, Teddington, 25; dissolved, 166; Frankfurt, 166; Grosvenor Square, 25; Military Mission to Denmark, 33, 34; Paris, 28, 45, 46; Rheims, 25, 32–3, 37–42, 43–6, 107, German surrender, 41–2, 106, 108, 110, 120, 127; South Kensington, 25, 33; Versailles, 25
Susloparov, General, 37, 40, 41, 44

Tedder, Air-Chief-Marshal (later 1st Baron), 32, 106, 107, 109–10

Thanksgiving Services, 61, 68, 86, 88, 95, 97, 129, 132–3, 158
theatres, 50, 58, 88, 138, 165
Thompson, Inspector, 32, 53, 79
Tito, Marshal, 113
Tizard, Sir Henry, 83
Truman, Harry S., 43, 45, 53, 108, 132, 136–7, 170

United Nations, 62, 84, 89, 105, 141, 143, 159

VE Day (8 May 1945), 28, 55, 59, 60–81, 82–93, 94–102, 103–15, 117–23, 127, 128, 135, 136–42, 145, 150, 174, 175
VJ Day, 172–3, 174
Vyshinsky, Andrei, 109

Wagner, Rear-Admiral, 26, 30
war criminals, 152–5; executions, 61; trials at Nuremberg, 43, 155
Wehrmacht, 17, 21, 26, 30, 36–7, 38; 11th Panzer Division, 21–2
Werth, Alexander, 127, 132
Wightman, Ralph, 91–2
Williams, Hubert, 94
Woodsford, Tom, 91
Woolton, Lord, 79
Wragg, Harry, 83

Younger, General, 131

Zhukov, Marshal, 108–9, 110
Zimmermann, Captain-Lieutenant Arnim, 120

INDEX OF PLACE NAMES

Compiled by Gordon Robinson

Alderney, 123
Alkmaar, 112
Altrincham, 63
Amsterdam, 20, 35
Armagh, 99
Ascot, 164–5
Australia: victory celebrations, 139
Austria, 21, 22, 23–4, 113–14, 115, 144, 150, 156

Bangor, Northern Ireland, 99
Bayeux, 112
Bedford, 61
Belfast, 90, 99
Belsen, 147
Bentheim, 148–9, 150, 152
Berchtesgaden, 21, 23
Berlin, 15, 16, 17, 28, 42, 43, 65, 66, 116, 144, 153, 170; German surrender, 106, 107–10, 127, 129, 135
Birmingham, 88
Bolton, 88
Bombay, 141
Bonn, 144
Bremervörde, 152
Breslau, 62
Brighton, 84, 100, 160–1
Bristol, 87
Brussels, 38
Buchenwald, 23, 145
Burma, 100, 142
Burslem: Victory Pageant, 92
Bury St Edmunds, 102
Bushy Park, Teddington, 25

Caernarvon, 94
Cairo, 141
Cambridge, 84
Canada: victory celebrations, 138–9
Canterbury, 86, 102

Cape Town, 140
Cardiff, 94–5
Caterham, 76
Channel Islands, 29; German surrender, 120–1; liberation, 116–26, 127; 'Operation Nest-Egg', 124–5
Cividale, 113
Cocanada, 142
Colditz Castle, 23
Compiègne, 154
Copenhagen, 33, 34–5, 103–4
Coventry, 86
Croydon, 82
Czechoslovakia, 21, 22, 62, 63, 133, 134–5, 173

Den Helder, 112
Denmark, 22; German surrender, 34; liberation, 33–5, 75; victory celebrations, 34–5
Dordrecht, 36
Dover, 84
Dresden, 135
Dublin, 51
Dunkirk, 29

Eastbourne, 82
Edinburgh: victory celebrations, 57–8, 96–7
Eire, 51, 159
Elbe river, 20, 21, 144

Finland, 50–1
Fittleworth, Sussex, 92–3
Flensburg, 18, 19, 28, 35, 38, 45, 51, 147, 152, 153, 154, 155
France: German surrender, 41–2, 106, 108, 110, 120, 127; victory celebrations, 49, 105–7, 134, 166
Fulwell, 87

Ghana, 174
Glasgow: victory celebrations, 58–9, 97–9
Grangemouth Docks, 57
Guernsey, 116–17, 119, 126; liberation of, 121–2, 123–4; Underground News Service (GUNS), 118

Hague, The, 105
Halifax (N.S.): celebration riots, 138–9
Hamburg, 16, 18, 19–20, 147, 148, 150, 153
Hamelin, 149, 151
Harleston, 90
Haverfordwest, 96
Hawkesbury, 53
Henley, 164
Holland: German surrender, 36–7; liberation, 20, 35–7, 75, 105; victory celebrations, 105, 112
Hove, 84
Hull, 85–6

India: independence, 174; victory celebrations, 141–2
Innsbruck, 23–4
Italy: German surrender, 29, 37; victory celebrations, 50, 113

Jersey, 116; liberation of, 122–5
Johannesburg, 140

Kenya: victory celebrations, 141
Kew, 60, 161
Kiel, 20, 33, 112, 113, 145, 150, 173
Kirriemuir, 56
Knutsford, 63
Konetopy, 135

Leeds, 88
Leith, 58
Linz, 21
Lisbon, 105
Liverpool, 87
Llanelly, 95
London, 32, 46, 96, 153, 161–2, 165–6; Arts Theatre Club, 164; Beefsteak Club, near Leicester Square, 64; Big Ben, 81; Bloomsbury, 78; Buckingham Palace, 54–5, 68–9, 71, 72, 78, 121; Charing Cross, 57, 78; Ciro's restaurant, 165; County Hall, 81; Dorchester Hotel, Park Lane, 165; Downing Street, 64–5, 66, 71; Freedom of City to Eisenhower, 166; Grosvenor Square, 25; Guildhall, 73, 166; Haymarket, 69–70; Horse Guards, 66, 72, 161; Houses of Parliament, 64, 67, 68, 72, 81; Hungerford Club, Charing Cross, 57; Leicester Square, 73; Liverpool Street Station, 52; Lyons cafés, 71; Mall, 68, 71, 76; Mansion House, 72, 166; Mayfair, 63–4; National Gallery, 73; New Zealand Forces Club, Charing Cross Road, 78; Oxford Street, 61; Paddington Green Hospital, 65–6; Pall Mall, 56; Parliament Square, 65, 66, 68, 81; Piccadilly, 64, 69, 70, 72, 77; Piccadilly Circus, 54, 55, 69, 76, 77; Pratts Club, 56; Prince of Wales Theatre, 165; Rainbow Corner, Shaftesbury Avenue, 69; Regent's Park Zoo, 161; Ritz Hotel, Piccadilly, 32, 64; Royal Exchange, 72; Royal Mint, 72; St Clement Danes, 81; St James's Park, 68; St John's Wood, 52–3; St Margaret's, Westminster, 67–8; St Martin-in-the-Fields, 57; St Paul's Cathedral, 55, 72, 86, 158; Savoy Grill, 73; Soho, 78; Somerset House, 72; South Kensington, 25, 33, 61; Strand, 52, 72, 73, 81; Tivoli, 73; Tower of London, 72, 161; Trafalgar Square, 57, 64, 69, 70, 73, 76; victory celebrations, 52, 56–7, 60–1, 63–81, 134; War Office, 73; Waterloo Station, 81; Wembley, 54; Westminster, 54, 71, 80; Westminster Abbey, 86; Whitehall, 54, 55, 64, 69, 70, 71, 72, 78, 161; Woolworth's, the Strand, 52
Londonderry, 99, 100
Lübeck, 33
Lüneburg Heath, 25; German surrender, 26–32, 120
Luton, 82–3
Luxemburg, 155

Malaya, 174
Maldon, 68
Manchester, 88–9
Mannheim, 112
Mecklenburg, 27
Melbourne, 139
Milan, 50
Moscow, 110, 127, 128, 172; Belorussian Station, 132; Gorky Street, 132; Kremlin, 128, 130; Lenin Library, 130; Moskva Hotel, 132; Red Square, 129, 130, 131, 132; St Basil's Church, 130; victory celebrations, 129–34
Munich: Amalienburg Palace, 74
Mürwick, 18

Nagasaki: attack on, 174
Nairobi, 141
Naples, 50
New Delhi, 141–2
New York: Astor Hotel, 138;
  Broadway, 137, 138; Macey's
  department store, 48; Palace Theatre,
  138; Statue of Liberty, 138; Times
  Square, 48, 49, 137, 138; victory
  celebrations, 47–9, 134, 136–8; Wall
  Street, 137
Newmarket, 83
Northampton, 89
Northern Ireland, 99–100; victory
  celebrations, 99
Northolt, 165
Norway: liberation, 75, 103–5, 177;
  victory celebrations, 105
Norwich, 86–7
Nuremberg, 43, 61, 155

Okinawa, 62, 143
Omagh, 99
Oslo, 75, 103–5, 177
Ottawa, 138
Oxford, 83

Paris: Montgomery's visit, 166;
  SHAEF, 28, 45, 46; victory
  celebrations, 49–50, 105–7, 134
Piddletrenthide, 91–2
Pilsen, 22
Plon, 17, 18
Plymouth, 84–5, 114, 119
Poland, 173
Poona, 141
Portland, 114
Portugal, 50, 105
Potsdam Conference, 170
Prague, 19, 22, 62, 134–5
Pwllheli, 94, 96

Rangoon, 142
Rethorn, 111
Rheims, 25, 32–3, 37–42, 43–6, 107;
  German surrender, 41–2, 106, 108,
  110, 120, 127
Richmond Park, 161
Rome, 50
Rostov, 128
Rotterdam, 20, 36, 112
Russia: aid from British Red Cross,
  127–8; victory celebrations,
  127–34

St Helier, 117–18, 122–3, 124, 125
St Peter Port, 117, 121
San Francisco, 37, 46, 47, 62, 136, 172
Sark, 123
Seaburne, 161
Segeburg, 111
Sherborne, 102
Singapore: Changi Jail, 143
Sissinghurst, 52
South Africa: victory celebrations,
  139–41
South Norwood, 82
South Shields, 100
Spain, 50
Stanmore, 102
Stendal, 107
Stockholm, 50
Stoke-on-Trent, 92
Sunderland, 87
Stratford-on-Avon, 89–90
Sunbury, 90
Swansea, 35–6
Sweden, 22, 50
Switzerland, 105

Tarakan, 62
Tarvisio, 113
Torgau, 20
Tours, 128
Trentham Park, Stafford, 92
Trieste, 50
Tunbridge Wells, 90
Turin, 50

Udine, 50
United States: victory celebrations,
  47–9, 134, 136–8
Utrecht, 36
Uxbridge, 100

Versailles, 25
Vienna, 144

Wageningen: German surrender, 36–7
Warley, 102
Warsaw, 22
Washington, 49, 136
Watford, 100
Weymouth Bay, 114

Yalta conference, 20, 21, 22, 144
York Minster, 86
Yugoslavia, 113

Zagreb, 75